JOIN FUTURE

bleep techno and the birth of british bass music

Matt Anniss

VELOCITY PRESS

First published by Velocity Press 2019
velocitypress.uk

DESIGN & TYPESETTING
Kieran Walsh

PHOTOGRAPHY
Vanya Balogh, David Bocking, Normski

ISBN: 9781913231002

CONTENTS

FOREWORD

When I first went to nightclubs, it felt as if bass didn't really exist. As an underage teenager sneaking into what were then mostly still known as "discotheques", the one common thread to the music - the majority of it being '80s electronic chart Pop - was the lack of bass. Of course, there were basslines and the thud of electronic drums, mostly via the then ubiquitous Linn drum machine, but nobody was feeling the bass. It was a while later, when I first went to a Dub soundsystem party, that I first noticed the air move, saw a speaker cone vibrate from the sheer power of bass and felt that sub resonate through my rib cage. It was an incredible sensation, and I instantly knew I was in love with low-end.

House music arrived and club systems got better and often bigger, but still there wasn't that much bass weight. One of my favourite early House tracks, still much loved to this day, is Phortune's "Can You Feel The Bass?" I'd flip out if I heard it played in a club but my inner monologue would ponder the question in the title and think, "Well, not really, no." This didn't mean early House records weren't sonically life-affirming (they certainly were) but production wise, at least initially, they weren't a huge sonic leap forward in their production methods.

As House music exploded across the UK, producers here started to take the new electronic strains coming out of the United States and added their own distinctive British twist to them. Artists such as Bang The Party, No Smoke, Baby Ford, Renegade Soundwave and A Guy Called Gerald amongst many others were releasing distinctive records that worked on the dancefloor as effectively as anything coming out of Chicago, New York or Detroit. Many of them added a distinctive bass flavour often lacking on US imports.

Then there was Unique 3. From Bradford, they were the first UK act to really bring the bass - particularly sub-bass - to UK electronic music in a way that it hadn't featured before. Britain's deep affinity with Reggae and the exposure of so many to severely bass-heavy Reggae soundsystems, particularly prevalent in Yorkshire, meant it was inevitable that bass was going to become a distinctive factor. Unique 3's huge (and now sadly somewhat forgotten) influence on what came out of the UK cannot be understated: Hardcore, Drum & Bass, Dubstep and current UK Bass variants all owe something to Unique 3's "bass-prints".

In their wake from the Steel City came Warp Records and the wave of Sheffield Bass, or Bleep & Bass or Bleep Techno (or whatever you want to call it) that begat a thousand imitators. Again, an often-overlooked character was majorly responsible for so much of this music, or at least how it sounded: the mighty Robert Gordon. Co-founder of Warp and remixer, engineer and producer extraordinaire, Gordon is as important a figure in dance music history as any legend one may care to mention. The records he mixed or produced had a massive impact on my then DJ partner, Brainstorm, and I. We were obsessed with bass, which along with these futuristic bleeps sounded unlike anything else, especially when blasting out of a huge soundsystem.

We were very fortunate that our Edinburgh club night UFO, which soon morphed into Pure, had possibly the most powerful system in the country. When the bass drop in LFO's "LFO" came in the whole building would quiver, glasses would fall off the bar, old dust would be dislodged from the ceiling and the music would be drowned out by shrieks and screams of bass derived delight. It really did feel like we had joined the future.

Records by Nightmares On Wax, Sweet Exorcist, Juno, XON, Ital Rockers and a legion of others will be with me as long as I live, and should so many years of sonic abuse one day render my hearing kaput, it's slightly reassuring to know that I'll always be able to feel the power of them as they shift masses of air through speakers with their sub-bass and low frequency oscillations.

Listening back to many of these records, and particularly anything touched by the hands of Robert Gordon, it is wild how well they stand up to this day, and how dynamic they are, something that is often missing in current productions. In my opinion, this is particularly prevalent when it comes to what gets called "Techno" today, which has seemingly paused any sonic progress in favour of sticking to a dogmatic kick-drum based template that few producers in that realm seem brave enough to break out of.

Of course, there is a lot of forward-looking, futuristic sounding dance music with interesting, imaginative and intricate drum programming, perhaps more deserving of being called Techno, being produced today. Much of it comes from that other English bass stronghold, Bristol. This perhaps indicates that bass awareness and progression may go hand in hand. And talking of Bristol...

Matt Anniss, author of this mighty tome, grew up in Sheffield and has lived in Bristol for many years, so he is a man who really knows bass. Matt and I first bonded over our love for this music, out-nerding each other on obscure Bleep & Bass 12" singles and nuggets of Bleep information. I have followed the progress of this book since it was merely an idea, and it is incredibly satisfying that it is finally here; it has been the dictionary definition of a "labour of love".

After reading Join The Future I can't imagine another human being who could have done a better job of telling this story and shaping it so that it is not merely a lot of fascinating information, but rather a living, breathing account where the personalities behind the interviews are brought vividly to life. Matt's love and passion for his subject shines through on every page. He also challenges some of the supposed orthodoxies of the history of the evolution of dance music in this country in the late '80s, a history many pivotal marginal voices have previously been written out of. Matt rightfully allows some of those forgotten voices to be heard at last.

Hopefully this book's very existence will lead to some new ears hearing and falling in love with this music. Perhaps some of those will be inspired to do it themselves and, in turn, "join the future" like so many of their predecessors did in the late 1980s and early '90s.

JD TWITCH September 2019

WEIGHT FROM THE BASS

'There are many imitators, but we are the true creators.'

LFO 'We Are Back', 1991

It is a bitterly cold Sunday night in February 2018, and just over 600 people have squeezed into a former industrial unit in Attercliffe, once the beating heart of Sheffield's steel industry. This is the Southbank Warehouse, one of the city's newest club spaces, and the excitable throng has gathered for that most modern of phenomena: a party and live internet broadcast by online dance music channel Boiler Room.

In keeping with tonight's self-consciously retro-futurist theme, the post-industrial space - an unashamed throwback to the formative years of British dance music culture in the late '80s and early '90s, when attending legally dubious parties in abandoned factories and warehouses was a rite of passage - is lit only by a handful of blue and red lights. Occasionally, projections light up a makeshift screen on one wall, while piercing green lasers fizz into life at crucial moments.

In the centre of this stripped-back pleasure palace of corrugated iron, steel and concrete is a hastily erected DJ booth. Stood over the turntables is Winston Hazel, a smiling 50-something who has been making Sheffielders dance since the dawn of the 1980s. Tonight, he's not the headline attraction - that honour goes to his sometime Leeds breakdancing rival, George 'E.A.S.E' Evelyn of Nightmares On Wax fame - but he's clearly the person the hometown crowd is most eager to hear.

As Boiler Room's MC introduces Hazel in the manner of a ringside announcer hyping the imminent arrival of a prizefighter, the assembled partygoers let out a wholehearted roar befitting a local legend. Hazel smiles, then presses play on the turntable to his left. Out of the venue's sizeable sound system comes the distinctive futurist shimmer of Ability II's celebrated early UK Techno anthem, "Pressure". As the spacey intro bubbles away and the drum hits get louder, the eager punters closely clustered around the decks shuffle forwards in anticipation. At the back of the room, propped up against a stack of industrial-strength speakers, I await the inevitable bass drop.

When it comes, the pulsating, bone-rattling assault of subsonic vibrations almost knocks me off my feet. The crowd surges forward virtually in unison, a messy throng of flailing limbs, spontaneous cheers and serotonin-fuelled momentary bliss. Were it not for the flashing smartphone cameras and live Internet stream, you'd be forgiven for thinking that we'd travelled back to the summer of 1990, when clubs, warehouses, fields, factories and forests reverberated to the sounds of Britain's first authentically homegrown dance music movement: Bleep & Bass.

Hazel is here primarily to celebrate the enduring legacy of that sometimes overlooked sound, a heavyweight style first forged in the bedroom studios, illicit after-hours 'Blues' clubs and sneaky raves of Bradford, Leeds and Sheffield. By any stretch of the imagination, this was an unlikely musical revolution spearheaded by young men who had grown up in some of Yorkshire's most notorious, poverty-ridden inner city suburbs.

Away from the media spotlight - to begin with, at least - these unassuming heroes crafted a futuristic style of dance music every bit as forward-thinking as the revolutionary sounds that had emerged from Chicago and Detroit earlier in the decade. Like their celebrated contemporaries across the Atlantic, Bleep's early pioneers created music that transcended cultures while instinctively reflecting the suburbs and cities they grew up in.

Back in the present, Winston Hazel is in his element. He's surrounded by a mixture of misty-eyed Sheffield scene veterans revelling in a rare chance to revisit their youth and eager young ravers who have discovered the genre's key records through more recent productions made in tribute. Fittingly, it's not long before Hazel unleashes the record that first drew up the Bleep blueprint, Unique 3's "The Theme". Raw, minimal and blessed with unspeakably weighty sub-bass, it remains a landmark record: a track equal in significance to A Guy Called Gerald's near peerless "Voodoo Ray", which had been released six months before it in June 1988. These two records, more than any other, proved that British dance music was finding its voice.

As his set progresses, Hazel unleashes a swathe of similarly important records that "Shaped the Future", as tonight's event is themed. There's Forgemasters' ghostly and intoxicating "Track With No Name", a record Hazel wrote and produced with his friends Robert Gordon and Sean Maher in early 1989, Nightmares On Wax's "I'm For Real" and "Aftermath", and the commercial and critical high point of Bleep, LFO's sublime "LFO". Naturally, each is greeted with a rapturous response.

Now peering down on the action from a mezzanine high above the dancefloor at one end of the warehouse, I'm struck not only by the timeless quality of these 30-year-old records but how powerful and intoxicating they still sound all these years on. And, boy, is the sub-bass heavy.

This, of course, was the key part of Bleep's revolutionary appeal. Before the style's inception, such obsession with low-end frequencies was a niche pursuit for Reggae soundsystem enthusiasts and, to a lesser extent, those raised on beatbox Electro. Since then, this obsession with heavy bass vibrations has become the defining characteristic of almost all new styles of electronic music birthed in the United Kingdom.

Behind the DJ booth positioned slap bang in the centre of Southbank Warehouse's now writhing dancefloor, Winston Hazel is doing his best to prove this point. Amongst a fine selection of mind-altering Bleep classics, the veteran DJ drops percussive, bouncy UK Funky records from the late 2000s, weighty '90s Dub-House, breakbeat-driven sub-bass wobblers and, as you'd expect, a string of recent records from Yorkshire bestowed with the same immense low-end pressure and futuristic outlook as those crafted at the height of the Bleep movement. Had he been able to find space for some early Jungle, '90s Drum & Bass, hazy East Midlands Deep House, a spot of Dubstep and a dose of UK Garage, none of it would sound out of place.

These British-developed styles have traversed borders, inspired countless producers in far-flung corners of the globe and, 30 years after the first Bleep & Bass white labels began appearing on the shelves of independent record stores in the north of England, become part of the densely woven fabric of worldwide dance music culture.

You'd be forgiven for not knowing the part Bleep & Bass played in the development of homegrown British dance music, or its role in what author and music scholar Simon Reynolds has dubbed, 'the Hardcore Continuum.' The written history of British dance music is a hotchpotch of facts, myths and often-repeated half-truths.

According to the now accepted narrative, British dance music first found a distinctive voice between 1991 and '93, when Hardcore and later Jungle marked a clear departure from the US-derived styles that had first made the UK move. To make matters worse, most people believe that it was in London where House and Techno first took root in the UK, despite plenty of evidence to the contrary.

It's true that Bleep & Bass did not develop in isolation, and that the influence from soundsystem culture was being expressed in different ways around the UK (think Street Soul and 'the Bristol Sound', to cite just two contemporaneous examples). It is also true that Reggae and soundsystem culture had previously inspired plenty of British musicians in the Punk and Post-Punk eras, particularly those who grew up in cities with sizeable Afro-Caribbean communities.

Even so, Bleep & Bass still provided a spark for all that followed, in the process lighting the blue touch paper on a revolution that shaped British dance music for decades to come. At a time when the nascent ecstasy culture was hitting its peak and electronic music production was suddenly within reach of even those on modest incomes, Bleep offered the inspiration for countless imitations and better-known musical mutations.

For three years, the sound travelled far beyond its humble Yorkshire roots, first spreading through the Midlands, South East and London, before taking on the world. By the tail end of 1990, successful Bleep records were being made as far afield as New York, Rome and, somewhat surprisingly, the birthplace of Techno, Detroit. Each time, local producers put their own spin on it, retaining core elements while moving the sound in new directions.

Along the way, there were top 20 chart hits, in-depth features in legendary British magazines, an NME front cover for the scene's best-known act, Leeds outfit LFO, and the elevation of Warp Records to internationally renowned dance label; Sheffield's answer to Nu Groove, Trax or Transmat. There were sound-alike and copycat records from future British dance music legends, national package tours featuring PAs from well-known Bleep acts, and a wealth of music that inspired mutations that are still being name-checked to this day. Amazingly, all of this can be traced back to three young men with some rudimentary electronic instruments, whiling away an afternoon in the spare bedroom of a terraced house in Bradford.

• • •

Less than four months after witnessing Winston Hazel's whistle-stop musical history lesson, I'm sat on stage at the Wardrobe Theatre in Leeds, blinking into the spotlights and trying my hardest to assess the size and make-up of the gathered audience. We're midway through the inaugural edition of the Inner City Electronic festival, and I'm hosting *Dub Roots*, a panel discussion focused on the impact made by soundsystem culture on the development of electronic music in the UK.

Seated to my left are two men who contributed much to the development of West Yorkshire's particularly weighty and potent take on Bleep: Iration Steppas main man Mark Millington and former LFO founder member Martin Williams. They're joined on the panel by Brighton-based dub maestro Prince Fatty.

So far, we've discussed how these three men first fell in love with Dub soundsystem culture and the positive impact on British music made by the 'Windrush Generation' of Caribbean immigrants and their descendants. There's been some discussion, too, of the nature of the scenes in Yorkshire and elsewhere in the UK in the period leading up to the emergence of Bleep between 1988 and '90.

Millington, a man who appears to have been born to hold a crowd with hilarious anecdotes, is naturally dominating the conversation. He makes a series of pertinent points about the influence of the Soul all-dayer scene, the role of dedicated Jazz-Funk and Electro dancers, and the way the 'Blues' - Jamaican after-hours speakeasies that were once a common feature of inner-city Caribbean communities - helped to shape the sound of Bleep & Bass.

I spot my moment. Turning to the crowd, microphone raised, I say that I have a statement I'd like to the panel to discuss. Looking up from my notes, I say: 'The roots of all contemporary British bass music can be traced back to Yorkshire in the late 1980s.'

Given that the audience is mostly made up of locals, some of whom have been drinking for the best part of six hours, I'm expecting a boisterous response. Instead, this statement is greeted with a mixture of gasps, laughter, groans and the occasional cheer. I mumble something about explaining this theory in greater detail in a forthcoming book called *Join The Future*, then turn to Millington. 'Mark, what would you say to that statement? Can the roots of all modern British bass music be traced back to Bradford, Leeds and Sheffield in the late 1980s?'

As he turns to face the crowd, his eyes widen and his face lights up. 'In a word, yes'.

INTRODUCTION

PART ONE

RHYTHM TAKES CONTROL

'We're a creation of the city that we grew up in. Britain's not like America - it's not segregated in the same way.'

RICHARD BARRATT aka DJ Parrot

CULTURE CLASH

POLITICS, CONFLICT AND COMMUNITY

'We're made to look like we're all drug pushers, criminals and pimps, and that's not how it goes. That's only a small minority of the population. The rest are decent, hard working people, or would be decent, hard working people if they could go and get a job if the rest of the people in Leeds would give them a job.'

Unnamed interviewee,
CHAPELTOWN: ONE YEAR ON, TV documentary, 1987

Behind Leeds train station is a high-profile waterfront development known as Granary Wharf. Accessed via the station's futuristic back entrance and a series of passageways beneath railway viaducts known as "the dark tunnels", the development is the epitome of 21st century urban redevelopment.

Back in the 1960s, '70s and early '80s, the area was a dilapidated, overgrown mess of abandoned wharf-side warehouses, failed business and once grand Victorian buildings that had seen better days. Today, the area is brimming with life. There are fashionable bars and restaurants galore, glass-fronted towers of luxury apartments, expensive chain hotels and smart office buildings hosting some of the biggest names in law and finance.

Take a 15-minute stroll up the hill, past the train station towards the city centre, and you'll notice other similarly dashing developments such as the Victoria Quarter, a high-end shopping centre housed in the kind of building you'd expect to see in Dubai, rather than a former industrial powerhouse in northern England. Reminders of those times remain dotted around the centre of Leeds, though, from a string of ornate Victorian shopping arcades and impressive civic buildings to converted industrial units and sizeable townhouses with still impressive facades.

Step off a train in the rival Yorkshire city of Sheffield, and you'd initially be equally as impressed. While the Steel City boasts less wealth than its near neighbour, it too has undergone considerable regeneration over the last three decades. The train station itself is an especially striking example - particularly now its grand Victorian pub has been painstakingly restored - but so too is the area surrounding the Victoria Quays canal basin (once home to Sheffield's second mainline railway station), the Peace Gardens and the oversized greenhouse that links it to the Millennium Gallery, the Winter Gardens. First-time visitors will also notice a swathe of impressive buildings owned and operated by the city's two universities, something almost as evident up the M1 in Leeds.

In some ways, it's as if the upheaval that marked the latter half of the 20th century, and in particular a 15-year period between 1975 and 1990, never happened. Yet stray a little further from the centre of either city, or that of their near neighbour Bradford, and you'll find plenty of examples of urban poverty; not just in the increasing numbers of homeless people sheltering in shop doorways or under road bridges, but also in working class suburbs that have seen better days. There, away from the prying eyes of tourists, shoppers and day-trippers, you'll find echoes of the crime, mass unemployment and lack of investment that characterized the cities' declines in the 1970s and '80s.

Visit Burngreave, Sharrow, Pitsmoor or The Manor in Sheffield, or Beeston, Hunslet, Bramley, Chapeltown and Harehills in Leeds, and you'll encounter significant levels of poverty, crime and deprivation. The exact social make-up of these communities may have changed, with more recent immigrants from Eastern Europe and Africa than South Asia and the Caribbean, but the issues of poor housing, lack of investment and youth unemployment remain.

Some of these areas, and others in those cities and beyond, still haven't recovered from the seismic events of the late '70s and '80s. There has been no economic miracle for Yorkshire's most deprived communities, just constant reminders of past glories and the continuing North-South divide.

* * *

The Yorkshire that Bleep's pioneers grew up in during the late '70s and '80s was very different from the one that their parents and grandparents had grown accustomed.

In the postwar period, Bradford, Leeds and Sheffield were no longer the industrial powerhouses they had been during the Victorian era - when they variously led the world in textile manufacture, steel production, engineering and tailoring - but their economies were still hugely vibrant. During the 1950s and '60s, all boasted full employment - or close to - and required immigrants from the Caribbean, India and Pakistan to bolster their workforce.

By the dawn of the 1970s, these immigrant communities were becoming a sizeable presence in the working class neighbourhoods of Leeds, Bradford and Sheffield. While racial tensions remained high in some areas - and the National Front and associated fascist groups maintained a threatening presence in British cities throughout the decade - there was a growing, if sometimes grudging, acceptance of this changing social fabric.

In 1971, 50% of Sheffield's workforce was employed in manufacturing, with the state-owned British Steel Corporation being one of the city's biggest single employers. Over in Leeds, Hepworths and Burton owned huge clothing factories. At one point, the Burton factory in Harehills had a workforce of 10,000. Bradford, too, still had a strong manufacturing sector, despite the decline of its once famed "heavy woollen[1]" textile industry.

As the decade progressed, these core industries, on which the cities had developed their identities over the course of centuries, were beginning to change. Britain no longer had an empire to which it could forcibly sell its wares, and its global domination of manufacturing and engineering was rapidly coming to an end.

The election of Margaret Thatcher's Conservative government in 1979 accelerated this process, primarily by taking policy decisions that would have not only devastating consequences in Bradford, Leeds and Sheffield but also many towns and cities in the Midlands, North East, Scotland and South Wales.

Sheffield, in particular, felt the full force of Thatcher's passion for privatization and free-market economics. From 1980 onwards, the "Steel City" became a focal point for an almighty clash of political cultures. On the left stood the staunchly socialist trade union movement, supported by the Labour-run City Council: on the right, the most ideologically driven Tory government to date.

The first great conflict occurred in 1980, with steelworkers striking for the first time in 50 years. During the 14-week strike, there were clashes between police and pickets outside Hadfield's privately owned Hecla Steel Works; within a year, 1,900 of the mill's 2,700 workforce had been made redundant. It was a similar story elsewhere in the city, with savage job cuts across the manufacturing sector. By the end of 1981, unemployment in Sheffield stood at 11.3%; within three years it had risen to almost 16%.

---

1   The 'Heavy Woollen District' actually encompasses a number of towns and villages in West Yorkshire including Dewsbury, Batley, Morley, Gildersome, Heckmondwike, Ossett and Mirfield. It was named in the 19th century when the area led the world in the production of wool cloth for clothing, including such specialities as "shoddy" and "mungo". The name now lives on in the world of sport, with "Heavy Woollen" cricket and football leagues and the "Heavy Woollen Derby" between Rugby League sides Batley Bulldogs and Dewsbury Rams.

The 1984-85 miners' strike, which brought the coalfields of South and West Yorkshire to a standstill (as well as those in South Wales and Nottinghamshire), intensified ill feeling between Yorkshire's working class and the Conservative government. The most famous standoff between miners and police, the so-called "Battle of Orgreave", took place in the no man's land between Sheffield and Rotherham, while the National Union of Mineworkers based its strike headquarters in the Steel City.

The loss of the miners' strike hit Yorkshire hard. In Leeds, a city that had long boasted an entrepreneurial spirit and affluent suburbs packed with naturally Conservative voters, the City Council quickly took steps to address the loss of its manufacturing base. Wisely, the Council focused on attracting new businesses in different sectors, most notably the growing financial services industry.

It was a different story down the M1 in Sheffield. There, the Labour-dominated City Council - whose elected councillors often tended towards the Militant end of the Labour party spectrum and insisted on flying the red flag over the Town Hall each and every May Day[2] - continued to oppose government policy at every juncture.

Blazing "us and them" rows broke out over all sorts of subjects, most famously the decision to cap rates, the local tax that paid for council services. Sheffield had traditionally charged high rates to city taxpayers, using the money to subsidize low public transport fares and ensure good quality services for all.

Pertinently, this included investing in arts and culture, with the council funding the opening of two recording studios and rehearsal spaces, Red Tape in the city centre, and the Darnall Music Factory. In addition, the council also paid to convert a former bus garage into a live venue and club space known as the Leadmill.

Gez Varley, later one of the founder members of LFO, once phoned Leeds City Council to ask why his home city had nothing similar to Red Tape. 'They said they didn't because it wasn't a growth industry,' he says. 'This was 1988. The music industry was the third biggest industry in the country at that point, and they didn't invest in it.'

Spending ratepayers' money on recording studios and music venues was the kind of socialist utopianism that was wholly at odds with the 'small state, low tax' ideology of Thatcher's government. As with previous conflicts between the Iron Lady and "The People's Republic Of South Yorkshire", the left's favourite hate figure came out on top.

---

2   More on the Sheffield political scene in the 1970s and '80s can be found in John Cornwell's entertaining, self-published compendium of council anecdotes, *Tomb of the Unknown Alderman and Other Tales From The Town Hall* (2006).

By the end of the decade, Sheffield had lost 10% of all its jobs, including 35,000 in the manufacturing sector alone. It was a similar story across Yorkshire, with long-term unemployment the net result. In 1989, some 61,853 people had been unemployed for 12 months or longer, 10,000 of which were under 25.

Some token efforts were made to offer opportunities to young people in inner city communities, with numerous schemes focused on unemployment hotspots such as Chapeltown and Harehills in Leeds. According to figures quoted in Yorkshire Television's 1987 documentary *Chapeltown: One Year On*, there were some 10,000 unemployed people in the area at the time; even more shockingly, 24% of the area's dominant ethnic minority community was without work.

Money was offered up by the government (Chapeltown and Harehills sat in the then Conservative held Leeds North East constituency, whose MP until 1987 was former Education Secretary Sir Keith Joseph) to fund a special "jobs taskforce", running out of a shiny new Job Centre on Chapeltown Road[3]. There were also several training centres set-up to teach unemployed youngsters, including the Tech North computer skills centre in Harehills (opened by a councillor who would later push through local licensing law changes to allow Leeds clubs to open later) and Side Step in the city centre. The latter would go on to play a key role in bringing together various future Bleep pioneers.

Given these high unemployment figures and a lack of investment in alternative industries, it's perhaps understandable that many in the region felt a sense of isolation and anger. Some felt abandoned by the government, others as if they were under attack from a Tory party fixated with the get-rich-quick attitude of "entrepreneurialism".

It was not uncommon for some on the left - and that was a high proportion of voters in Yorkshire's cities, if not the leafy suburbs and adjacent rural areas - to accuse the government of punishing them for having the audacity to vote Labour. Even if you sit on the right of the political spectrum, there's little arguing that those in the North suffered more than most during the Thatcher years[4].

Curiously, the curse of long-term unemployment may have inadvertently provided the perfect conditions for a musical revolution to take place - not just in Yorkshire, but also elsewhere within Britain. Today, we're used to benefit claimants being punished if they fail to find work within a prescribed amount of time; back in the mid-to-late '80s, the government was nowhere

---

3   *Chapeltown: One Year On*, Yorkshire Television, 1987 (https://player.bfi.org.uk/free/film/watch-chapeltown-one-year-on-1987-online)
4   Other areas hit hard included Scotland and South Wales, both Labour Party strongholds in the 20th century,

near as harsh on those out of work. They tended to be left to their own devices, assuming they at least made a token effort to find work, and could, therefore, eke out an existence in any way they saw fit.

'During the '80s, the benefits system effectively allowed working class kids to be bohemian,' says Richard Barratt, better known as Sheffield music scene veteran DJ Parrot. 'In the past, bohemians had always been well-to-do, because to live and just make art all day, you had to have money coming in from somewhere. For working class kids, that option had never been there before.'

Barratt points out that the benefits system had previously helped fuel the rise of DIY culture during the Punk and Post-Punk eras, and played a part in allowing other sub-cultures, such as New Romantic in London, to flourish. Those with ideas and a desire to be creative could feed off the prevailing individualism and 'get up and go' ethos of society at large, even if they did strongly oppose Thatcherite ideology.

'You'd get football lads who wanted to be entrepreneurial, people who wanted to take up DJing or just dress in a certain way and sleep all day and go out all night,' Barratt says. 'That provided so much oxygen and energy for making things, particularly music. It wouldn't be allowed to happen like that now.'

It's certainly true that the explosion in dance music and rave culture that happened in the latter half of the 1980s was partially fuelled by those who bought into Thatcherite ideals - or at the very least the "get up and go" attitude espoused by her followers. From former City boys promoting giant raves off the M25 to 20-somethings setting up record labels or distribution businesses, there was no shortage of closet "Thatcherites" amongst Britain's rave generation.

Not that many in Yorkshire were that way inclined, at least openly. Aside from high levels of youth unemployment and widespread inner-city poverty, there were other issues for them to contend with.

As a result of their clashes with striking miners and steelworkers, confidence in the police was at an all-time low. Tensions were strained further by perceived racism within local police forces, an issue brought into sharp focus by the Chapeltown race riots of 1981 and 1987.

Chapeltown had a long history of clashes between the police and the local black community, with widespread violence first erupting on bonfire night, 1975. The local action group, the Chapeltown Community Association and the associated Chapeltown News magazine had spent years warning of possible trouble due to the heavy-handed tactics of West Yorkshire Police. In fact, in 1972, the United Caribbean Association, another local campaigning group, had set out their worries to the Parliamentary Select Committee on Race and Immigration.

'Harassment, intimidation and wrongful arrest go on all the time in Chapeltown,' they wrote. 'Black teenagers returning from youth centres to their homes in groups are jostled by the police, and when the youths protest, police reinforcements with dogs are always ready just around corners... We believe that policemen have every black person under suspicion of some sort of crime and for that, every black immigrant here in Leeds mistrusts the police because we think that their attitudes are to start trouble, not prevent it.[5]'

By the 1980s, these issues had only intensified, and it didn't take much for tensions to boil over. The 1981 riot - one of a number up and down the country in predominantly black neighbourhoods such as Brixton in London, Toxteth in Liverpool and St Pauls in Bristol - was sparked by the particularly aggressive arrest of a black teenager, with the ensuing carnage only intensified by looting and violence, nominally in support of Chapeltown's black community, by white teenagers and young men from the nearby Gipton council estate.

Given this history, it was not all that surprising when Chapeltown burned once more on the night of 22 June 1987. Again, the clashes between police and local youths erupted as a result of the arrest and brutal beating of a black teenager.

Paul Edmeade, later to go on to be part of early Leeds Hip-Hop outfit Breaking the Illusion, remembers the aftermath. 'I went to a school that was just by Potternewton Park,' he says. 'I remember we all ran down at break time to look at the damage [caused by the riot] because we'd heard it the night before. We all went down, and it was like, "We've smashed all our own shops up." We didn't get it. But your bigger siblings were at the forefront of it and were talking about trouble with Babylon [the police] and why they did it.'

The mistrust between police and Britain's black communities was not new, and in many ways was indicative of wider issues with racism in society. Although attitudes were changing, it was not uncommon for the sons and daughters of Caribbean immigrants to receive abuse from some of their white counterparts.

'I wouldn't say that there was racism in Chapeltown, but in town there definitely was,' says Iration Steppas Soundsystem main man Mark Millington. 'Down the road by the train station - Boar Lane - there were a lot of pubs, so for us guys to go to Bradford or Huddersfield by train, we had to find a way of going round them. If we went down Boar Lane, we'd have got called names and threatened.'

Club promoter Tony Hannan, who launched one of Leeds' earliest dedicated Acid House parties in the summer of 1988, has similar memories. 'Leeds was a very rough city in the '80s,' he says. 'You got all the black kids

---

5   Farrar, Max: *Rioting or Protesting? Losing It or Finding It?*, in *Parallax* (Volume 18, Issue 2, Summer 2012. (http://maxfarrar.org.uk/wp-content/uploads/2012/06/Rioting-or-Protesting_-final-14-Feb-2012-1.pdf)

hanging out at the Merrion Centre and all the white kids hanging out on Boar Lane near the train station, down that area. When those two groups met, there were massive fights. There was a lot of racial tension in Leeds[6].'

Yet despite these simmering tensions, race relations within the communities themselves were nowhere near as bad as they had once been. Although newly arrived immigrants from Pakistan and Bangladesh were sometimes treated to abuse from white neighbours, multiculturalism was slowly on the rise across the UK.

This was certainly the case when it came to younger members of inner city communities. In the mixed working class neighbourhoods of Bradford, Leeds and Sheffield, young people of all ethnic backgrounds freely mingled. They attended the same council-run schools, hung out together afterwards, and began to form friendships. Some were drawn together, too, by a shared passion for black American music. It was this, as much as their shared experience of economic hardship (and later dole culture) in the "forgotten North", that would ultimately lead to the Bleep & Bass revolution.

---

6   Some members of Leeds United's hooligan "firm", the Service Crew, had ties with the National Front. It was apparently rare to see racism directed towards black members of the crowd at Elland Road, at least according to lifelong Leeds United fan Mark Millington.

THE
DANCE

ALL-DAYERS, ELECTRO AND REGIONAL RIVALRY

'When I go to a club, the most important thing is for me to get a sweat on.'

MARVIN OTTLEY Elite dancer, quoted in *The Face*, 1989[1]

Britain in the 1980s was a divided country. Everywhere you looked, conflict was rife, from the government taking on trade unions and protesting marchers clashing with police, to "hooligans" kicking off with rival supporters in pubs and football stadiums.

Given this backdrop, not to mention the lack of job prospects and prosperity for many in post-industrial towns and cities, it's perhaps unsurprising that many young people sought recreational release. Some found this in political protest, others by joining bands or following fashion. Many chose to join one of the many sub-culture "tribes" surrounding musical movements, such as "Two-Tone" Ska, Goth, Indie Rock or New Romantic.

For most of those involved in the formative stages of the Bleep & Bass movement, their chosen release was dancing, and their "tribe" one of the many organized crews that were popping up across the Midlands and the North of England. If you weren't dedicated enough to want to dance competitively, you could still represent your suburb, town or city by hopping on a coach, heading to a big event and dressing like your local peers.

'The dancers were kids who through the week were being racially abused - there was no education, they had shit job prospects, and everything was a pressure cooker just pushing them in,' says long-serving British Electro-funk DJ Greg Wilson. 'When they went out to dance, they were somebody.

---

1   *The Face* (UK edition), November 1989. The feature focuses on the "drillers" and "footworkers" who were active on Leeds club scene, citing links between dancers at the Northern School of Contemporary Dance and two clubs in particular: Ricky's and the Warehouse.

Dancing was absolutely crucial to the well being of the community and to your status within the community, particularly for the kids who pushed it further and were in a Jazz-fusion crew, or went into breakdancing later.'

Dancing had long been the pursuit of choice for those in northern working class communities whose musical passions sat outside the mainstream. One route in was via the white-dominated Northern Soul scene of the '60s and '70s, which elevated obscure black American Soul records - and the DJs that discovered them - to cult status.

In black communities, many grew up surrounded by music, from Reggae, Ska and Rhythm & Blues, to Soul, Funk and, in the latter half of the 1970s, Disco. Many of those interviewed for this book told of being encouraged to dance with relatives at home, or being taken to gatherings where strutting your stuff with family and friends was par for the course.

'I grew up sharing a bedroom with an older brother who was the best dancer in Bradford,' says Kevin Harper, later to become a keen breakdancer and DJ. 'He played all the latest music and I got to learn some of the moves. To this day people still stop him on the street and tell him that he's a legend.'

If you didn't have parents or siblings who could school you, then you needed to make extra effort to access the music you loved. As Winston Hazel suggests, being a fan of underground black dance music could be an exasperating experience. 'I remember wondering when I was growing up why I couldn't hear 'our music' - contemporary underground black music - on the radio or in clubs,' he says. 'I remember walking down the street with my portable stereo thinking to myself, "Wouldn't it be great if this music were playing out of all the shops on Fargate?' When I told my mates at school I was into Funk, they said, "Don't tha mean Punk?" I didn't understand why people didn't know the music I liked.'

Outside of specialist radio shows and certain low-key events held in community centres, the only place to hear the latest underground tunes at the turn of the '80s was either to buy them from specialist record shops - assuming you had the disposable income to do so - or to make a pilgrimage to one of the few clubs dotted around the North that had a similar music policy.

Helpfully, thanks to the influence of the earlier Northern Soul scene, the North of England already had a network of clubs where black American music dominated, as well as a programme of Sunday and bank holiday all-dayer events that attracted dancers from all over the country.

The roots of the all-dayer scene - up north, at least - can be traced back to the demise of legendary Northern Soul hotspot the Golden Torch in Stoke. Famous for hosting amphetamine-fuelled all-nighters that attracted up to 1,300 people a time (despite boasting an official capacity of 500), "the Torch" had its license revoked in 1973. In the years that followed, the number of Sunday all-dayers across the Midlands and the North increased dramatically.

'There were early all-dayers at both the Blackpool Mecca, mainly in the smaller Highland Room, and in Stoke,' remembers Colin Curtis, formerly resident DJ at the Golden Torch until its closure. 'I worked in Newcastle Under Lyme doing regular Thursdays and Sundays, which developed into all-dayers. The Mecca thing spread because we ended up doing all-dayers at Cats Whiskers in Burnley and in Blackburn, Leeds and Bradford.'

These all-day parties, where alcohol was served for just a few short hours and closing time was called at 10.30pm, were often held in historic, pre-war ballroom complexes. Often, these would feature a grandiose main hall where Northern Soul was played, and a smaller offshoot room focused on dancefloor Jazz or what purists called 'Modern Soul'.

'When I started the biggest all-dayers were at the Palais in Nottingham and were run by the West Midlands Soul Club,' says Jonathan Woodliffe, a Northern Soul enthusiast who would later play a significant role in the development of the all-dayer scene as a DJ and venue booker. 'The all-dayers there were absolutely fantastic. It was all Northern Soul - mostly 1960s, but some '70s music as by that time in 1975 obscure new releases were being played on the Northern scene.'

Famously, the inclusion of 'modern' Soul records - Philadelphia Soul, Jazz-Funk and early Disco, primarily - was a bone of contention on the Northern Soul scene. When Ian Levine and Colin Curtis started mixing up stomping 1960s scene staples and fresh black American dance records at their weekly Highland Room residency at the Blackpool Mecca, it resulted in a split in the previously united scene.

'From '73 onwards the music changed in America, and it really gave us a fantastic armoury of records to play,' Curtis says. 'We'd decided that there were records that were as good, if not better, than the Northern Soul records we were playing at the time. Along was coming a new form of dancefloor music that we were very excited about.'

One man who bought into what Levine and Curtis were trying to achieve was Neil Rushton, a Midlands-based DJ and promoter who had previously trained as a newspaper journalist. When he started doing regular all-dayers at the Ritz, a historic old Mecca ballroom on Whitworth Street West in Manchester, Rushton very deliberately booked DJs from both the Highland Room and the more purist Wigan Casino. It was here, in a venue famed for its bouncy dancefloor, that the future direction of the British all-dayer scene would take shape.

'It wasn't the place where the schisms [in the Northern Soul scene] became apparent or developed - It was actually where everything met together,' Rushton told journalist and author Bill Brewster in 1999[2]. 'When I had the opportunity to promote the Ritz, there were a lot of great new records

2   Brewster, Bill: *Interview: Neil Rushton*, DJ History Archive/Red Bull Music Academy (http://daily.redbullmusicacademy.com/2017/07/neil-rushton-interview)

around. I didn't want it to be just the '60s Soul that I loved but I didn't want it to be just the current stuff, either. The reason why it worked so well wasn't because the battle lines were drawn, it was actually because it was the first place to combine it. We were the first venue to take the blinkers off.'

To begin with, not all of Rushton's punters were ready for Ian Levine and Colin Curtis's brave new world. 'It all crystallized at those all-dayers,' Levine explained to Bill Brewster in 1999[3]. 'All the Blackpool crowd came because me and Colin played and all the Wigan crowd came because Richard Searling DJed. It was like two football crowds: Manchester City and Manchester United. All of these Wiganites with their singlets and baggy pants were shouting, "Fuck off! Get off! Play some stompers!" It was all getting quite nasty.'

Despite the early animosity, the Ritz all-dayers quickly became must-attend events for Soul enthusiasts from across the country. By 1977, the growing dominance and appeal of "Modern Soul" and Jazz-Funk had forced other Northern Soul promoters to open second rooms to cater for those whose tastes extended further than solid gold 7" singles. At the Ritz, the number of died-in-the-wool Northern Soul dancers was beginning to be outnumbered by those with broader horizons.

'Eventually, you did have a situation where there would be people from Wigan pilled out of their heads from the night before, barbed out at the Ritz, and they'd be picking arguments,' Neil Rushton told Bill Brewster. 'But it was never as bad as at the Blackpool Mecca. At the Mecca you had a guy from Wolverhampton running a banner through the venue saying, "Ian Levine Must Go." There was never a fight at the Ritz all-dayers.'

It was the mixture of people and sounds that made the Ritz so important. 'You had a clash of cultures, a clash of people's opinions on music and a very interesting dancefoor would result from that,' Colin Curtis says. 'You'd have traditional Northern Soul dress versus Hawaiian shirts and plastic sandals. There was a definite visual change: the bowling shirt versus the Hawaiian shirt if you will.'

Crucially, the racial make-up of the crowds was also changing. 'By the time I left Blackpool Mecca I would say that on an average Saturday night in the Highland Room, there would be six black people,' Curtis says. 'On an all-dayer, at that particular time, there would be a dozen. I went to Manchester, and within six months I was playing to a 70% black crowd. That crowd started coming to venues like the Ritz and Rafters, so from '78 onwards the all-dayers had changed. The mixed race attendance increased dramatically.'

---

3   Brewster, Bill: Interview: Ian Levine, DJ History Archive/Red Bull Music Academy (https://daily.redbullmusicacademy.com/2016/01/ian-levine-interview)

The attendances at the Ritz, and other venues on the all-dayer circuit across the North and Midlands, such as Tiffany's at the Merrion Centre in Leeds, and the Hummingbird and Locano in Birmingham, began to be swelled not only by serious black dancers from the wider region, but also those prepared to travel up from down south.

Many of those London-based dancers were, of course, regulars on the southern Jazz-Funk all-dayer circuit, which was dominated by the Chris Hill-founded 'Funk Mafia' collective of DJs. The club where they cut their teeth, though, was called Crackers - a seedy, 200-capacity West End venue that had a reputation for attracting the capital city's most expressive and talented dancers.

'Mixing freestyle Jazz moves and *Soul Train*-style steps such as The Bump, the dancers at Crackers were serious,' wrote Stephen Titmus in a 2013 Red Bull Music Academy feature outlining the story of the 200-capacity basement venue. 'This was competitive. Battle dancing. Unless you had real moves, you couldn't even get near the floor. For mere mortals, this meant much of the time was spent at the bar or near the back.[4]'

Amongst the young upstarts aiming to topple London's finest fusion dancers - Trevor Shakes, Richard Baker and IDJ amongst them - were future DJ heroes such as Carl Cox, Fabio, Paul 'Trouble' Anderson, Terry Farley, Norman Jay (quoted in Titmus's piece comparing Crackers to legendary New York club space the Paradise Garage) and Cleaveland Anderson. Jay and Anderson were amongst a number of keen London dancers who would regularly make the pilgrimage to Neil Rushton's Ritz all-dayers.

'The Ritz was really good - everyone would descend on Manchester,' Anderson told Bill Brewster in 1998[5]. "On the back of that all-dayers started popping up everywhere. Every week we were on the coach. One week it would be Manchester, the next Birmingham, Nottingham or Leicester. There would always be some all-dayer to go to.'

Attending an all-dayer was a serious business for those involved, especially the dancers. Not only that, it was a genuine lifestyle choice. 'The preparation from one event to the next was over the whole week. It was all about what look you'd turn up in the next week,' says Winston Hazel, who attended his first all-dayer in the Jazz-Funk era. 'It was all about 'showing out' for the girls and showing off the dance style to make it look more elaborate. You wore your clothes to enhance your dancing, and your personal clothes style matched your style of dancing. It was a really important element of all-dayers. It's one of the things that drew people together, to see who would come with what next.'

---

4   Titmus, Stephen: *Nightclubbing: Crackers*, Red Bull Music Academy Daily (https:// daily.redbullmusicacademy.com/2013/03/nightclubbing-crackers)
5   Brewster, Bill: *Interview: Cleaveland Anderson*, DJ History Archive (courtesy of Red Bull Music Academy/Bill Brewster and Frank Broughton)

The crowds at all-dayers were a mixture of enthusiastic youngsters obsessed with music and fashion, dedicated dancers, and those in professional Jazz-dance and Jazz-fusion crews. 'The improvisation was amazing, especially in the Jazz room,' Hazel says. 'The Funk room featured improvised dance, but a lot of the dancing there was inclusive, so you'd get a lot of girls and guys dancing together. Then the battles would break out, which was basically Jazz-fusion moves, which got a little bit more eccentric each time you went.'

At the time, the North and Midlands boasted some of the most talented and dedicated Jazz dance crews around. Representing Manchester were the Jazz Defektors, Foot Patrol and Fusion Beat, while Leeds sported the Elite Dancers and the Meanwood Posse. For a period, Nottingham's Groove Merchants also featured significantly.

Each of these crews featured dancers who worked hard perfecting their individual style. Some favoured a 'floorwork', 'footwork' or 'drilling' style - characterised by speedy footsteps and minimal upper body movement - while others drew greater influence from Mambo, Swing, ballet or contemporary dance.

'This was at a time when all dancing was "upright", essentially, except for spinning a bit, but not on your back or anything,' Hazel remembers. 'You wouldn't even comprehend someone spinning on their back or their head in this period. It was more style and pattern over style and fashion.'

The all-dayer scene was the natural stomping ground for these crews of semi-professional, Jazz-inspired dancers. Having dazzled in their local clubs during the week, the Sunday all-dayer offered them the chance to take on all-comers in what Hazel describes as, 'respectful tribalism.'

'You had some crews like the Convicts, Brute Force and a few others who were, in terms of freestyle dancing, the funkiest on the scene to my mind,' Hazel says. 'I always looked up to them and thought, "Wow." These people would meet on the dancefloor ultimately, and their styles were off the scale. The improvisation was amazing.'

These dancers were, by today's standards, surprisingly clued-up musically. They were also very demanding, preferring the latest sounds to those embraced by their older siblings and parents. Helpfully, in Colin Curtis and Nottingham's Jonathan Woodliffe (popularly known as DJ Jonathan), the northern all-dayer dancers had two of the most forward-thinking around.

'DJ Jonathan was brilliant,' Kevin Harper says. 'He always had the freshest records. When he went to play at all-dayers at Venn Street in Huddersfield, I'd always make sure I was there to hear the hottest records.'

Woodliffe, who had graduated to DJing at all-dayers in the late 1970s, was slavishly dedicated to sourcing new records. 'I was just interested in playing all the new records coming through,' Woodliffe says. 'If something had come out that week, I'd have it. By the early '80s, through working at

Rock City full-time, I had a lot of income. If I went to a record shop and spent £150 on records for the week, so be it. At that time, it was a lot of money. Colin Curtis was probably doing the same thing in Manchester.'

Curtis, along with Manchester contemporary Hewan Clarke, could not only claim a big following on the all-dayer scene, but also as time progressed a packed weekly session at a club called Berlin on King Street West. Here, the duo would alternate between more purist Jazz for the footworkers and contemporary Funk and Soul. 'This session became the focal point for the scene in the North,' wrote Mark 'Snowboy' Cotgrove in his comprehensive history of Jazz-dance in the UK, *From Jazz-Funk & Fusion to Acid Jazz*[6]. 'Hewan would start the evening off with Jazz, and dancers would get their early to practise their moves - including Hewan, who was a rated dancer.'

The nature of Curtis and Woodliffe's up-front record collections made them cult figures amongst the North's dancers. 'What Jonathan Woodliffe and Colin Curtis did for the northern all-dayer scene was immense,' Winston Hazel says. 'There were other DJs who were equally good, but they were the DJs that the all-dayer crew followed. If Jonathan or Colin played anywhere, people would travel. They had the funkiest dancers wherever they played, all the new styles.'

* * *

By 1982, the newest, freshest musical style was New York Electro, a sound built around heavy bass, killer drum machine grooves and sparse, almost minimalist production. To those brought up on more traditional forms of popular music, Electro records sounded like they'd been beamed to Earth from another dimension.

It's difficult to overstate the importance of Electro and the associated Hip-Hop culture, to what happened in British dance music over the following years and decades. It was a style of music that had been inspired, in part, by the exotic, Far Eastern futurism of Yellow Magic Orchestra, the post-Krautrock electronic hypnotism of Kraftwerk, and the synthesized pop of British New Wave (some of which, we shouldn't forget, was made in Sheffield). It also drew heavily on P-Funk - itself an inspiration for many young, black Britons - and the next generation Jazz-Funk of Herbie Hancock.

More than anything, though, it was a New York phenomenon. It grew out of the block-party Hip-Hop scene in the Bronx, with all that entailed. There were DJs recycling drum breaks from Disco, Funk and Rock records, hype men rapping over beats and "B-boys" and "B-girls" battling for dance supremacy.

---

6   Cotgrove, Mark: *From Jazz-Funk & Fusion to Acid Jazz: The History of the UK Jazz Dance Scene*, Straight No Chaser Publishing, 2009.

There were arguably two records that sparked Britain's love affair with Electro and Hip-Hop culture. Perhaps the most important, in terms of the spread of the sound at least, was Malcolm McLaren and the World's Famous Supreme Team's "Buffalo Gals." While it may have been a novelty record, it introduced a generation of Brits to scratching and breakdancing (courtesy of an eye-catching promo video featuring NYC's Rock Steady Crew) and climbed to number nine in the singles charts.

'I came from a Reggae and Ska rudeboy background and was interested in soundsystems, but that changed in 1982 when "Buffalo Gals" happened,' explains George 'E.A.S.E' Evelyn, later to produce a string of key early Bleep records as part of Nightmares On Wax. 'The explosion in breakdancing and scratching was a huge thing.'

McLaren famously got the idea for the song after attending a New York "block party" thrown by Afrika Bambaataa. If anything, it was Bambaataa's "Planet Rock" single, released the same year, that would go on to have a much more significant influence. It was both devilishly simple and hugely far-sighted.

"Planet Rock" made extensive use of samples from Kraftwerk's "Trans Europe Express" and "Numbers", but derived its power from the unflinching heaviness of its distinctive drum track. This was provided, as has been well documented, by Roland's groundbreaking TR-808 Rhythm Composer.

The "808" first went on sale in 1980, and quickly grew in popularity thanks to its relatively affordable price tag (a snip at $1,195, compared to the $5,000 being demanded for the industry standard Linn LM-1 drum machine). The pre-installed percussion sounds varied in quality - think spacey cowbells, hissing cymbals and tinny handclaps - but included a kick-drum that was deep and relatively rich. With a bit of tweaking, the bass kick-drum could also be made to oscillate at impressively low frequencies, resulting in ludicrously heavy bass. This would become known in some circles as the "808 boom". It was this "boom" that helped make early New York Electro records, and similarly minded Funk and Boogie releases, sound like the heaviest, most crucial music on Earth.

That was certainly how many British teenagers felt about Electro. In hindsight, the sound's appeal was not just the music itself - however futuristic and groundbreaking it may have been - but also the culture that surrounded it. Put simply, there was something for everyone. There were trademark clothes and accessories to make you look the part and a musical culture that made the DJ - and in some cases their mic-wielding MCs - the centre of attention.

Arguably more important, to begin with at least, was the accompanying breakdancing scene. Many who had cut their teeth throwing Jazz-fusion shapes at all-dayers naturally embraced breakdancing, with its tricky-to-master freestyle moves, fashion-conscious dress sense and ingrained battle mentality.

By the summer of 1983, Electro and breakdancing were beginning to dominate the northern all-dayer scene[7]. The focal point of the scene was undoubtedly Nottingham's Rock City club, which boasted one of the heaviest and most impressive soundsystems in the UK.

'We had this brilliant sound system, this amazing lighting rig with a laser, and two giant video screens either side of the stage,' says Rock City resident DJ Jonathan Woodliffe. 'The DJ console was just off the dancefloor with bassbins underneath it. There were also bassbins around the edge of the dancefloor, and the rest of the system was flown [from the ceiling], pointing down on the dancefloor. Around the bars, you could hear it, but on the dancefloor it was really rib-rattlingly loud.'

Such a heavy system suited the booming 808 bass and punchy drum machine rhythms of Electro. Since Electro was becoming increasing popular in Nottingham and he was already playing those records to appease the footworkers who turned up week in, week out, Woodliffe made a decision to push the sound more. To begin with, that meant playing more American Electrofunk on Friday nights, but it wasn't long before the club's weekly Saturday afternoon 'kids disco' (an event where under-age teenagers were allowed in and no alcohol was served) had morphed into the UK's most popular breakdancing event.

'We decided to do a Hip-Hop and Electro session for under-18s that quickly turned into a really big event,' Woodliffe says. 'We had this enormous polished dancefloor that was perfect for breakdancing. Myself and another DJ called Master Scratch would play. I could do a bit of trickery on the decks at the time - not a lot, but Master Scratch was better. So he'd cut things up and play breaks he'd found and discovered. I was more interested in playing the newest records that were coming through from America.'

Rock City's Saturday afternoon Electro sessions quickly began to draw in wannabe breakers from far and wide. 'I used to visit Rock City every other Saturday - Nottingham was the place to be[8],' says Pat Scott, who would make a regular pilgrimage over from Lincolnshire with friends Tim Garbutt (later to find fame with early '90s act Utah Saints) and future Gadget Show host Jason Bradbury. 'No matter what age you were, you could go to Rock City on a Saturday afternoon, and it was free to get in. That's where the battles started to happen.'

Although Scott was not in a seriously competitive crew, plenty of others around the North and Midlands were. Each town had its own serious breakdancing crew, while major cities like Leeds, Sheffield and Bradford often

---

7   Further information on the northern all-dayer scene, and the companion scene down south, can be found in *Britain's First Dance Music Boom: The Soul All-Dayer Scene 1975-86*, an in-depth feature I wrote for Red Bull Music Academy Daily in 2017 (https://daily. redbullmusicacademy.com/2017/07/all-dayer-feature_
8   For further information on the strength of Nottingham's Electro/breakdance scene, and the people who populated it, see Sam Derby-Cooper, Claude Knight and Luke Scott's excellent documentary film, *NG83: When We Were B-Boys* (NG83 Productions, 2016).

boasted several. Sheffield, for example, had Steel City Breakers and Smac 19, Bradford the Solar City Rockers, and Leeds the Chapeltown-based Connect 4.

'I was in Connect 4 juniors when I was 13,' laughs Paul Edmeade. 'Connect 4 was Joseph Mills, Junior Pattison, an old school rapper called Speedo and a guy called Longers. It was hard to get out to parties at that age, so there were a few older breakers like George Evelyn and Kevin Harper that I didn't meet until I started making music a few years later. I was a lazy breaker and quite shy. I think that's why I took up DJing and learned how to scratch.'

Relative youngsters like Edmeade had not come through the earlier Jazz-Funk all-dayer scene - in contrast to future northern House and Techno luminaries such as Winston Hazel and Gerald Simpson aka A Guy Called Gerald - and were amongst the most enthusiastic Electro disciples. It probably helped that Electro was far easier to get into than some other underground styles of electronic dance music, thanks in no small part to the work of British music entrepreneur Morgan Khan.

He'd already exploited the potential for compilations of black American dance music with his Street Sounds series, which contained 12" versions of key contemporary Funk, Disco, Soul and Boogie hits and could be picked up cheaply in high street chain stores such as Woolworths, HMV and Our Price. When Khan launched the Street Sounds Electro series in 1983, the first volume - containing such essential classics as Newcleus's "Jam On Revenge" and West Street Mob's "Break Dance Electro Boogie", as well as a rather more forgotten tune inspired by PacMan - it simply flew off the shelves. More volumes quickly followed, and Britain's youth went breakdance crazy.

'Electro was marketed in such a way in this country that everybody could get to hear it,' says Richard Barratt aka DJ Parrot. 'It went beyond being a ghettoized type of music. There were breakdance crews, of course, but also kids in the schoolyard - white as well as black - were still trying B-boying and rolling about on lino.'

Where once teenagers would hang around on street corners with no distinct purpose, spontaneous breakdance battles began to break out in shopping centres, parks and community halls. Accompanied by the obligatory portable cassette player or, if you could afford one, ghetto blaster, would-be "breakers" would try out their moves at every opportunity. There were similar scenes in cities across the globe, from Rome and Rio to Paris and Tokyo.

It was through their love of Electro and Hip-Hop culture that a significant number of Bleep's pioneers - and many others who would later play a huge role in the emerging British House and Techno movements - were first drawn into the wider music scene. LFO's Mark Bell and Gez Varley first met as rivals during a Saturday afternoon breakdance battle at the Merrion

Shopping Centre, while Nightmares On Wax's George Evelyn and Kevin Harper were drawn together through their involvement in Bradford's Solar City Rockers crew.

'I think it was around 1983 when I went over to Bradford and met Kevin [Harper] for the first time,' says George Evelyn. 'Although I was from Leeds, I was going there to join Solar City Rockers. After going to one of their practice sessions in a sports hall, which they'd hired for 50p, I ended up going back to Kevin's house. He was the first person I'd seen scratch live, in front of my own eyes. He did it on his mum's hi-fi. I said, "You've got to teach me how to do that, man!" We got pretty tight after that through the way we were hungry for music and hungry for scratches. We were obsessed with finding out where the cuts on our records came from.'

It was a similar story down the road in Sheffield, where Steel City Breakers and Smac 19 had a fierce but friendly rivalry. Members of the latter could regularly be seen showcasing their moves in JD Sports, while it was not uncommon to see representatives of both crews going head to head on Fargate (close to the now famous "fountain down the road", as immortalized in Pulp's song "Disco 2000").

Smac 19's reputation was so high, in fact, that in 1985 they were invited to judge a breakdancing competition on Yorkshire Television's now forgotten weekly music programme, Sounds Good, alongside, somewhat bizarrely, Sheffield boxer Herrol 'Bomber' Graham. The first televised heat featured Steel City crew Positive Force against Bradford's Solar City Rockers, minus members George Evelyn and Kevin Harper. 'We were a few men down so never stood a chance,' Evelyn laughs. 'I do remember watching it on television though.'

Smac 19's "unofficial spokesman" and crew DJ was Winston Hazel. 'We were seen as the main South Yorkshire crew because we'd been doing it longer than most,' he remembers. 'During that competition I was sat with the presenter, Martin Kelner, commentating on what was happening. It was very basic! It was at a time when breakdancing had stopped being outlawed by the media and was a bit more accepted as part of the changing youth culture of the time. We jumped at any opportunity to get on telly.'

Solar City Rockers, Smac 19 and other Yorkshire crews regularly featured in organized breakdancing competitions at Rock City and over the Pennines in Manchester. The latter was home to the North's best known breakdance crew, Broken Glass, whose 1984 single "Style Of The Street" (produced by Greg Wilson, alongside members of Magazine and A Certain Ratio) was a key moment in the development of the UK Electro scene.

Competition from inside and outside Yorkshire created a hardened battle mentality and (mostly) friendly rivalry between those involved. This rivalry would continue, on the growing northern club scene and beyond, over the years that followed.

CHAPTER THREE

RIDDIM IS FULL OF CULTURE

SOUNDSYSTEMS, BATTLES AND THE 'BLUES'

"The fruits of those [interlocking social] networks are evident amongst a whole generation of young black and white people who have grown up alongside one another and shared the same streets, classrooms and youth clubs. They are visible everywhere in cross-cultural affiliations and shared leisure spaces, on the streets, around the games machine at the local chip shop, in the playgrounds and parks, through to the mixed Rock and Reggae groups. As a result of these, nothing is quite as "black and white" as it seems."

SIMON JONES *Black Culture, White Youth,* 1988

Under overcast skies, people of all ages and ethnicities are streaming into Potternewton Park in Chapeltown. As they've done on each August Bank Holiday Monday since 1967, the people of Leeds are gathering to celebrate Caribbean culture at one of Britain's oldest carnivals.

It's early afternoon at the 2018 edition and things have yet to really get going. The sweet and sticky smell of char-grilled jerk chicken rises from oil barrel barbecues dotted around the park's winding paths, while the sounds of 21st century Soca, Dancehall and Reggae drift over from the flatbed trucks parked up on nearby Harehills Avenue. DJs and dancers, many of whom have headed to this corner of Leeds from as far afield as Birmingham,

Leicester, Manchester and Bristol, idly stand around the trucks impatiently waiting for the costumed "masquerade" parade - an annual tradition for 51 years - to finally get underway.

They'll need to wait a little longer. Before the troupes of costumed dancers can take to the streets they will be presented to the crowds - a mixture of stoned students, veteran ravers, proud parents pushing prams, wise old West Indian sages and crews of excitable teenagers - in front of the festival-sized main stage recently erected within the park's natural amphitheatre.

To the untrained eye, the dancers' dazzling, over-the-top outfits are a sight to behold. Designed to be representative of aspects of Caribbean life - think birds, butterflies, animals, coral reefs and mythological characters - these kaleidoscopic costumes can trace their roots back to the earliest days of Trinidadian carnival culture in the 19th century. Yet prior to Trinidad and Tobago gaining independence from Britain in 1962, carnival celebrations were condemned or outlawed; they were, after all, anti-establishment in nature, with the associated drinking and musical merriment laced with a heavy dose of satire at the expense of the colonial authorities[1].

When the first wave of post-war Caribbean immigrants stepped off the HMT Empire Windrush at Tilbury Docks on 21 June 1948, they brought with them music and cultural traditions that were initially alien to their new British neighbours. With suspicion and racism rife, it would take a number of years for these traditions to be paraded before the public, despite the presence on the passenger manifest of several leading Calypso musicians (musicians Lord Kitchener, Lord Woodbine, Lord Beginner and Mona Baptiste) and Sam Beaver King, a future Mayor of Southwark who was an early enthusiast for carnival-style celebrations in London.

In fact, over a decade would pass before these Windrush generation pioneers - now settled with more friends, family and fellow islanders by their side - felt confident enough to organize community celebrations that mirrored Trinidad and Tobago's "mas" bands and parades. There were small-scale indoor events in London from 1959 onwards, but it would take a while longer before Notting Hill's annual outdoor carnival would be established. In fact, the first serious celebration took place in 1966, though it was a fete celebrating not just Caribbean culture but the whole of the community.

In fact, it was Leeds' ex-pat Caribbean community that would host Britain's first dedicated "West Indian Carnival" - an event organized by, and for, the city's British Afro-Caribbean community. The groundwork was laid in 1966 when two students - Trinidadian Frankie Davis and Jamaican Tony Lewis - joined forces to put on a "West Indian Fete" at Kitson College. 12

---

1   Farrar, Guy; Smith, Tim; Farrar, Max: Celebrate! 50 Years of The Leeds West Indian Carnival (Jeremy Mills Publishing, 2017)

months later, the Leeds West Indian Carnival was born, complete with a celebratory costume parade that danced down the hill from Chapeltown to the city centre.

That first carnival was a modest affair, but by the 1980s it had grown into a vibrant annual celebration that drew in participants - particularly dancers, steelpan bands and Calypso performers - from Yorkshire, the Midlands and North West. Musical satire at the expense of the British authorities still featured, but it would be the organizing committee's 1983 decision to involve local Jamaican style soundsystems - complete with selectors and MCs - that would shape the future of the event and better reflect the nature of the music scene within Yorkshire's sizable Afro-Caribbean community.

Today, it's the off-route street corner soundsystems manned by local crews that attract more partygoers than the parade, steelpan bands and costume competitions. You'll find these impressive looking "sounds" rising from the overgrown front gardens of Victorian terraced houses, sitting resplendent in the middle of blocked-off side streets and - as one ingenious crew did during the 2018 edition - nestling beneath bus shelters on Chapeltown Road, the main thoroughfare that heads from Leeds City Centre up towards Hyde Park, Woodhouse and the leafy suburb of Roundhay.

The selectors and soundmen skulking behind sizable speaker stacks don't always stick to the script passed on by their forefathers. These days, their musical selections don't just reflect the sub-bass heavy pulse of Jamaican music, but also later British-pioneered styles of dance music that owe their existence to the wide-ranging cultural impact of soundsystem culture. As darkness falls, you're just as likely to hear Jungle, Drum & Bass, Trap and Grime as much as Dub, Roots Reggae and Lovers Rock. While the rhythms and exact musical make-up differs, each of these varying expressions of soundsystem culture has one defining feature: the richness, warmth and heaviness of the bass.

* * *

The story of how soundsystem culture took root in Britain is one that's been told many times before, with focus falling mostly on the London-based pioneers who introduced it to the UK. Yet while they would provide the foundation, the culture's spread and long-lasting influence was as much the product of those outside the capital city as within it.

According to British Reggae historians, the first man to fire up a Jamaican style soundsystem - albeit a rudimentary one - in the UK was "Duke" Vincent Forbes. It was 1954 when he began playing Calypso and Ska records using one turntable and custom-built valve amplifiers and speaker boxes. His simple but popular system would become the blueprint for bigger, louder and more prominent sounds operated by mic-sporting Reggae, Rock-steady and later Dub "selectors" such as Lloyd Coxsone (who began building his rig in 1962) and Jah Shaka.

London was naturally the hub of soundsystem culture in the UK during the 1950s, '60s and '70s, but by the time the 1980s rolled around the city's dominance was being rivalled by similarly strong scenes elsewhere. There were notable outposts in Birmingham (clustered around the Handsworth and Aston neighbourhoods), Bristol (St Pauls and Easton), Manchester (Hulme and Moss Side), Nottingham (St Ann's) and Liverpool (Toxteth).

In fact, any town or city that boasted a significant British Afro-Caribbean community had its own soundsystems and associated events, with once mighty industrial cities, where work had been plentiful for immigrants in the first three decades after the Second World War, playing host to the most vibrant scenes.

Yorkshire's scene was particularly strong during the '70s and '80s. While Chapeltown in Leeds arguably led the way, there were similarly significant communities of soundmen and selectors in Bradford (mostly in the West Bowling, Manningham and Heaton suburbs), Sheffield (Pitsmoor and Burngreave) and, most surprisingly of all, Huddersfield.

There, the number of custom-built sounds was, for a town of its size, surprisingly high; at its height, the town boasted over 30 systems, an astonishing figure fleshed out in delightful detail in Paul Huxtable and Mandeep Singh's 2014 book *Sound System Culture: Celebrating Huddersfield's Soundsystems*[2]. These sounds would regularly battle against regional rivals from Sheffield, Bradford and Leeds at the local West Indian club, known as "Venn Street" due to its location, and at the lesser-known Aravark Club[3]. These "sound clashes" were replicated in many other towns and cities throughout the country, with rival "soundmen", selectors and vocalists taking it in turn to try and get the best response from the crowd.

This kind of competition was an ingrained part of soundsystem culture - a tradition that had made its way over from Jamaica, where sound clashes and battles between record-playing soundsystem operators were far more popular than concerts. It was a tradition that expressed itself in Hip-Hop culture in New York - thanks, in part, due to scene founder DJ Kool Herc being a Caribbean immigrant who owned his own soundsystem - and would later play a vital role in the development of numerous styles of British dance music.

Rivalry was not confined to the soundmen, either. Like the Soul and Electro all-dayer scenes, where dedicated dancers would battle for supremacy using Jazz-dance moves, soundsystem-powered events in community centres and local Caribbean clubs also attracted competitive dancers. They

---

2   Unknown author: *Notting Hill's Got Nothing on Huddersfield* (Vice, 2014)
3   Sword, Henry: *Retracing The Roots of British Soundsystem Culture* (Vice, 2016)

didn't breakdance or showcase their footwork moves, of course, instead choosing to style out their own take on "skanking" - a Jamaican pioneered dance style that had become more widely recognized thanks to the popularity of the "Two-Tone" Ska revival that swept Britain in the early 1980s.

Like the contemporaneous Post-Punk movement, this revival was the inevitable result of societal changes, most specifically a generation of black and white teenagers who had grown up living side by side in British towns and cities. The West Midlands was the birthplace of "Two-Tone", but there were plenty of young musical fusionists to be found elsewhere. To them, there were no boundaries and joining the dots between Punk, Dub Reggae and American dance music made perfect sonic sense.

• • •

It would be a little longer before Bradford, Leeds and Sheffield would give birth to a futuristic new spin on soundsystem culture, though the seeds were being sown from the late 1970s onwards.

Chapeltown in Leeds may not have been able to boast the same number of soundsystems as Huddersfield, but its scene was arguably even more vibrant in the '70s and '80s. There, soundsystem dances and sound clashes took place in a handful of venues within the neighbourhood. 'We had to do our own thing within the community,' says Mark Millington of Leeds' leading soundsystem crew, Iration Steppas. 'You couldn't have a black dance in town, so that's why we had the community centres to do them in, as well as certain warehouses that allowed us to do our thing with soundsystems in the '70s and '80s.'

Within Chapeltown, action revolved around the Community Centre on Reginald Terrace, the West Indian Centre on Laycock Place, a former Synagogue on Francis Street that was variously called the International Club and the Phoenix Club, and the Trades Hall on Chapeltown Road. Soundsystem sessions also took place in the backroom at the Hayfield Hotel off Chapeltown Road, a historic pub that was eventually demolished in the early 2000s after becoming a magnet for gang-related violence.

'There were soundsystem sessions every week at the Community Centre,' Millington explains. 'We had our own local sounds who would play regularly, but there were also big events that included Jah Shaka, Tubby, Saxon and even Coxsone - many sounds from out of town that people might know played there. When they got bigger, Saxon would play the Community Centre on their own without someone like Shaka also being on the bill. Those sessions were roadblock!'

In the Jamaican tradition, each particular soundsystem would have its own specific musical niche. Some would be light and soulful, showcasing Roots Reggae or Lovers Rock (Kooler Ruler, one of the first sounds to play at Leeds West Indian Carnival in 1983, led the way locally in this regard), while others would prioritize the bass-weight and heavy dancefloor rhythms of Dub. Key Leeds sounds at the time included Chapeltown-based Ambassador, Genesis, Magnum 45, Ras Claart, Emperor and Jungle Warrior, as well as Mess-I and Messiah from Hyde Park (an area better known for its student population, but also host to British Afro-Carribeans thanks to its proximity to Chapeltown and Harehills).

'The North was quite strong in the '70s and '80s for Dub,' Millington remembers. 'Leeds was mainly a Dub town at that time. The Community Centre in Chapeltown was the big thing at the time, but Venn Street in Huddersfield and Palm Cove in Bradford were also important. It was like a circuit - something would be happening every weekend at one of those places and you went there to support the dances. We were very entertained, and that's where we got our inspirations from'.

The circuit, as Millington describes it, also included Bensons and Checkpoint in Bradford, where he'd later DJ on Sundays, occasionally with his cousin's local sound, Conquering Lion. Like a lot of local soundsystem DJs, Millington got his records from what has become a Leeds institution: Sir Yank's record shop on Gathorne Road. A tiny, ramshackle place run out of a tiny building at the back of a row of back-to-back terraced houses, Sir Yank's has somehow survived to this day.

'It was the main Jamaican import place at the time,' Millington explains. 'Sir Yank had a garage and used to sell out of that, or his house. I'd go to Sir Yank's straight from school and stand outside hearing music play. If you liked a certain record he put on, you'd stick your hand up and be like, "Yeah! I want one of these!" Sometimes he'd have ten copies of something, sometimes one, so you had to be there to grab one, or they'd all be gone. It was a great place to meet and listen to music.'

• • •

Sir Yank's customers were not only soundmen and selectors who lugged their heavy equipment down to local community centres for evening dances, but also those whose sounds resided in the Blues - unlicensed, all-night social clubs located in the backrooms and basements of residential houses within Chapeltown and Hyde Park.

'There were so many Blues - I think Leeds had more than London at that time,' Mark Millington says. 'They were all around the streets of Chapeltown. They had local sounds and DJs but some also brought in sounds from out of town on Fridays, Saturdays and Sundays.'

Blues, or shebeens as they'd previously been called, had first emerged within the Caribbean communities of major British cities in the 1950s. They'd initially sprung up due to a need for spaces to listen to music, dance and play cards or dominoes in an era where racism was still rampant and regular pubs and clubs could be no-go areas for those without white skin.

'I think that was one of the reasons it was allowed to go on,' says George Evelyn, then a Hyde Park teenager who maintained an interest in Dub and Reggae music despite his devotion to breakdancing. 'As long as the Blues were there, the police knew where everybody was. If it's self-contained in a few places in one neighbourhood, it's easier to control. It kept things under wraps to an extent because there was somewhere for people to go. People were occupied and entertained.'

Due to their illicit, word-of-mouth nature, Blues came and went regularly. 'It was an open thing - anyone could do a Blues,' Mark Millington says. 'Once you had drinks, music and the authority of the property owner to run that Blues, it was no big thing. Anyone could run them, and lots of people did.'

Blues were more often than not named in honour of their proprietor, a member of the local community with an interest in soundsystem culture and an entrepreneurial spirit. In Chapeltown, that meant Blues with names like Duke's, Cliff's, Maxi's, Sonny's and Streeger's; in Sheffield, it was CJ's, Pinky's, Mandeville's, Brace's, Chatoo's (held in a prefab building in the back garden of a terraced house off Chesterfield Road) and, the most famous of all, Donkey Man's.

These infamous owners would often work the door, leaving hosting and bar duties to a strong female member of their family. Each Blues would boast a soundsystem, which had either been built specifically for the space or was carried in for each all-night session. There would usually be a small homemade bar selling a limited range of drinks (think rum, Red Stripe beer and Coca-Cola) and occasionally a kitchen dishing up traditional Jamaican food. Entrance was at the discretion of the owner and was usually via a side door or backdoor. Crucially, the Blues often opened at 2am, around the time when city centre clubs were closing, and went on through the night.

'Some of the Blues, like Darkie's near Sir Yank's, would take up most of a house, while others were just the ground floor or cellar,' remembers Gip Dammone, then an aspiring promoter of Jazz-dance clubs (he would later go on to be a successful restaurateur and club owner). 'There were lots of Blues in Chapeltown around that time [in the mid-1980s], and it was mostly Reggae music you'd hear. You'd see lovely, incongruous things, like all these dreads hanging out and then two little women sat to the side drinking Babycham at six in the morning. There would be all sorts of people in there - they were like social clubs.'

Dammone, a white Yorkshireman of Italian heritage, regularly visited Blues such as Darkie's alongside other workers from the restaurant, club and pub trade. 'In the 1970s and '80s the whole Leeds restaurant trade would go to Chapeltown after work because it was safer,' he says. 'We were a bit scared of going into town after work - there was a lot of violence. For the most part, I found it friendly in Chapeltown in those days. It had quite a vibrant scene.'

Aside from Dammone and his colleagues, the Blues was also a draw for members of the music community. 'When I lived in Wakefield I'd travel over to Chapeltown or Bradford to the Blues quite a lot,' says Leeds promoter Dave Beer, one of the key figures behind the city's long-running Back To Basics club nights. 'The Blues were the only place you could buy weed. It could be dangerous territory sometimes and you had to have big balls as a skinny white kid to go down there.'

It was a similar story down the M1 in Sheffield, whose Post-Punk "Industrial Funk" musicians regularly headed to the Blues after gigs or studio sessions. 'Some members of the band were constantly at Donkey Man's Blues,' says producer Mark Brydon, who at that point in the 1980s was riding high as a member of Steel City band Chakk. 'I always found it very friendly. We used to knock on the door and ask whether we could come in. I used to spend evenings with my head in the bassbins of their big soundsystem listening to proper Roots Rock Dub Reggae. There was no bother - nobody hassled us and we could have a draw and listen to music.'

Brydon and his Chakk bandmates shared a house close to another notorious Blues house, CJ's in Broomhall. 'It wasn't somewhere you'd go regularly,' Brydon says with a smile. 'It was somewhere you felt privileged to be allowed in. It was probably the fact that our faces were seen so much around the neighbourhood that got us in. I think going to Donkey Man's and CJ's definitely informed the way that our records sounded, because we learned so much about good bass and bad bass from those Blues. It's true that the Blues really influenced the way records were being made.'

The outlaw nature of the Blues, which often switched location from one house to another on the rare occasions that the police decided to take an interest in their activities, did scare off some potential attendees, though not Brydon or Leeds' Gip Damone and his friend DJ Lubi.

'I remember one night I was in Darkie's with my brother Simone and we got into some trouble for roaching up this fag packet that we thought someone had discarded on the pool table,' Dammone says. 'So we're smoking this joint and a guy appears - he looked like a general with square shoulders on his jacket and he was carrying a cane. He was giving us the evil eye and started talking to us aggressively because it turned out we'd ripped up his cigarette packet. We knew the cook, so he took him into the kitchen and had a word. When he came back out again he was all smiles, but we passed him the spliff and scarpered.'

That was not the only occasion that Dammone had to flee a Blues in a hurry. 'Another time a guy came into the Blues that Simone and I were in wielding a cutlass,' he laughs. 'I got out of there pretty quickly and ran like fuck!'

● ● ●

By the mid-1980s, the musical purity of the Blues as a haven for Roots, Dub and Reggae was beginning to be challenged by a new generation of DJs and dancers. While some loved Reggae, others were more excited by the potential of Jazz-Funk and emerging styles of American dance music such as Electro, Hip-Hop and House. 'I remember one time at Darkie's, where a Jazz dancer called Doville had arranged for Manchester DJ Hewan Clarke to play,' DJ Lubi remembers. 'Hewan was already there when we walked into the basement, which was lit by red lights at either end of the room. Hewan was standing there in the DJ booth, which was encased in wire mesh. They must have got two turntables in for that one because they normally had one. Hewan played everything - Soul, Rare Groove, Electro, Jazz-Funk and Reggae. We were meant to play but just got some beers and stood next to him in the DJ booth. A few looked at us suspiciously, but it was fine because we were with the DJ.'

Events like this were still a rarity, though, and it would take the efforts of a young DJ with ambitions to build his own soundsystem to really change things. This was Mark Millington, who along with his friend Sam Mason was well known for wandering around the neighbourhood with a "sound" made out of two connected ghetto blasters.

'Everybody knew me as "music man",' Millington says with a chuckle. 'Me and Sam would always be walking around with our ghetto blasters. People said to me, "why don't you build your own sound?" I'd say, "I can't be arsed because it costs money and I'm on the dole". Eventually, I was persuaded to do it, and that turned out all right.'

It would take a while before that sound, Ital Rockers, would be built. By that time Millington was a respected DJ with a Sunday residency at Checkpoint in Bradford - assisted by an elder local Reggae musician and wannabe producer Homer Harriott. 'When we played at Checkpoint I used to play Soul mainly,' Harriott says. 'When House came in from Chicago, Mark started buying those records. Before we played as Ital Rockers at the community centre it had always just been Reggae on those Sunday sessions, but we changed that.'

By early 1987, Millington had started building what would become the Ital Rockers soundsystem. 'It was never a major sound,' Harriott says. 'It was a cross between a home hi-fi and a soundsystem. It had big [speaker] boxes, but they weren't as big as a regular soundsystem's boxes. Musically Mark was talented and could compete on the strength of his selections, but at that time not on the strength of his sound.'

The Ital Rockers soundsystem soon became a regular sight in venues around Chapeltown, particularly the Hayfield Hotel, the Trades Club and the community centre on Reginald Terrace. While Millington would stick to Reggae - and Dub specifically - at some gigs, he was just as excited by the possibilities offered by the new American styles of House and Techno, which he saw as some futuristic form of Dub.

'Ital Rockers was a party sound - I played everything,' Millington asserts. 'That meant Lovers, House, Garage, Soul, Hip-Hop, Reggae, Dancehall and Dub. I did this thing once a month at the Hayfield Hotel with my little soundsystem. I'd be playing Dub and Dancehall, then get on the mic and say, "We're switching". I'd then play House and stuff like that.'

Not all of the drinkers at the Hayfield Hotel were all that keen on Millington's desire to mix up the sounds they were hearing. 'I took a lot of flak,' he says. 'Man would say: "take that shit off" and "keep to rub-a-dub!" There was a sound at the time called Jungle Warrior and their soundmen and DJs were often at the Hayfield when I was playing. As soon as I started playing House they'd leave or go outside, then the dancers who wanted to hear that sound would come in. The Jungle Warrior guys hated House and Hip-Hop, but later down the line, they embraced it. It took a lot of people years to realize that to be a DJ you had to be versatile in what you played.'

Millington was a trailblazer in Leeds, but he was not alone. There were others across Yorkshire committed to mixing up styles, though they were more often found DJing in regular clubs than in community centres and Blues. 'For some reason, I didn't give a fuck,' Millington says. 'I believed in what I was doing. A lot of people tried to drag me back to just playing Reggae but I stuck to my guns. I'm proud of myself when I look back on it. I can say that I created a pathway for a lot of people. The Dub scene has now had evolutions through the introduction of House and Hip-Hop influences.'

To the west in Bradford, another DJ crew - one without a soundsystem of their own - was making waves. Formed by Ian Park and cousins Patrick Cargill and Kevin 'Boy Wonder' Parker during their time in breakdance crew Solar City Rockers, Unique 3 were renowned for mixing up Hip-Hop, Electro, Jazz-Funk, Reggae, Dub and House. They played regularly at local community venues such as Checkpoint and Benson's, building a decent following among dedicated dancers and regular punters.

'Unique 3 was a big name coming out of Bradford at the time,' Millington remembers. 'They played really good music. People were saying things to us like, "Unique 3 think that they can kill Ital Rockers!" It was this big Bradford and Leeds rivalry, I suppose.'

The rivalry was such that Unique 3 decided to challenge Millington and the Ital Rockers crew to a sound clash - an old-fashioned soundsystem battle for supremacy at a club on Manningham Lane in Bradford. 'It wasn't a big deal at first, but the closer it got, the bigger it became,' Millington grins. 'We took it really seriously'.

So seriously, in fact, that Millington enlisted the help of Homer Harriott to create some "specials" - exclusive tunes that would never leave his collection, a la the dubplates cut for leading soundsystem DJs in Jamaica - to try and best their Bradford rivals.

'I'd just started putting a little studio together with a TEAC four-track, a Yamaha drum machine, a Juno 106 synthesizer and some other little bits of gear,' Harriot remembers. 'Mark, our mate Maz and me could all sing so we'd get on the mic as well. We started making little dub versions of tracks like you would for a Reggae dance, but in a House style.'

These 'specials' were largely covers of popular House tracks, with new lyrics and vocals making fun of their West Yorkshire rivals. 'One of them was a cover of Hercules "Seven Ways To Jack",' Harriot says. 'We included us singing lyrics that said what we were going to do to Unique 3. So "Seven Ways to Jack" became "Seven Ways to Destroy Unique 3". Like, "Number one, go in the studio. Number two, create some dubplates." Near the end of the dance, we'd always want to end with a bang, so we'd have a few "specials" to drop. That's where I started to get more interested in making dance music.'

When it came to the overhyped sound clash in Bradford, those 'specials' did the business. The set-up of the clash, which took place in the autumn of 1987, featured Unique 3 at one end of the room using the house system, with Millington and Harriott on the Ital Rockers soundsystem at the other.

'We killed them at that clash,' Millington laughs. 'I remember that "Seven Ways To Kill Unique 3" kicked up the place - it went crazy! There was another one we did called "Ital Rockers In The House" and that went down really well. People still ask me for that tune to this day. The thing is, Unique 3 didn't prepare for that clash like we did. I was the soundman in them days, so I knew about dubplates and clashes. We went there as if it was a real soundsystem clash and they turned up with just their latest tunes from Chicago or whatever. Having stuff from Chicago didn't mean jack shit when we had dubplates!'

It was a sign of things to come. 12 months later, Unique 3 would respond in the best possible way by unleashing a thunderously bass-heavy record that set the ball rolling on Britain's Bleep & Bass revolution. It was a challenge that Millington, Harriott and many others in Sheffield, Leeds and Bradford simply couldn't resist.

HOUSE PARTY

YORKSHIRE'S CHANGING CLUB SCENE 1985-1991

"I didn't feel like I needed to maintain the culture of my parents, it felt irrelevant to me at the time. They'd created a niche for themselves in the city as West Indians coming to the UK, a niche that supported their needs and the needs of their peers. Although I existed within the 'black ring of security' - a protective ring of culture that we existed within as young West Indian kids - we quickly tried to create our own existence here. We knew the difficulties our parents faced, but our attitudes were, 'That's not happening to me, man'."

WINSTON HAZEL talking to Red Bull Music, 2017[1]

While some young black Britons were making moves within the soundsystem culture inherited from their parents, others were far more focused on the potential of cutting edge club culture, and specifically the freshest American dance music. Some, like Winston Hazel, had already immersed themselves in the vibrant all-dayer scene, cutting their teeth dressing up and throwing shapes to Jazz-Funk, Boogie and Electrofunk. For these dedicated dancers with a passion for music, getting involved in the club scene in their respective cities was a logical next step.

1   Muggs, Joe: A Chat With Bleep Pioneer Winston Hazel, Red Bull Music, 2017
(https://www.redbull.com/gb-en/winston-hazel-sheffield-dance-pioneer-interview)

That's not to say that being a young black DJ was easy, though. Halfway through the 1980s, many city centre clubs were still no-go areas for those with darker skin, with owners generally keener to appeal to young white youth than the sons and daughters of Windrush Generation immigrants.

Hazel had seen this first hand. 'You couldn't get access to the venues,' he says. 'There was a racial issue in that a lot of clubs didn't want to be associated with events that had a lot of black guys and girls. The long-standing Jazz-Funk clubs, like Dollars, Rebels and Crazy Daisy in Sheffield - late '70s, early '80s venues - went into decline because pop culture became more attractive to the venues. There was less chance of you being able to go to a venue and say, "I'd like to put on a Funk and Soul night." They'd give you a week night when people just didn't go out.'

Hazel eventually secured regular DJ gigs at Turnups and Maximillians, venues that were either aimed at a black crowd or that put on regular events to appeal to the Afro-Caribbean community. 'The guy that owned Maximillians at that time also owned Shades on Ecclesall Road, which is where my mum and dad used to go to hear Reggae bands,' Hazel remembers. 'Maximillians was on Charter Row and later became a club called Kiki's. I used to do an '80s Funk and Soul set as part of a night that had a commercial DJ doing most of it. He gave me 20 or 25 quid to play the latest Funk and Soul.'

Thanks to his links to the breakdance crews and the Jazz dancers who populated the all-dayer scene, Hazel was a smart booking for promoters who wanted to draw a young black crowd to their events. Like the DJs he looked up to on the all-dayer scene - particularly Colin Curtis and Jonathan Woodliffe - Hazel was obsessed with getting the freshest new dance records from the USA. Where he played, the dancers on the Sheffield scene would follow.

'The black crowd, especially the younger men and women, didn't accept that '70s Funk and Soul was Funk and Soul,' he says. 'They'd created this distance between what they liked and what was actually Funk. I had a good upbringing in that before I got into the more electronic Funk stuff, but my crowd wouldn't accept anything '70s or old.'

One regular visitor to Winston Hazel's sets in 1984 and early '85 was Richard Barratt, later to take up DJing himself as DJ Parrot. 'When I went to Turnups on a Wednesday night to check Wini's set there would usually only be one or two white faces in there, mainly girls,' he says. 'The black crowd following him always wanted to move onto the next dance. It was about new dances and new fashions - you moved forward all the time. The idea of moving back to what your parents liked was an anathema - it was like, "We don't do that, we move forwards".'

Another occasional visitor to Turnups was Luke Cowdrey, later to become a Manchester institution as one half of DJ duo the Unabombers. 'At that stage, I wasn't old enough to get into most places,' he laughs. 'I think my first experience of Winston Hazel was at Turnups, hearing him play Change records - that kind of pre-House records that Greg Wilson calls Electrofunk and the Cockneys call Boogie. The electronic side of that sound, the instrumentals and the dubs, became a big thing in Sheffield.'

Cowdrey fell head over heels in love with the sound and quickly became an obsessive clubber. One of his favourite early hangouts was a cramped backdoor club called Mona Lisa's, which was above Maximillian's but accessed through a car park round the back of the building. It was a slightly tatty and run-down place whose décor hadn't been updated since the 1970s. That meant flock wallpaper, paintings of bare-breasted women with impressive afros, a low ceiling and a DJ booth hidden in a cupboard to the side of the dancefloor.

'I used to go to this night there called Wigwam,' Cowdrey remembers. 'It was run by a guy called John Stacey, who I think played at The Haçienda as well. It was quite mixed what he played, but quite a lot of Industrial Funk like Cabaret Voltaire, New Wave, some American dance music. The crowd was sort of a mish-mash of students, black lads who were Jazz dancers, footworkers, trendies, people like Gypsy John, who was dressed head to toe in Vivian Westwood and, funnily enough, a few football lads.'

By November 1985, Wigwam had long gone. In its place came a new weekly night run by Richard Barratt, now beginning his journey as DJ Parrot, and a couple of other Wigwam regulars, most notably event promoter Matt Swift. This was Jive Turkey, an event that would radically change the complexion of Sheffield's club scene and, over the years that followed, shape the sound of the city's growing love of dance music more than any other night.

For the first few weeks, the club was quiet. Soon, though, Winston Hazel was invited to share resident DJ duties with Barratt and things began to click into gear. 'It slowly built up over time,' Barratt says. 'It wasn't like 50 or 60 at the first one and then thousands the next week. Before we started, the scene was quite segregated, but it began to get more mixed over time. The black and white crowds began to come together. The thing is, Sheffield's never had a lot that's 'going off'. If you've got the thing that's 'going off', you're going to get everybody. There was just nothing else.'

Like most successful DJs at the time, Barratt and Hazel played a good mixture of music, with the former embracing older Funk and Soul as well as contemporary sounds such as Electro, Hip-Hop and the New York style of sparse, stripped-back dance music that would now be called 'Proto-House'[2]. Hazel kept up with the latest black American dance music - a trait that later bagged him a job as the dance music import buyer at local store FON

---

2   Examples of records now considered 'Proto-House' from NYC include Serious Intention's "You Don't Know", Visual's "The Music Got Me", Colonel Abrams "Music Is The Answer", Subject's "The Magic, The Moment", Pushe's "Don't Take Your Love Away" and Cultural Vibe's "Ma Foom Bey". All were made between 1983 and '86 and came backed with sparse, stripped-back instrumental 'dubs' marked out by extensive use of razor-sharp drum edits and copious amounts of delay. For more information, see my piece for Red Bull Music Academy Daily (http://daily.redbullmusicacademy.com) entitled 'The Birth of House in New York City'.

Records - and was conscious of the forward-thinking nature of the smartly dressed battle dancers and footworkers who made up a big portion of the Jive Turkey crowd in the early days.

'You had to have the newest records,' says Jonathan Woodliffe, resident DJ and venue booker at Rock City in Nottingham, another club that the footworkers from the Midlands and North would regularly travel to. 'The mix of people we had, black and white, didn't come down to get drunk and hear music. They came down with a change of clothes, drank water and wanted to hear new music.'

It was a similar story up in Bradford, where Unique 3 - whose DJ line-up in 1985 included Kevin 'Boy Wonder' Harper and guest George 'E.A.S.E' Evelyn, both of whom had come through the Solar City Rockers breakdance crew - played to crowds of dedicated dancers at Benson's and Checkpoint, whose second room boasted Latin Jazz and Jazz-Funk provided by Dig Family resident DJs Lubi and Chico.

To the east in Leeds, the footworkers, drillers and Jazz dancers divided their time between nights like Dig and the Cooker at the Coconut Grove on Merrion Street (both run by Lubi, Chico and Gip Dammone, whose family owned the three-floor venue[3]), events in Chapeltown at the Trades Club, West Indian Centre and the Phoenix Club on Francis Street, and the city's most hyped venue: the Warehouse.

Opened in 1979 by the late Yorkshire-based American entrepreneur Mike Wiand, the Warehouse was a club like few others in the UK at the time. Wiand, who had already made significant sums running a chain of burger restaurants, was keen to open something that matched the quality of clubs he'd visited in Spain and his native USA.

'What you have to remember is that most clubs back then weren't what they are today,' Wiand told the *Yorkshire Evening Post* back in 2010[4]. 'Most of them had soundsystems that were terrible, the lighting sucked and the music they played was so behind the times. At the time most DJs used to play 7" records and interrupt the end to introduce the next record, whereas in Marbella when I visited the DJs played 12" records and mixed them. It attracted a cool, alternative, mixed crowd and I was pretty sure from the ten years I'd spent in Leeds that there was the same cool, alternative crowd out there.'

When it opened, the design and décor of the Warehouse had more in common with New York clubs such as the Paradise Garage and Studio 54 than the down-at-heel venues the city was known for. While the soundsystem

---

3   The Coconut Grove was a restaurant and event space that took up two floors, with a 300 capacity club space known as Ricky's in the basement. The only way to get between the three floors was via the fire exit. The three-floor complex was sometimes referred to as the 'Merrion Suite'; it later changed ownership and was renamed the Gallery.
4   McPhee, Rob: *The Warehouse: Leeds Night Club Memories*, Yorkshire Evening Post, 28 May 2010 (www.yorkshireeveningpost.co.uk/news/latest/the-warehouse-leeds-nightclub-memories-1-2246028)

couldn't match the Richard Long designed masterpiece at the Paradise Garage, it was far superior to all of its Yorkshire rivals. Like the 'Garage', the Warehouse's DJ booth was high up above the dancefloor at one end of the room, with a stage on the ground floor. Curiously, the bass cabinets were embedded below the stage.

By the mid-1980s, the Warehouse had a reputation for being the go-to place in Leeds. Its management, DJs and door staff were welcoming to black dancers as well as white ones, resulting in an interesting mix of Indie kids, Goths (the Sisters of Mercy being the city's most famous band at the time), Hip-Hop kids, serious black dancers and students. The club's music policy initially reflected this mixture of dancers.

'Ian Dewhirst was the main DJ there to begin with and he'd play everything,' says Dave Beer, then a tour manager for the Sisters of Mercy with a growing interest in black American dance music. 'You'd hear classic Funk and P-Funk Allstars to Gil Scott-Heron and obscure Indie tunes. He catered for different crowds, and that's where the creativity came in. He used to take influence from different styles and mash them together'.

Dewhirst had come through the Northern Soul scene and was a pivotal figure on the Soul all-dayer circuit. He was also keen to mentor younger DJs and put particular effort into teaching one of the club's pot-washers, Roy Archer, how to DJ. 'Ian taught Roy by getting him to do minute-mixes, so every minute he'd have to mix a new tune in,' says Martin Williams, then a Soul boy from Chapeltown with DJing ambitions of his own. 'Roy could do it as well. He was a really good DJ. We used to go down to the Warehouse to hear him play.'

Although the Warehouse was a major draw for some, it never boasted the volume of footworkers, drillers and Jazz-fusion dancers as some other key venues and events in Yorkshire around 1985 and '86. These spats-clad dancers tended to gravitate towards events where they could hear the hottest new music coming out of the United States. By the tail end of 1985, that meant Chicago House.

'Those early House records were the right tempo for what those Jazz dancers wanted,' Jonathan Woodliffe says. 'As DJs we didn't think, "That's a House record!" We just listened to it, bought it and played it on its merits. It was like a breath of fresh air because we were hearing something that was different again. America had yet again come up with something else for us to play.'

Woodliffe was one of a handful of early adopters of House music in the Midlands and North of England, alongside Leeds' Steve Luigi, at that point resident DJ at Ricky's below the Coconut Grove on Merrion Street, and Jive Turkey's Parrot and Winston Hazel. Between them and a handful of younger DJs who quickly embraced the sound - think Unique 3, DJ Roy, DJ Martin,

Mark Millington of Ital Rockers, Nottingham's Graeme Park, Manchester's Mike Pickering and influential West Yorkshire selector DJ Hutchie - House music became a regular feature in clubs and on the all-dayer circuit.

'I remember going to one of the Funk and Soul all-dayers in 1986 and hearing Adonis's "No Way Back",' says George 'E.A.S.E' Evelyn. 'I thought: "What the fuck is this?" You could body pop to House records, fusion to them, footstep to it or battle to it. That was how those tracks threw down. But from 1985 to late '87, the word "House" never came into it. They were just club tracks.'

The growing dominance of House music within the Jazz-dance community of the Midlands and North became increasingly obvious to those who were DJing at Jazz-focused club nights. 'I saw it with my own eyes,' says DJ Lubi, then resident at Dig and the Cooker. 'Sometime in 1986 one of the dancers who regularly came down to Checkpoint [in Bradford] asked if he could put on a night with a Latin Jazz band playing and a DJ they'd provide. So we played with our little Latin Jazz band, mostly doing covers of Chick Correa tunes, and they were getting down to it. Then I started to DJ with my usual Jazz records and nothing was working. Then their crew DJ came on and threw down this jacking House tune and the place went bonkers. I thought, "Things have changed". Those guys had moved onto a new thing.'

Given the footworkers' love of the fresh and the new, it wasn't all that surprising. 'When House cane in it was just another step on from Electro and everything else,' Richard Barratt says. 'It was a new dance that had come in. It was a new style and a new sound.'

Luke Cowdrey, who moved to Manchester midway through 1986 but remained a regular at Jive Turkey, remembers the first time he saw the footworkers battling to House music. 'I distinctly remember these black lads from Sheffield and Manchester footworking to Adonis's "No Way Back", Chip-E and loads of other DJ International records,' he says. 'I saw these lads throw down their keys in challenge. The footworkers who danced to Jazz loved House and did exactly the same dancing to it. I can honestly say I was born again at that moment.'

To begin with, fresh House records were played as part of a wider palette of sounds, not just at Jive Turkey in Sheffield but also up in Huddersfield[5], Leeds and Bradford, across the Pennines in Manchester, and down the M1 in Nottingham. 'As a DJ it was all about being versatile,' says George Evelyn, who by early 1987 was DJing alongside Kevin Harper as Nightmares On Wax. 'A good DJ was someone who had versatility. That really came from the selector in Jamaican soundsystem culture. You can have all the skills in the

---

[5]   There were regular Soul style all-dayers at the West Indian community centre on Venn Street, as well as the soundsystem battles and Reggae sessions mentioned in the previous chapter.

world, but can you select? Can you read the club in a way that you can select the right record, flipping from one sound down into Hip-Hop, up into Funk or what became known as House? The DJ had to have depth.'

Nightmares On Wax held a residency at a night called Downbeat at Ricky's. It had started as a student night. With footworkers and members of Leeds bands such as Age of Chance also in attendance, it had a typically mixed crowd in the early days. 'The Jazz dancers were always at our clubs and on our dancefloors,' Evelyn remembers. 'We had a bunch of people who would come down, including more famous local dancers like Edward Irish and Marvin Flowers, and challenge each other. Circles would appear on the dancefloor. If we were playing Jazz-Funk, they'd be doing fusion dancing. If we were dropping House they'd be 'drilling' to it. If you talk about that period from 1984 to '87, it was totally drillers music. It certainly wasn't rave.'

The popularity of Chicago House in the Midlands and North initially dwarfed the micro-scenes elsewhere, even in London, the city that is most frequently associated with helping to spread the sound across the UK. 'For a period of time I lived in London, and it was really difficult to find anyone who played House,' says Glyn Andrews, later a member of Warp-signed act Tuff Little Unit. 'I fell in love with House after somebody gave me a tape of Trax Records stuff - Mr Fingers "Mystery of Love" was mind-blowing. Parrot and Winston used to play House a lot, but in London, it was rare to hear it in the clubs then. The only way I could hear it was on Jazzy M's show on pirate radio[6].'

Aside from the gay clubs, few DJs in London were championing House music in the same way as their compatriots in the Midlands and North. 'The music played at places like the Electric Ballroom in Camden, where Paul 'Trouble' Anderson was resident DJ, was a little different again to what we were seeing in Nottingham,' Jonathan Woodliffe says. 'Paul played a lot of Electro but also a lot of Go-Go[7]. Island Records had invested a lot in licensing those records [from Washington D.C. labels] to try and break them in

---

6   Jazzy M, real name Michael Shinlou, is an often-overlooked figure in London's House music story. When Chicago House began landing in the UK, he added a section dedicated to the sound to his show on LWR (London Wide Radio). Called "The Jackin' Zone", this featured a mix of original Chicago material and demos by UK producers. By 1988 he'd made the move into production, becoming an in-demand remixer. A year later he established the OhZone record label, which went on to release some important early UK House and Techno tracks. Although well regarded in London at the time, he never became quite as famous UK-wide as the likes of Danny Rampling and Paul Oakenfold. The same fate also befell Lawrence "Kid" Batchelor, who championed House from 1987 onwards. He also co-produced one of the earliest UK House singles, "I Feel Good All Over", as part of the influential trio Bang The Party.
7   Go-Go fused elements of Funk, Hip-Hop and R&B, with the sound marked out by distinctive "dotted" rhythm patterns that were markedly different from the two-step bounce of Electro and the four-to-the-floor grooves of Disco and House. Island Records founder Chris Blackwell was a big fan and even funded a film inspired by the Washington D.C. Go-Go scene starring Art Garfunkel, the largely forgotten - and rather terrible - Good To Go (1986).

the UK with the aid of people like Pete Tong. It was never a flavour that went anywhere. In London, it was little clubs with 200 or 300 people and the DJs might play a few House records.'

Luke Cowdrey has similar memories of Go-Go being rejected by the serious dancers who made up a significant portion of the crowds at Jive Turkey. 'Between 1986 and '87 when Go-Go was big in London alongside Rare Groove, Sheffield was quite militantly House,' he says. 'I distinctly remember Parrot or Winston playing Trouble Funk's 'Good To Go' and all the black lads leaving the dancefloor in disgust. There was a guy from London there and he turned to the person next to him and asked, 'What's happening'. The reply he got was: "We do House music up here".'

As supporting evidence for the importance of House music in the Midlands and North in that period, Woodliffe cites the Trax Records tour to the UK in 1987. It happened on the back of some mainstream media exposure for the sound and a string of chart hits for both original Chicago cuts and copycat UK records[8].

'On that tour, they did three dates: the Limelight Club on Shaftesbury Avenue in London, Rock City and The Haçienda in Manchester. When the Trax Records crew - Marshall Jefferson, Adonis and Larry Heard included - came up to Rock City on a Sunday for an all-dayer. The night before they were in London and they said it wasn't very busy. Rock City sold out that day - 1700 people.'

Amongst the crowd at Rock City that day were many from the Yorkshire scene, including Leeds lads Paul Edmeade (later to become part of the city's first signed Hip-Hop crew, Breaking The Illusion) and Martin Williams. When the tour headed to Manchester, the Haçienda was similarly packed.

'It was March 1987 - before day one of Shoom and Spectrum in London,' Luke Cowdrey says. 'Marshall Jefferson, Adonis and Larry Heard were all there - it was like meeting the Gods. It was just as packed at the Haçienda as it was at Rock City. There's a whole narrative where people were jacking to militant drum machine music up here before they were down south. In some ways, it doesn't matter who started it, but in that period the 'triangle of House' in the UK was Sheffield, Manchester and Nottingham. By the time things kicked off in London, where it was seen as a new thing, up here it was just a continuation of what had been happening.'

● ● ●

---

8   Arguably the greatest of these early British US-style House records was Hotline's Rhythm King-released "Rock This House" (1986). It was made by two producers from Huddersfield, Tony Powell and Trevor Russell, and was naturally very popular on the Northern club scene.

By that point in 1987, Britain's underground clubs were on the cusp of a seismic shift - one that can be traced back to an unusual network of people whose founder members Cowdrey first encountered on a memorable day in 1984 or early '85. On this particular day, Cowdrey was ambling down John Street in Sheffield towards Bramall Lane stadium, home to his beloved Sheffield United FC. In front of him on the pavement was a small group of people he recognized from attending United matches.

'They were the early members of what became the Blades Business Crew [hooligan] firm,' he says. 'This lot were totally different. They were three or four years older than me. One or two had long hair, and one was wearing a headscarf. They were dressed in pastels, baggy clothing, sunglasses and beads. A couple of them were wearing Walkmans. Some were wearing designer clothes - Chevignon, Chipie. Being a peacock myself, I was obsessed with them.'

Fashion had, of course, long been an essential part of youth culture in the UK, not least on the Northern Soul and Jazz-Funk circuits. It was hugely important to many who followed football teams around and got into fights, as had taking a keen interest in music. Even so, the group Cowdrey encountered was like nothing he'd seen before. 'This was after the whole scally, Fila, trendy sportswear late-1970s thing that the Scousers and Mancs had started,' he says. 'This was most definitely an '80s thing.'

One of the ringleaders of the group - and the one Cowdrey associates with it the most - was a character named Tony Canetti: 'He was an infamous Sheffield lad that I've later discovered was considered an international grafter - he travelled around Europe relieving the premium shops in Milan, Rome and Paris of their goods. They were getting everything - they were like the Paninari[9] on acid.'

Canetti and his cohorts were part of an extended network of international grafters and sneak thieves - mostly British working class men interested in football, music and fashion who would criss-cross Europe robbing, working odd jobs and hustling to get by. In the summer, they could often be found on Ibiza - an island with significant liberal and counter-cultural heritage that was beginning to become a destination both for the world's beautiful people and working class Britons.

'As unemployment grew in Britain, a new breed of tourist reached the island,' Matthew Collin wrote in *Altered State*, his peerless history of Acid House and ecstasy culture. 'These weren't backpackers or two-week package tourists, but bright, inquisitive youths for whom the prospect of

---

9   Paninari was an Italian cultural movement that began in Milan in the early 1980s and became recognized worldwide thanks to media coverage in the middle of the decade. If you were a 'Paninaro', you were obsessed with designer clothing, western - and particularly British and American - music and the conspicuous consumption associated with Thatcherism and Reaganism. To begin with, the Paninari met in sandwich bars and burger joints.

slaving for low pay or subsisting on the dole had little appeal. They went to Tenerife in the winter and Ibiza in the summer, maybe with a stopover in Amsterdam.'

This network of young white working class grafters, including people from Sheffield, Manchester and Huddersfield, was well connected. Some had travelled further afield, discovering a little-known drug called MDMA on trips to San Francisco (the drug, later to be nicknamed ecstasy, had been popular in the Bay Area's world-renowned gay clubs) at the turn of the 1980s[10]. By the time people like Tony Canetti and his friends from Sheffield began making trips to Ibiza around 1984, MDMA had already reached the island.

'When they congregated in Ibiza they shared their swag, which was mostly clothing,' Luke Cowdrey says. 'Inevitably, there was also MDMA. So there was this weird melting pot of villains, grafters, sneak thieves and football hooligans, all dressing in a really bizarre way and arriving in Ibiza where, with a mixture of ecstasy and acid, a new scene was developing.'

This scene was centred on Amnesia, a club opened in the hippy-era that had previously been a hangout for the rich and beautiful. Most of those who initially went to dance at the open-air club to the sound of resident DJ Alfredo in 1984, '85 and '86 were Spanish or Italian, with the northern grafters and a handful of adventurous Londoners the only Brits on site. By the time more suburbanite Londoners began travelling to the island in 1987 - encouraged by British DJ Trevor Fung, who had set up a bar in San Antonio along with his cousin - Canetti and his cohorts from Sheffield and Manchester were an almost permanent fixture in Amnesia throughout the summer.

'As [DJ, cultural historian and early Ibiza regular] Nancy Noise has pointed out, those boys from Sheffield brought what we now know as the Balearic look to the island,' Luke Cowdrey says. 'This is three to four years before Acid House exploded in the UK in 1988. I'm also told that at Amnesia, a corner of the club was named after one of the boys from this Sheffield firm. A whole corner of the club!'

Of course, the MDMA-fuelled experiences of those British clubbers while dancing in Amnesia would have a profound effect on UK club culture. A handful of DJs - Nicky Holloway, Paul Oakenfold, Danny Rampling and Nancy Noise being the most famous examples - were inspired enough by their experiences in the summer of 1987 to return to the UK and put on events in London such as Shoom and Future[11].

---

10   For more details on the development of MDMA as a drug and its route into Ibiza and later the UK, see Chapter 1 of *Altered State*.
11   Future was one of Paul Oakenfold's key nights at Heaven. Alongside Shoom it promoted the "Balearic Beat" sound of the White Isle. Nancy Noise's reflected on her role in the event and the Ibiza story in a 2017 *Boy's Own* article (https://www.boysownproductions.com/zine/2017/4/17/future-perfect)

This motley crew of Brits, many of whom had come through the Jazz-Funk all-dayer scene, embraced Alfredo's unique musical approach - think contemporaneous House records mixed with off-kilter Pop records and throbbing European dance music - and began to popularize both the "Balearic Beat" and US House music in the capital city. By now, you should all know the story; it's been re-told in books and magazines and on television documentaries countless times.

What's not discussed quite so much is how the game-changing travelling grafters from the North of England were already familiar with House music. During the times they were in their home cities, they were regulars at key clubs in Sheffield and Manchester, where dressing differently and rocking your own look was par for the course.

'Jive Turkey was quite dressy, so I'd be borrowing shirts to get in,' Sheffield DJ Chris Duckenfield told journalist Bill Brewster in 2008[12]. 'It seemed odd to me that it was dressy and yet musical as well. I'd never seen that before: fashion and music. At House parties, people didn't really dress up.'

More importantly in the grand scheme of things, by 1987 the number of House records being played at underground Northern club nights dwarfed any other kind of music.

'Sheffield and Manchester by that point had a cockiness and confidence about the House sound which was already ingrained in our culture,' Luke Cowdrey says. 'When those Sheffield lads were going to Amnesia in Ibiza in 1986, they were already familiar with House. It was part of our culture - a continuation of the appreciation of weird electronic music that had been in the city's DNA since Cabaret Voltaire and the Human League started in the 1970s.'

It wasn't long after the Sheffield and Manchester contingents returned from Ibiza in 1987 that the first ecstasy tablets started appearing in the city's clubs. 'I remember when I was first offered 'X', as it was called then, at Jive Turkey,' Richard Barratt says. 'I asked this football lad who was offering them out how much they were. He said they were £25. I said, 'That's more than the weekly Giro cheque most of the people in here get!".'

Of course, the trickle of ecstasy pills into the UK would soon become a flood, fuelling the biggest cultural movement since the 1960s. 'MDMA changed everything,' Cowdrey says. 'There was a seismic shift in a story that had been developing for three years in the North and Midlands. Ecstasy was the Viagra of House music.'

* * *

---

12   Brewster, Bill: *Sheffield DJ Chris Duckenfield on Warp Records, Swag and "Killing Jive Turkey"*, Red Bull Music Academy Daily

It's hard to overstate the effect that ecstasy and House music had on clubs across the UK between 1988 and '92. It was just as keenly felt across the Midlands and North as it was elsewhere across the UK. It was particularly dramatic for those who had little interest in taking drugs and whose entry into the scene had been earlier in the decade via Electro, Hip-Hop or Jazz-dance.

'I remember the Warehouse being the stomping ground for the Hip-Hop heads in Leeds, but then we started noticing things like guys dancing with their tops off,' Paul Edmeade says. 'We didn't understand ecstasy and what it was doing to the scene to begin with. We genuinely didn't know why there were these guys were dancing with their shirts off.'

Ralph Lawson, then a student in Leeds with a passion for the Balearic House sound becoming popular in London, remembers there being a "changeover" point in mid-1988. 'It was an interesting moment because there were two sets of crews in the Warehouse and the DJs had to cater for both. There were still some Hip-Hop heads and serious dancers wanting to get a circle going when Hip-Hop tracks were played. At that point, the House heads would be standing around. They'd have taken a pill and wanted the music to go more up-tempo and electronic. So the DJs would play a couple of House tracks and then switch back. The two sets of people didn't mix that well, and it was obvious that there was going to be a split.'

The rise of Acid House culture in 1988 swept up people from many different social backgrounds. Perhaps the most significant change for the scene in the North and Midlands, though, was the sheer volume of students and white working class people - many of whom were part of that now celebrated sub-sect of House-loving football hooligans known as acid casuals - who were joining the scene-founding black dancers in the clubs.

'Acid House was so fresh and new when it broke and that excited all these kids, many of whom were on the dole,' says Leeds club promoter Tony Hannan. 'They were like, 'Wow, what is this?' Like me, they were looking for something to brighten up their lives other than going to football and fighting, which was a big part of youth culture in the 1980s.'

Hannan had been a trainee at Leeds United before he got into dance music via trips to the Haçienda in Manchester, down to Jive Turkey in Sheffield and to the Garage in Nottingham, where Graeme Park was still resident DJ. Hannan wanted somewhere closer to home where he and his friends could dance, so he joined forces with local DJ Mark Alexander and launched his own club night, Kaos.

'We started with a bank holiday party at Ricky's in August 1988,' Hannan says. 'It was mental - hot, sweaty and packed: a proper Acid House club. After about six months I decided to do a monthly Tuesday night at the Warehouse. Kaos ran for about two years there. That gave us the chance to bring in DJs like Paul Oakenfold, Sasha, Mike Pickering, Graeme Park and Brandon Block. As the Warehouse also had a stage, we got people such as Orbital and Dream Frequency in to do live PAs.'

Ever the entrepreneur, Hannan also threw some bigger parties at universities in Leeds and Bradford. When Acid House began to mutate further in 1991 with the onset of speedier Hardcore records, Hannan ended Kaos - via a 3,000 capacity blow out at the Gallery, the club that replaced the Coconut Grove and Ricky's in 'The Merrion Suite' of venues - and launched another, Soak, at the Corn Exchange.

'That was much more focused on good American House music,' he says. 'Creating a club on the ground floor of the Corn Exchange every Saturday was tricky. We had three hours after the shops closed to get everything in and set up before we started.'

If Kaos was the club that dragged many Leeds United supporters into Acid House culture, Joy played a similar role for many of the city's students. It too was on a Tuesday night at the Warehouse, thought its DJs were much more inspired by what was happening down in London. 'There was definitely a rivalry between Kaos and Joy,' says Ralph Lawson, who came on board as a resident DJ after meeting one of the men behind the party, Nick Saunders. 'Our crowd was much more student-heavy whereas theirs was all Leeds people. They were getting big names whereas we got slightly lesser-known people from London.'

Down the M1 in Sheffield, key local venue The Leadmill had jumped on the Acid House bandwagon by launching the Steamer, a midweek night whose resident DJ team included Haçienda hero Graeme Park. 'It was on a Wednesday night to begin with,' remembers long-serving Sheffield DJ Pipes. 'Graeme was technically a better DJ than anyone else we'd heard, certainly better than Parrot and Winston. He would use doubles to extend fast Hip-Hop tracks like Big Daddy Kane's "Long Live Kane".'

Despite the addition of new rival nights, Jive Turkey was still riding high. After a spell at the City Hall Ballroom, where they boasted one of the UK's only remaining dedicated Jazz rooms alongside the increasingly House and Techno-centric main room, Richard Barratt and Winston Hazel's night was back in familiar surroundings. What had previously been Mona Lisa's had now reopened as Occasions.

'People would say, 'I'm going [to] Occasions",' Pipes says. 'Later in the '80s and early '90s it got nuts in there. There would be like 700 or 800 people crammed into this 300 or 400 capacity venue. The music was always varied but when Acid House took hold, there would be more of that stuff. You knew there would be a section where they'd play fast Hip-Hop tracks or Rare Groove, before mixing back into the more minimal House and Techno tracks. The black footworkers would still be there, dancing to the 'heads down' footworking music. During those deeper House and Techno tracks your head would be down and you'd be focusing on dancing.'

As the years rolled by, competition for dancers in Sheffield got fiercer, with a new generation of DJs - Asterix and Space (AKA Chris Duckenfield and pal Richard Benson) - pushing heavy sounds from Europe and London (Hardcore Techno, basically) in clubs such as the Limit.

'When we got an opportunity to play there, The Limit was a Rock club,' Duckenfield told Bill Brewster. 'We played everything from Soul II Soul to Belgian New Beat to this week's new Detroit records with a lot of cheesy rave stuff thrown in. The night just went nuts, but it also crippled a little bit the comfy scene that was going on in Sheffield at that time in the late '80s and early '90s.'

Similar happened up in Leeds, where Orbit in Morley[13] dished up a diet of blistering UK, European and American Techno to a crowd who wanted it hard and fast. There were naturally those who kicked against it too, with Dave Beer, Ralph Lawson and the late Alistair Cooke launching the now legendary Back To Basics night in November 1991.

'That whole rave scene around Hardcore was disrespectful to me,' Beer says. 'We launched Back To Basics for people in long trousers and sensible shoes. It was for the more discerning clubber. I know that sounds a bit pompous and up its arse, but maybe we were. It struck a nerve with a lot of people who were feeling the same. We wanted a bit more quality from all angles, from the surroundings to the décor to how people were and how they looked.'

Beer would go on to become one of the most successful club promoters[14] and venue owners in the UK. So too would Leeds rival Tony Hannan, who joined forces with infamous DJ Brandon Block to launch Up Yer Ronson in 1992. In the years that followed, Back To Basics, Up Yer Ronson and another Leeds night, Hard Times, would help to kick-start the 'superclub era' of British clubbing, with the city they lived in being celebrated across Europe for the strength of its club scene[15].

* * *

In contrast, those in Sheffield didn't aim for a similar level of success, even if Jive Turkey did become a 'destination club' during its final years at the City Hall Ballroom in the early 1990s. They were far happier having a thriving underground scene with its own distinctive vibe.

---

13   The Orbit launched in 1991 and went on to become one of the key purist Techno nights in the UK for over 15 years. The music played by its resident DJs was far more intense than consistently found at other clubs in Yorkshire.
14   At one point, Mixmag dubbed Beer the "King of Clubs".
15   Leeds mid-1990s position as a clubbing hot-spot was helped by the local council's decision to allow venues to open until 6am as long as no alcohol was served after 2am (the time when most clubs across the UK had to close).

'In Sheffield, we celebrate the stoic and understated,' Luke Cowdrey explains. 'We didn't need the affirmation of Factory Records or media people in London. If you stuck your head above the parapet and shouted your mouth off, people thought you were a bit of a dick.'

Whereas the scenes in Nottingham, Manchester and Leeds were in looser, baggier and more loved-up in varying degrees, Sheffield's danced to a different groove. 'It was raw,' Luke Cowdrey says. 'A basement, a red light and a feeling. Detroit records, Chicago records - rough, uncompromising, drum-machine driven House and Techno. It was probably a lot more serious than what was going on elsewhere in many ways. Sheffield was very loyal to that sound and felt that the Balearic thing happening elsewhere was cheesy. It was pure energy. That was the sound, and it became a unique thing in the same way that Detroit had a distinctive sound.'

So distinctive was this sound, in fact, that Steel City dancefloors went off to a completely different set of peak-time anthems. 'At that time I was going over to Manchester a lot and I didn't realize at the time that a lot of the stuff played in Sheffield was very much just Sheffield stuff,' Chris Duckenfield explained to Bill Brewster. 'Parrot and Winston would pick up on tracks and make them big where they weren't really big anywhere else, which fascinated me.'

This distinctive Sheffield sound was particularly prevalent in the events that took place outside of regular club venues. There was a thriving warehouse party scene in the lower Don Valley, right in the heart of the city's once-mighty steelmaking district. 'These parties were called Hush Hush,' Duckenfield explained. 'Parrot and Winston would play in these disused warehouses. Because of the environment they felt a little bit off the leash as DJs, so they'd go a little more wild [musically] than they would in the clubs.'

Sheffield also boasted a number of Acid Blues: Reggae style all-night venues that kicked off when clubs shut at 2am. The two key Acid Blues were CJ's in Broomhall and Donkey Man's in Pitsmoor. 'They were dark, sweaty, hot and raw,' Pipes remembers. 'You never went alone, and you'd be looking over your shoulder a lot of the time. You had to keep your wits about you. CJ's had a fairly loose policy about who would DJ. If you turned up with your crate of records, they'd let you do an hour or whatever.'

Musically, these after-hours Acid Blues reflected the raw, stripped-back heaviness that marked out the developing Sheffield club sound. 'As the story progressed, places like CJ's and Donkey Man's had DJs who played that hyper-Hardcore sound that me and Wini weren't really into,' Richard Barratt says. 'They had people like Asterix and Space and Easy D playing those sorts of records. Hardcore certainly wasn't non-existent in Sheffield.'

Given their illicit, unlicensed nature and the money to be made from drug dealing, these Acid Blues often attracted some shady characters including members of rival gangs. This led to some pretty hairy moments. One night Barratt was DJing at Donkey Man's when an infamous local character pointed a gun at him.

'Somebody had been shot at CJ's with the same gun a couple of weeks before,' he remembers. 'I just started hearing these bangs, looked up from the decks and this psychopath was blasting plaster off the walls with a sawn-off shotgun. It was getting late - or early, depending on the way you look at it - and there weren't many people there so I thought I'd stop playing. Next thing I know he's by the decks. He said, 'Paz, play another record'. He opened up his coat, and there was the sawn-off shotgun pointing at me. I didn't think he wanted to shoot me, but I was a bit worried about it accidentally going off because I knew it was loaded. So I said, 'Yes Kenny,' and put another record on!'

Two weeks later, the local 'psychopath' in question used the very same gun to shoot someone in the face outside another Sheffield Blues. 'It was a proper manhunt,' Barratt remembers. 'It was on the front of the Sheffield Star every day for weeks. Eventually, they caught him. The thing is, that argument wasn't about drugs or dealing - it was something trivial that got out of hand. You just couldn't reason with this guy.'

* * *

If anything, Chapeltown in Leeds had an even worse reputation for gang-related violence than Sheffield's Pitsmoor or Burngreave. In fact, so bad was its reputation in the late '80s and early '90s that students were advised not to venture there at all. For those who were interested in underground dance music, like Ralph Lawson, this was rather difficult. After all, by 1989 the Astoria on Chapeltown Road was home to a number of the city's leading Acid House events.

'It was crazy at that point because we'd had a write-up in *i-D* as one of the North's best club events,' says Drew Hemment, a friend of Ralph Lawson who was quickly becoming one of Chapeltown's most prolific DJs. 'We had big numbers and it was a big rave - the whole thing was just mental. I remember crazy things, like getting my records out of the car outside and 12 guys pulling knives on me. I had knives to my throat and my records disappeared. We had a warehouse party later that night, so I went down there totally distraught. When I got there, I found that one of the local junkies who used to be at the back of the room during the Blues I DJed at had fought off four people and carried my records to the warehouse party. Stuff like that happened all the time.'

Hemment was by then a recognizable figure in Chapeltown as resident DJ at Twilight, a Thursday, Friday and Saturday night Acid Blues that utilized numerous locations across the notorious inner-city suburb. Twilight was initially set-up by local soundsystem crew Jungle Warrior - the very same outfit who had previously been critical of Mark Millington's efforts to play House during his Ital Rockers events at the Hayfield Hotel - and DJ Mikey Luton. When Luton fell out with Jungle Warrior and set up a rival Acid Blues at the previously Reggae-only Sonny's, Martin Williams (DJ Martin) and Drew Hemment (DJ Drew) took their place behind the decks. Williams lasted two or three nights before handing the reins to Hemment for good.

'While I was doing Twilight we went through dozens of houses,' Hemment remembers. 'There would be times when we would cruise around, find an empty house and break into it on a Friday afternoon. We could then set it up for the weekend. We also had a couple of long residencies in the same house. Every place we used was seedy as fuck.'

One of these long residencies was at a place on Francis Street opposite the Phoenix club. 'You'd go into this house and the living room was stripped back to bare floorboards,' Ralph Lawson remembers. 'There were decks and a big, stacked soundsystem at one end. It was Jungle Warrior's Reggae sound that was used in Twilight. The guys running it were Dub guys who had cottoned on quite early that House music was becoming big. The sound was set up to play Reggae music, which meant big bass cabinets and a sound EQed for bass-heavy music. What you were feeling when you were in there was bass.'

Hemment played a mixture of Belgian New Beat, Acid tracks, Chicago House and what Lawson refers to as 'orbital rave music' - breakbeat-driven Hardcore tracks and piano-heavy House anthems that were big at the infamous illegal raves that took place in locations just off the M25.

'My background was Hip-Hop and I loved beats and basslines,' Hemment admits. 'To me, there were a lot of touchpoints between Hip-Hop and the breakbeat heavy UK records of the period. I'd play right through the night and into the morning, sometimes until lunchtime. At that point the hookers would show up to take over the house during the day. We'd have nothing to do with them, but it was like a change of shift.'

A similar blend of bass-heavy House, Techno and Breakbeat Hardcore was all the rage at Sonny's, where Mikey Luton, George 'E.A.S.E' Evelyn, Christian Cawood and Kevin 'Boy Wonder' Harper were regular DJs. 'It became one of the key after-hours spots,' Evelyn says. 'I ended up playing at Sonny's for almost two years, and it became the main lynchpin of the underground in Leeds. At the same time as I was doing that and playing Italian House, Breakbeat hardcore, rave records and local stuff, the illegal raves were happening over the Pennines in Blackburn. To me, Blackburn was the epicentre of that illegal rave thing up North.'

The increasing importance of the unlicensed, illicit rave scene did have an adverse effect on the numbers of dancers heading to the Acid Blues. If something was happening in Yorkshire or Lancashire, dancers were drawn to that rather than the local Blues.

'There came a point, maybe around the end of 1989, when many of my regulars weren't coming down on a Saturday night,' Hemment admits. 'They told me they were going to these raves in Blackburn. So one night I made a call to close Twilight so we could all drive over the Pennines to one of these raves. I rocked up to the party with a bag of records and said, "I'm Leeds, are you going to let me on?" Amazingly, they did.'

By his own admission, Hemment got 'swept up' in the illegal rave circuit, becoming increasingly active on the scene. His initial involvement was as a DJ, but he quickly became embroiled in the organizational side as well. It was at a time when anti-rave hysteria in the tabloid press was reaching its peak and the Conservative government was instructing local police forces to squash the growing free party movement.

'It was wild for a period before the police cracked down hard,' Hemment says. 'The town of Blackburn went wild and the police couldn't control it or contain it. It was beyond the rule of law. Then the police cracked down massively and there were huge riots. There was one at Nelson where the police burst in and kicked the shit out of everyone.'

The warehouse party at Nelson, to the north of Burnley, was the biggest one yet attempted by Tommy Smith and Tony Cleft. They'd initially started small by taking over a club in Blackburn in late 1988 and running an after-party in an abandoned building. By the time they saw 10,000 people squeeze into the warehouse in Nelson on 24 February 1990, they'd run scores of events around the area, with attendances growing by hundreds or thousands at each successive rave. Their parties had become so successful, in fact, that they'd become a target for gangs of organized criminals from Scotland, Liverpool and Manchester.

'It all went dark and a lot of gangster stuff started happening,' Hemment sighs. 'A lot of us involved in the Blackburn and West Yorkshire raves were idealistic - we felt like we were changing the world and caught in this very special, incredible moment. But behind the scenes, there were a lot of people making a lot of money.'

The Nelson rave fell a few short weeks after the Lancashire Evening Telegraph had begun a campaign to rid the North West of raves. When the night came, the police were ready, with over 200 officers in riot gear ready to descend on the location. 'I was sitting on the roof taking in the beauty of it all when I spotted a blue wave coming in,' Smith told Matthew Collin in *Altered State*. 'When I looked closer it was a wave of shiny blue riot helmets. They waded into everyone.'

With Greater Manchester Police determined to arrest and imprison those behind the raves, Smith and Croft headed over to their friend Drew Hemment's territory in West Yorkshire. In early July, following the high profile raid on a rave beneath a motorway bridge near Wakefield a few weeks earlier[16], Hemment made his move. 'The rave was called B-Rave New World and it took place at this horse riding place north of Leeds,' he says. 'We got the crowd there but the police were waiting for us. When we arrived, we basically charged the police out of there. They took my decks, so I got a lift into town and picked up replacements. Once we brought them back and got the music going, the crowd went mental!'

It was less than two weeks later when Smith put on his first big rave in West Yorkshire. It was called Love Decade and took place just outside of Gildersome, a picturesque village to the South West of Leeds. 'It was carnage,' he says. 'That's where the police really cracked down hard. There was fighting like you wouldn't believe and one of the biggest mass arrests in British legal history.'

In total, the police arrested 836 ravers that day, though only eight were ever charged with offences. Almost as many were injured in the melee. The incident became so infamous that it featured prominently in a feature in *The Face* written by local dance music journalist Vaughan Allen[17]; initially, he'd just been commissioned to write about Yorkshire's vibrant club scene and the growing number of local producers who were championing the thrilling Bleep & Bass sound.

Dave Beer is another with vivid memories of the events at Gildersome. 'By the time we got to Gildersome we'd already had serious trouble at Nelson near Manchester,' he says. 'It was horrible because the police were dealing with us just like the miners in the Miners Strike. They were blatantly attacking all of the partygoers. Everyone was pilled-up and loved-up and just wanted to dance. I remember seeing the police coming down the hill like Romans, banging their shields and coming down in groups, wading in with truncheons and just hitting everyone. It was absolutely crazy but nobody was moving. People were just going, 'Fuck it - we're not moving. We've got nowhere to go. What are you going to do about it?' The police had other ideas.'

---

16   According to Vaughan Allen's feature on the 'Yorkshire House sound' in the October 1990 edition of *The Face*, there were 231 arrests at the Horbury Lagoon rave near Wakefield. 224 of these people were released without charge. Amusingly, one of those arrested was an off duty police officer from Bradford.

17   Allen cut his teeth on *Leeds Student* while at university, where future Select magazine Editor Andrew Harrison encouraged him to do a series of big articles on the importance of Acid House in 1988. He later became *i-D* magazine's Yorkshire correspondent, writing numerous articles on early Bleep pioneers. In fact, he wrote more about the sound at the time than any other journalist.

In hindsight, the response of the authorities to raves was extremely heavy-handed, particularly considering that most who've ingested MDMA are less likely to cause trouble than those who've been sniffing cocaine or heavily drinking. In the years that followed, the government's response to raves would only get harsher[18], though it was still pretty heavy in 1989 and 1990. For those involved, a police raid on a party could be a frightening experience.

George Evelyn remembers one particular rave in Blackburn where the police prepared for a raid by cutting off the power and blocking off the only exit - a small doorway at one side of the building. Pandemonium followed. 'The first thing I remember is the weight hitting my chest as the crowd surged forwards,' Evelyn says. 'Someone climbed up into the rafters and somehow managed to get the metal shutters of this warehouse up. As we all ran out, I remember thinking, "just don't fall," because it wasn't that long after the Hillsborough disaster. As we ran out, the police were trying to stop people with their shields. We managed to burst through and run up this hill. It was scary, man. The police were so ready for this rave - they came in big numbers to crack heads. It just shows that the government aren't about understanding things - they're just about the force of the law and that can be dangerous.'

---

18   The UK government first legislated against raves via a private members bill introduced by Conservative MP Graham Bright in March 1990. Although officially titled the Entertainments (Increased Penalties) Bill, it was often referred to in the press as the "Acid House parties bill". It was passed in July 1990, eight days before the Gildersome rave. The government further tightened legislation against free parties and raves via the more famous Criminal Justice and Public Order Act of 1994. Its strict definition of a rave (a gathering of 100 or more people with the intent to dance to 'music with repetitive beats') was strict and inspired countless protests and demonstrations from within the UK dance music community.

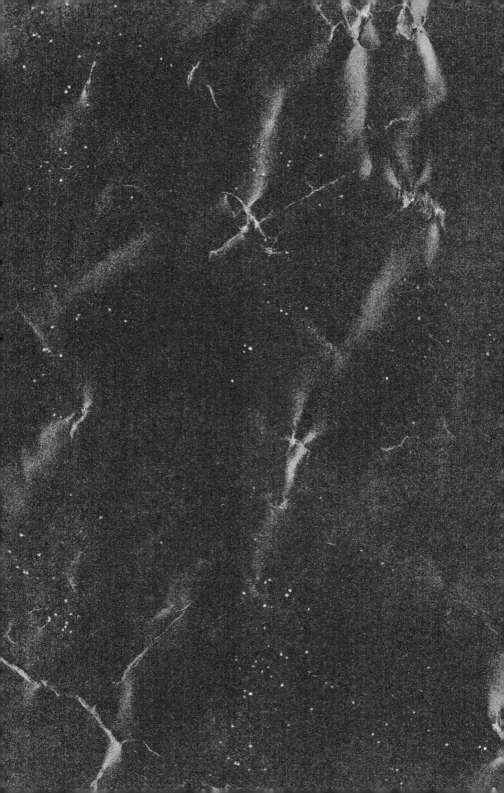

PART TWO

PIONEERS OF THE HYPNOTIC GROOVE

'Bleep records sounded like nothing else and they were uniquely British. They had a funkiness that came from Electro, as well as the influence from Detroit Techno, but they were totally unique thanks to the inspiration that came from Dub. Bleep & Bass was like nothing else, and it was ours.'

RICHARD SEN

BLOW YOUR HOUSE DOWN

A GUY CALLED GERALD AND THE TRANS-PENNINE EXPRESS

'There was a real connection with Sheffield.
You felt this trans-Pennine thing [was going on].
We used to drive over the Snake Pass a
lot to go to parties or work in the studios.'

GRAHAM MASSEY 808 State

Zigzagging its way over the 500-metre High Peak hills that separate Glossop to the West and Ladybower Reservoir to the East, the Snake Pass is one of Northern England's most dramatic roads. Renowned for its inclement weather and frequent winter closures, the road has been one of the key arterial roots between Lancashire, South Yorkshire and the North East Midlands for centuries.

Close to the road's highest point is a small lay-by; a patch of gravel just big enough to accommodate a couple of cars. Pull over here while driving in a westerly direction and you're greeted with the kind of astounding views that take the breath away. On a clear day, you can see far further than the town of Glossop in the near distance, its limestone cottages and former cotton mills dwarfed by the seemingly endless sprawl of Greater Manchester further to the west.

CHAPTER FIVE

^ A GUY CALLED GERALD

The road's popularity as a trans-Pennine route has little to do with this stunning vista though, but rather its relatively short length. The Pass itself is barely 15 miles long, though traversing its blind summits and hairpin bends seems to take an eternity. At night, when the headlights of approaching cars dazzle around each tight corner, driving becomes an especially hazardous occupation.

Despite its reputation as an accident blackspot, the Snake provides the shortest route between Sheffield and Manchester[1]. During the 1980s it was a vital connector of the growing club scenes in these two very different cities: the immigrant-embracing workhouse of the world to the west and the belligerent, staunchly socialist Steel City to the east.

To begin with, the trans-Pennine travellers were the Jazz-dancers and footworkers[2], alongside a smattering of Yorkshire DJs drawn to the greater availability of obscure import records in key North West record shops[3]. Later, it was young Acid House evangelists heading to jack at Jive Turkey or take in the life-changing atmosphere of Manchester's most infamous venue, The Haçienda.

Quite a lot of rubbish has been written about the Haçienda over the years, but there's no doubt that it played an important role in the North's dance music story. Before the onset of Acid House's Second Summer of Love in 1988 and the media-promoted Madchester movement that followed, the core crowd at The Haçienda's sometimes sparsely attended club nights included some of the city's best footworkers and Jazz dancers. They initially attended to dance to the heavy sounds provided by Hewan Clarke, a popular DJ who also made regular appearances at Berlin, Legends, the Gallery and Blues-style after-hours spot the Reno, but decided to stick around when he left and a new set of resident DJs took over.

They were particularly prominent on the dancefloor in the first few years of Nude, The Haçienda's Friday dance party helmed by resident DJs Mike Pickering and Martin Prendergast. The most visible of all was Samson, the de facto leader of Foot Patrol - a zoot suit-sporting collective who earned the reputation of being one of the UK's leading Jazz-dance collectives during the period. They later made multiple TV appearances showcasing their impressive moves, but in 1985, '86 and '87 were more often dominating the

---

1   Those living to the north of Sheffield could traverse the Woodhead Pass, the main signposted route between the two cities, while inhabitants of West Yorkshire would use the M62.
2   These would travel anywhere across the North to dance, though the North West scene, where DJs such as Colin Curtis and Hewan Clarke provided the soundtrack at a network of small clubs dotted around Greater Manchester and Merseyside, was the strongest of all.
3   After picking up records in Liverpool, record distributors' "import vans" would first visit Hot Wax in Newton-Le-Willows, a store owned by key local DJ and collector, Kev Edwards, before visiting Spin Inn and Eastern Bloc in Manchester and travelling onwards to Sheffield. Winston Hazel remembers making early morning trips to Hot Wax in order to get "first dibs" on imports fresh off the van.

dancefloors of underground black clubs like the Playpen: the venue where Colin Curtis and Greg Wilson claim that House music was played for the very first time in Manchester[4].

'When I arrived in Manchester, I went to Berlins to hear Colin Curtis and Hewan Clarke, and to the Playpen for Stu Allan's sets,' Luke Cowdrey says. 'That's where you'd see the likes of Foot Patrol dancing to both Jazz records and House records. Between Colin, Stu Allan and Mike Shaft, I was hearing all of the important records from the Jazz-Funk and House scenes.'

Greg Wilson, who had stepped away from DJing to pursue a production and management career in 1984, believes that it was Foot Patrol that helped popularize dancing to House within the Jazz-dance community.

'Look at the video footage of them dancing at the Mastermind Roadshow in Moss Side in 1986,' he asserts. 'It was Foot Patrol who put the kind of fusion style of dancing to House music. That was the original way that House was danced to before everyone was herded together on the dancefloor. Mike Pickering says that the most precious times he had at The Haçienda were between 1986 and '88 when he was playing Electro, Hip-Hop, House and Street Soul all together on one night. That was when the serious black dancers were still there.'

As ecstasy began sweeping through Manchester in 1988, Foot Patrol and their Jazz-dance contemporaries became marginal figures on the dancefloor. Ironically, the death of their dancefloor dominance was caused, in part at least, by a groundbreaking, scene-shifting record made by one of their friends.

● ● ●

One Sunday night in early 1988, Aniff Akinola was sat in his Manchester home listening to Stu Allan's popular radio show on Piccadilly 261[5]. Like the dancers who flocked to the Playpen when he DJed, Allan had been an early adopter of both Hip-Hop and House music. By the time Akinola tuned in on this particular Sunday in 1988, Allan had finished his Hip-Hop hour and was midway through a 60-minute mix of new House tracks.

'I knew Stu quite well at that time,' Akinola remembers. 'I often used to go down to the station while he was doing his show and bully him about playing crap records. He played some brilliant music, but some crap too. I thought he often missed the good ones.'

---

4   The pair made the claim in an online documentary entitled "Return To Legend", which can be watched on YouTube (https://youtu.be/lzmEEv3DW7M)

5   Allan inherited the Piccadilly 261 show from another important Manchester DJ and a friend of Akinola's, Mike Shaft.

Allan was undoubtedly an influential figure within the Manchester scene. Alongside Simon Barker on Radio Lancashire[6], he was one of the few radio DJs who pushed the latest cutting-edge American dance records. Crucially, Allan was also open to playing demo recordings submitted by listeners, giving over a portion of his broadcast to showcase these unsigned sounds.

Akinola always listened to this particular part of the show intently. He was a producer himself and had recently been recruited by local Indie-Rock imprint Skysaw Records to help launch a new sub-label that would tap into the North West's growing club scene. While Skysaw's owners saw the freshly minted Rham! Records as being an outlet for Hip-Hop, Akinola and his Chapter production partner Colin Thorpe had other ideas.

'Because we were so interested in Mantronix, we wanted to make Electro tunes,' Thorpe says. 'Electronic Soul was the thing - hard bottom, soft top. You know, crunching low-end with sweetness on top. Happily, the guys from Skysaw went along with it.'

There was already a Chapter & Verse[7] record in the works, but Rham! Records needed more material. So when Stu Allan began his famous demo section, Akinola was listening intently. It wasn't long before something caught his ear: a loose, alien-sounding, Electro-influenced track that Allan had introduced as an Acid House track made by someone calling himself "Housemaster G".

As the track's clanking bassline and intricately programmed drums crackled across the airwaves, Akinola got progressively more excited. 'I thought, "What the fuck is this?" I jumped on my bike and rode straight down to the studio,' he remembers. 'I knocked on the door and Stu let me in.'

Once inside the studio, Akinola demanded to know more about this tape played by Housemaster G. 'Stu said to me, "That track's alright". So I said to him, 'Give it to me!" He handed over the tape. Luckily, there was a phone number scribbled on the inlay.'

He called the number and arranged to meet the tape's creator a couple of days later at a house in Moss Side. When he arrived, he was shocked to be greeted by a face he recognized from the local club scene: a 21-year-old dancer called Gerald Simpson.

● ● ●

---

6   Barker's show was called On The Wire. It featured a heavily electronic, mostly British mix of new music. During the mid to late 1980s, there were a number of spin-off On The Wire events at the Ritz on Whitworth Street West. These featured live performances from acts including Tackhead Soundsystem, A Guy Called Gerald, 808 State and, on one famous occasion, a heavily pregnant Neneh Cherry.

7   Thorpe and Akinola were "Chapter", with "Verse" being their vocalists, Debbie Sanders and Paulette Blake. The quartet released seven singles and two albums between 1988 and 92.

Like so many of his generation, Gerald Simpson was turned on to the possibilities of music and sound before he'd even reached his teens. Born to Jamaican parents and raised amidst the council estates of Moss Side, Simpson's early musical experiences revolved around Sunday gospel sessions at a local church, and the vibrant soundsystem culture that had been ever-present in the neighbourhood for decades.

'I grew up in a really diverse place, but it was really safe,' he told *Sound on Sound* magazine in the summer of 2015. 'If someone had a party, you'd be able to hear it and go over [to their house]. There would be a soundsystem playing and you could just kind of hang out. The sounds were pretty powerful and they were all homemade. People built their own amps and speakers and I found that interesting. I wanted to be part of it.'

This interest in sound, speakers and electronics led the youngster to try and create his own soundsystem by connecting speakers together. 'Somehow I acquired a load of car speakers,' he explained to Bill Brewster[8] in 2003. 'One thing I noticed is that the more speakers I connected together, the quieter it got. I also used to do crazy stuff like pull things apart. When I was quite young, if I couldn't unscrew something, I'd put a knife in the fire and then melt the plastic off it.'

When Simpson later acquired a bass guitar and amplifier as a teenager, he disassembled the amp, studied how it worked and then re-built it with a 'little reverb' inside. Given this interest in electronics, it was perhaps unsurprising that Electrofunk and Hip-Hop hit him hard when the records first started appearing in the early 1980s.

'There was a bloke who would come into school with a ghetto blaster and sell tapes,' Simpson told *Sound on Sound*[9]. 'Later on, he started an Electrofunk soundsystem. Anything electronic like that used to make my ears prick up, so I wanted to get one of these drum machines. Everyone was getting into records and stuff, and I was like, "Nah, I want that machine that makes them beats". I wanted to do it myself.'

While daydreaming about acquiring a drum machine, Simpson explored his other growing passion: dancing to Electro and Jazz-Funk. His first experiences on the dancefloor were at youth clubs dotted around Manchester, where Hewan Clarke was amongst the DJs. He saw with his own eyes the miraculous moves and dazzling shapes thrown by local dance troupe the Jazz Defektors; naturally, he wanted to follow in their footsteps.

'The Jazz Defektors were a big thing for us, and we used to follow them around in a way,' Simpson explained to Brewster. 'There were other crews as well and they were more important to us than the DJs. I mean, we knew

---

8   Fully credited, this unpublished interview formed the basis of a feature I wrote for Red Bull Music Academy Daily in 2017 (https://daily.redbullmusicacademy.com/2017/02/guy-called-gerald-voodoo-ray-feature).

9   Doyle, Tom: Classic Tracks: A Guy Called Gerald – Voodoo Ray, *Sound on Sound*, July 2015.

Hewan and Colin Curtis and it was a really big thing if they came into Spin Inn [while we were there]. We'd look at what they were buying and dream of owning these Japanese Jazz fusion imports they were getting.'

Such was Simpson's love of dancing that he went on to get formal dance training as a teenager. 'I learned contemporary, Jazz and classical,' he explained to *Sound on Sound*. 'It was really interesting for me because it made a connection between movement and sound.'

When he started making music as a teenager, it was inevitably aimed at dancers. 'The training made it easier for me because I wanted to make stuff that people would wanna dance to,' he said. 'It's almost like synesthesia where you see colours to music - you can see colours to a sound. While I'm making music I'm thinking of movements all the time.'

By this point, Simpson had saved up enough to get his first little drum machine, a cheap and cheerful Boss Dr Rhythm DR55 with four pre-set percussion sounds. It was enough to create little jams with his bass guitar, but naturally, he wanted more; while others in his peer group daydreamed of acquiring records, Simpson made trips to second-hand equipment stores Johnny Roadhouse and A1 Music to ogle Roland drum machines and synthesizers. Thanks to shifts at McDonald's after he left school, he was finally able to afford a TR-808 - the drum machine that defined Electro and Hip-Hop in the period - in 1986. He was on his way.

• • •

When Aniff Akinola stepped into Simpson's mother's house in early 1988, "Housemaster G" had his collection of second-hand Roland machines set-up on the kitchen table. The 808 took pride of place, alongside a Tascam four-track tape recorder, a TB-303 bass synthesizer - the machine Chicago act Phuture used to create the wild and mind-altering that would become the defining feature of jacking Acid House records - and two SH-101 monophonic synthesizers[10]. While this small collection of kit was enough to create raw Hip-Hop, Electro and House tracks, you could hardly call it advanced.

Nevertheless, it was this set-up that helped Simpson get noticed - not just by Akinola but also by others in the Manchester scene. Determined to do something with his music, he regularly headed to local record shops to drop off tapes. 'I'd go into Eastern Bloc and I'd be saying to the guys behind the counter, "I've got all these machines that make music",' he said to *Sound on Sound*. 'They were like, "Yeah yeah". So I played them one of my tapes and they said, "You do this yourself? We've got a basement downstairs you can use".'

---

10   Monophonic synthesizers are so called because they can only play one note or sound at once. Polyphonic synthesizers can reproduce multiple sounds at once, allowing the musician to play chords, or basslines and lead lines simultaneously.

This connection led Simpson to start working on tracks with the shop's owner, Martin Price, local DJ (and warehouse party promoter) Andy Barker and Graham Massey, a trainee studio engineer better known for his role in Factory Records signed outfit Biting Tongues[11].

'There were all these kids that came into Eastern Bloc on a Saturday,' Massey remembers. 'At the time we all wanted to make Hip-Hop tracks. Andy [Barker], Darren [Partington] and Shine MC were one group, Spin-masters. Gerald and MC Tunes were Scratch Beatmasters[12], and then Andy, Gerald, Martin and me would jam as The Hit Squad MCR. There was also another group, Shine Four. We used to put on gigs at the Boardwalk with Ruthless Rap Assassins. They were a cut above everyone else really.'

While there was a record showcasing these acts[13], funded by 'asking one of the Eastern Bloc staff members to raid their Burnley Building Society account', it was the Acid House jams they'd do at the end of their late-night studio sessions that offered a glimpse of things to come.

'Although we were making Hip-Hop, between us we had the equipment to make Acid tracks, including a TB-303,' Massey remembers. 'Once we put that one record out, we'd use any spare bits of time to make tracks - Acid jams done in Gerald's loft or at studios when we had a little bit of spare time.'

As a result of these sessions, 808 State was born. Initially comprised of Massey, Martin Price, Andy Barker and Gerald Simpson, the outfit debuted with the wild and heavy 12" single "Let Yourself Go" - a thunderous fusion of layered Latin percussion[14], raging TB-303 acid lines and some suitably solid samples. Far-sighted debut album "Newbuild" quickly followed[15]; while it was not a runaway success at the time, the LP hit hard on the other side of the Pennines and remains one of the purest expressions of Chicago style Acid House ever created in the UK.

---

11   Massey joined Biting Tongues as a guitarist in 1980 and remained with the ever-changing collective until 1989, when they finally disbanded.
12   Simpson and MC Tunes (real name Nicky Lockett) initially started the project as a soundsystem and turntablist style DJ duo earlier in the decade.
13   Entitled "Wax On The Melt", the three-track, white label EP featured a cut-and-paste, sample-heavy Hip-Hop cut by Hit Squad MCR called "Line Of Madness", the beatbox Hip-Hop slammer "Only The Dope" by the Shure Four and Gerald and MC Tunes' heavy, Electro-influenced "Back To Attack".
14   "Let Yourself Go" was made in the wake of Manchester's first local House anthem, T-Coy's Latin Jazz-influenced "Carino". T-Coy was comprised of Mike Pickering, his sometime Quando Quango bandmate Simon Topping and keyboardist Ritchie Close. The band's Latin-influenced output was particularly popular with Foot Patrol and other local Jazz-dance crews.
15   According to Massey and Barker, "Newbuild" was recorded in a weekend.

Simpson continued jamming with 808 State throughout 1988, contributing drum programming to what would become one of British dance music's most enduring, end-of-night anthems, "Pacific State[16]". Yet by the time it became a huge hit in 1989 on the back of its appearance on the "Quadrastate EP", Simpson had cut his ties with Massey, Price and Barker.

'People say he left the band and went solo, but that's not accurate,' Massey says. 'He didn't go solo because he was always solo. If you know Gerald, you know he was always autonomous - in those early days the group was quite casual, and different people would be involved at different times. When we did gigs, who would be on stage performing as 808 State depending on who was around on the day.'

* * *

While all this was taking shape, Aniff Akinola and production partner Colin Thorpe[17] were rushing to get Simpson into the studio. By now, the young producer had provided Akinola with more demo tapes. One track particularly caught Akinola's ear. 'Most of Gerald's tapes were long, continuous improvised jams, but the second tape he played had four or five separate demos on it including the basis of "Voodoo Ray",' he remembers. 'There was just a bassline and some beats and little else, but I knew that had to be one of the tracks we made in the studio.'

In May 1988, Akinola, Thorpe and Simpson assembled in Moonraker, a studio owned by folk musician Mike Harding, and got to work. In attendance was engineer Lee Monteverde, whose obsession with clean-sounding dance-pop songs from the likes of Madonna and the Pet Shop Boys would play a significant role in the way the tracks turned out.

'He really showed me how to get clarity in things and how to record properly,' Simpson explained to *Sound on Sound*. 'We made sure that any of the stuff that was down on tape didn't have any noise on it. I wanted everything to be clean, and the space around it to be clean, so that when it came to doing the stereo imaging, everything was clean and in its own space.'

Simpson brought his machines into the studio so he could use the previously programmed parts. He'd already been experimenting at home with layering up SH-101 parts on his Tascam four-track, so was excited by the opportunity to do this further using the studio's professional 16-track mixing desk.

---

16   When "Pacific State" was released, Gerald Simpson was not initially credited as one of the writers despite the drum programming carrying his distinctive, Electro and Jazz-Funk influenced swing. It resulted in a bitter legal battle, initiated by Simpson and his manager, which resulted in the credits being amended on later releases and reissues.
17   The two first met at Berlin in 1986 and were introduced by mutual friend Colin Curtis. He believed dancer and music obsessive Akinola would make good music with aspiring producer Thorpe.

'I wanted to create a tapestry on tape,' he explained. 'By using two SH-101s I was trying to do something I was later told is called "heterodyning", which is where you use two tones to create a third imaginary tone. It's like an audio illusion, with almost a metallic sound coming from it in some places.'

Thorpe and Akinola were pleased with how the groove-based track was shaping up but felt it needed something else. In collaboration with Simpson, they came up with two innovations that would take "Voodoo Ray" to the next level. First was sampling up two quick snatches of dialogue contained on one of the spoken word records Simpson had brought with him: a Peter Cook and Dudley Moore comedy album. One featured Cook saying 'voodoo rage', the other Moore shouting, 'later'.

'Neither me or Lee [Monteverde] knew how the AKAI S-950 sampler I'd borrowed worked,' Thorpe laughs. 'So when we were getting it into the sampler Lee accidentally cut off the end, so "rage" became "ray". We thought, "Actually, that sounds even cooler".'

The other innovation was to utilize a vocalist they'd been working with on Electro-Soul tunes, a local singer called Nicola Collier. 'She really didn't like House,' Akinola remembers. 'We weren't getting much out of her, and her relationship with Gerald was a bit terse anyway. I went to the toilet and left them to it. While I was in there I had an idea for this vocal melody she could sing, so rushed back into the studio, sung it to her and jumped back on the mixing desk. Because of the tone of Nicola's voice, it just worked.'

According to Thorpe, Simpson wasn't keen on the vocal but went along with it. Once they'd laid the vocal refrain down, it was chopped up and loaded into the sampler. 'The S-950 had a button on it that said "reverse", so we pressed that and it sounded good,' Thorpe says. 'None of us knew how to program the S-950, so Gerald sat there pressing the button all the way through it, so that's where the stab pattern comes from. The whole record is basically just a series of experiments.'

Mixed live by Simpson - 'We went outside and kicked a football around in the car park, then went we went back inside he and Lee had completed six different mixes[18]' - the resultant track was hypnotic, spellbinding, intoxicating and like no Acid House record ever made before.

31 years after it was completed, "Voodoo Ray" remains an astonishing record. Propelled forwards by weighty 808 kick-drums and clicking percussive patterns influenced by Simpson's love of Jazz-Funk, Electro and Latin Jazz, the track's sharp TB-303 acid lines twist and turn around a clanking, metallic bassline. The now instantly recognizable vocal elements, progressively

---

18   Akinola claims to still have this tape in his possession; amongst the six versions is an instrumental mix without Collier's vocal or the Pete and Dud samples.

layered to increase the density and intensity, are in turns beguiling, haunting and euphoric. It may now be one of the most recognizable House records ever made, but the track has lost none of its charm or power.

Three other tracks were completed during the Moonraker sessions, making up a four-track EP that has held up remarkably well. These are similarly weighty, inspired and off-kilter, particularly the jacking "Escape" and sleazy, Foot Patrol-friendly "Blow Your House Down". It's a testament to Simpson's skill, and the assistance he received from the slightly more experienced Akinola and Thorpe, that his unique vision was realized so impressively.

Interestingly, Akinola says that while they were convinced of the EP's quality - and particularly the greatness of "Voodoo Ray" - they were initially in the minority. 'I knew very early on that it was a brilliant record, but we soon found out that not many other people liked it,' Thorpe says. 'A lot of DJs who got it early said that it was too "British" - the fact that it didn't sound like it came from Chicago and Detroit was a problem for them.'

When the test pressings of the record arrived in Manchester a few weeks later, Akinola gave copies to Hewan Clarke, Colin Curtis, Mike Shaft and Mike Pickering. Simpson had already done his bit by taking the first acetate down to Legend and The Haçienda to get it tested out over the soundsystems.

'The first time I heard it at The Haçienda, it really blew me away,' Simpson told *Sound on Sound*. 'What interested me was that compared to a lot of the stuff around at the time, the bass was more protrusive.'

• • •

It would take some time before Britain fell under the spell of "Voodoo Ray"[19], despite the first 500 white label copies selling out in under a day[20]. It naturally got support from some key DJs in Manchester, eventually becoming a chant-along anthem at The Haçienda. In some ways, that was rather fitting; after all, it was the Jazz dancers and footworkers who first inspired the venue's DJs to play House records.

'A lot of people assume that Gerald was influenced by The Haçienda and that he had some great conversion to House after visiting this great cathedral of dance music,' Greg Wilson says. 'In reality, it was Gerald and his contemporaries that brought House music to the Haçienda in the first place.

---

19   "Voodoo Ray" peaked at number 12 in the charts in the summer of 1989.
20   It was June 1988 when the first copies hit Spin Inn. Multiple re-presses of the original EP followed, as well as a licensed American release by Warlock Records featuring new reworks by Frankie Knuckles. Simpson's own remix - under the alternative Ricky Rouge alias - was released in early 1989.

People like Foot Patrol were the ones dancing to it right from the offset at clubs like the Playpen, the Gallery and Legend. By then it was embedded in the culture of the North in a way it wasn't in the South.'

Yet "Voodoo Ray" was in no way typical of the House sound that was, at the time, spreading like wildfire through the clubs of Manchester. It was a raw, industrial-strength outlier that stood in sharp contrast to the looser, baggier and more loved-up sound[21] being peddled by Nude residents Mike Pickering and Graeme Park, Jon Da Silva at the Haçienda's midweek night Hot, and a swathe of up-and-coming DJs dedicated to the more Balearic side of things: Justin Robertson, Moonboots, Jason Boardman and others. With chief cheerleaders the Happy Mondays and their associates cheering on from the sidelines with bags of ecstasy tablets in the back pockets, Manchester became the clubbing capital of the UK in 1988 and 1989.

'What had started from Nude and Berlin had developed into a huge counter-culture where people were travelling from all over the country,' Luke Cowdrey says. 'Manchester had become more populist, and the numbers attending clubs were huge. There were lots of white kids on MDMA feeding into the scene. Parties like Most Excellent had a much warmer, more euphoric kind of fusion of sounds than you got on the other side of the Pennines.'

The rush towards Manchester's most celebrated dancefloors didn't come from the black dancers that had been the backbone of Manchester's early House scene, but rather a mixture of excited students, white working classic Mancunians, and football lads from both sides of the Pennines[22]. Instead, Gerald Simpson's contemporaries found themselves marginalized in their home city, relegated to clubs such as PCR and Precinct 13 as well as trips over the Snake Pass or M62 to parties in Sheffield, Leeds and Huddersfield.

'Going to "House music all night long" is when The Haçienda lost the black crowd,' Greg Wilson says. 'The black crowd went back to styles like proper Hip-Hop, which became Hardcore, then Jungle and, later, Drum & Bass. They didn't want it just one way with a straight 4/4 [drum pattern] but wanted to bring in their own groove and approach to groove.'

---

21   There was one notorious club that bucked the trend and gravitated towards heavier Acid House and blistering American and European techno: the Thunderdome, a former Rock club in the impoverished Miles Platting area just north of the city centre. It attracted a far more working class crowd from the poorer areas of the city and was promoted by some of the city's most infamous acid casuals – Eric Barker, Jimmy Sherlock and John Kenyon. The Spinmasters (AKA 808 State's Andy Barker and later member Darren Partington) were amongst the resident DJs. Greater Manchester Police eventually got the Thunderdome shut down after a series of gang-related shootings outside.

22   Amongst those to make the weekly pilgrimage was Kaos and Up Yer Ronson promoter Tony Hannan. He remembers football fans from different clubs sticking together, leading to enclaves around the dancefloor representing Manchester City, Manchester United, Leeds United and others. The first "corner" was reserved for the Happy Mondays and their extended entourage.

That desire for more complex rhythms and music they could jack, foot-step or "drill" to was still being satisfied in the clubs in Yorkshire, or at least those whose resident DJs embraced "Voodoo Ray" the minute copies became available in Spin Inn and, a few weeks later, Crash in Leeds, Fourth Wave in Huddersfield and FON Records in Sheffield.

The dance music buyer in FON was, of course, Jive Turkey resident Winston Hazel. Along with many other DJs and future music producers in Yorkshire - and, to be fair, plenty of other places in the UK[23] - he was blown away by Gerald Simpson's mind-mangling masterpiece.

'The thing about "Voodoo Ray" is that it doesn't sound like it comes from anywhere in particular,' Hazel muses. 'To us, it sounds like it could have come from Sheffield, certainly more than it sounds like it came from Manchester.'

His then DJ partner Richard Barratt, another enthusiastic supporter of the record, agrees. 'By the time "Voodoo Ray" came out, Manchester was changing from what it had been,' he says. 'Their scene went to Piano House, Balearic and quite ravey European stuff. On our side of the Snake Pass, maybe because we were a bit behind, there was still that core of dancers around who went back through Electro to Jazz-Funk.'

It didn't take long for those dancers and DJs across the Pennines to make their moves in response to "Voodoo Ray". Across West and South York-shire, a swathe of would-be producers were scrambling to buy second-hand TR-808 and TR-909 drum machines, AKAI samplers and SH-101 synthesiz-ers. The stage was set for the birth of a brand new movement: Bleep & Bass.

---

23   Coming at a time when dance music culture was booming and music technology was becoming cheaper, the uniquely British sound of "Voodoo Ray" would prove extremely influential. It's my personal opinion that it should be counted as one of the single most impor-tant British records ever made; certainly, its impact is in some ways comparable to Lonnie Donegan's "Rock Island Line" or some of the early Beatles records – tracks which sent young Brits scurrying to form bands in the 1950s and '60s.

CHAPTER SIX

ONLY THE BEGINNING

UNIQUE 3 AND THE BIRTH OF BLEEP & BASS

'Every revolution was first a thought in one man's mind, and when the same thought occurs to another man, it is the key to that era.'

RALPH WALDO EMERSON [1]

Whether social, political or cultural, all revolutions need a moment of ignition: an act of significance that inspires others, either to rally around a cause or merely to provide a response. This moment may not seem immediately significant, but in hindsight provides a clear moment when momentous change became a distinct possibility.

In the case of what would become Bleep & Bass, that moment occurred in late summer 1988 in a terraced house in Bradford. There, three men - Ian Park, Patrick Cargill and David Bahar - had gathered to make music. It was not the first time they'd got together to jam out tracks inspired by their love of Electro, Hip-Hop, Soul, Reggae and Acid House, but they were still in an exploratory stage. A handful of tracks had been finished so far, with more in the works.

Part way through this particular session, the sound of feedback could be heard buzzing through Bahar's sizeable monitor speakers. 'When the feedback came through, it shook the house in the low register,' Bahar says. 'I was a massive fan of bass and wanted the dirtiest, wildest bass sound I could find. This was heavy, so I plugged a microphone into the mixer and recorded it onto tape. When we later went into a professional studio, I took the tape of that feedback tone with me.'

---

1   Emerson, Ralph Waldo: History, from Essays: First Series, 1841

^ **UNIQUE 3** by Normski

At the time, this ultimately far-sighted act seemed insignificant; after all, that raw, rumbling tone may never have got used. Yet, a few weeks later, it became the single most significant feature of the three producers' most impressive collaborative track yet: an insanely raw, sparse and weighty concoction that would send shockwaves through the Yorkshire club scene and, later, the world: Unique 3's "The Theme".

• • •

Like so many others in this book, Unique 3 can trace their origins back to the breakdance era. Ian Park and Patrick Cargill were enthusiastic members of Solar City Rockers, a Bradford crew renowned in the region for their weekly battles with city rivals Beat Street Boys. The collective also included Cargill's cousin Kevin Harper and someone who travelled from out of town to practice sessions and battles, Leeds-based teenager George Evelyn.

All four were obsessed with the emerging Hip-Hop sound. Park, Harper and Evelyn were wannabe DJs, while Cargill fancied himself as a bit of a mic man. They were all recognizable faces around Bradford, not least because they often rocked matching crew tracksuits (black Adidas with yellow and red trim, topped off with the kind of oversized peak caps popularized by Grandmaster Flash).

'Ian was the quiet one,' remembers Bradford-based DJ Lubi. 'When I was DJing at Checkpoint in 1984 and '85 he used to come up and ask me about records. Sometimes he requested records - it was usually Bob James or Roy Ayers. He was softly spoken, very polite and always seemed to be talking about music.'

Taking the name DJ Cool Cutz (and later simply Cutz), Park began making appearances behind the decks at Checkpoint and other key Bradford spots alongside Harper (Boy Wonder) and hype man Cargill (Jam Master P, later shortened to MC JMP). They were collectively known as Unique Three. Quite how prevalent and popular they were to begin with is hard to define[2], though there's little doubt about their skills and party-rocking credentials.

'Ian and Kevin were really good DJs,' David Bahar says. 'Patrick was a good dancer and as a rapper, he had the tone of a black American from New York. He was always one of the tallest guys in the club - a real ladies man. For a brief time they were managed by a local Jamaican guy who owned a shop selling hair products to the Afro-Caribbean community.'

When Harper decided to join forces with Evelyn as a DJ duo and move to Leeds in 1987, Unique Three had an uncertain future. Enter Adrian 'Edzy' Collins, another local lad with an interesting history. 'I ran away from home to London when I was 15 years old,' Collins explains. 'I managed to blag a

---

2   In one interview, Adrian 'Edzy' Collins told me that it's a stretch to say that they were performing a lot.

job at Pineapple Dance Studios in Covent Garden, even though I was under-age. I was lucky to fall in with a circle of people who were putting on warehouse parties - not the Acid House era raves, but that scene that existed beforehand in London[3].'

Through working the door at some of these parties and becoming an avid listener to pirate radio stations such as Kiss, Collins got a taste for DJing. When he was kicked out of Pineapple Studios, Collins returned to Bradford and sought work as a DJ.

'The first DJ job I got was at a Reggae club called the Palm Cove,' he remembers. 'I was DJing as Mixmaster Edzy. It was through that I crossed paths with Ian, who at that time was playing out as DJ Cool Cutz.'

The two quickly became friends. 'We weren't DJing together then, though we did quite regularly play on different floors at the same Bradford venue,' Collins says. 'On those nights we'd be bombing up and down the back fire escape, mid DJ set, to borrow records off each other.'

Following the break-up of the original Unique Three, Park and Collins started DJing together. 'We bagged a daft Thursday night in town,' Collins explains. 'We couldn't think of a better name, so just decided to slightly alter the name he'd been using with Kevin and Patrick.'

Thus, the outfit was reborn as Unique 3, with Cargill continuing to handle microphone duties. 'Jam Master P, or JMP for short, had by far the best voice I'd heard from a UK rapper,' Collins says. 'By then we'd decided to pull all of our individual music projects together.'

Collins came from an impoverished background and was used to hustling to get by. He saw music, DJing and Yorkshire's growing underground club scene as a possible money-spinner - a way to earn enough to get by and, if they were successful, become a little more comfortable. In early 1988, he began putting on a weekly event at a club called Rio Campus on Barry Street slap bang in the centre of Bradford.

While the venue was initially better known for hosting Rock gigs, Unique 3 were given the opportunity to host a Sunday club night they called the Soundyard. It ended up running until the tail end of 1990, with guest performers and DJs from the UK and US occasionally joining Collins, Park and Cargill on stage. 'Me and Ian used to DJ on four decks,' Collins remembers. 'On a typical night we'd play sets including '80s Funk and Soul, Disco, Hip-Hop, Electro, early House and Acid.'

---

3   This warehouse party scene began in the mid-1980s and revolved around events thrown by people such as Noel and Maurice Watson, the Dirtbox crew, Norman Jay and Judge Jules, and Wag promoter Chris Sullivan. Musically it was mixed, though the events – and the pirate radio shows hosted by many of the key DJs – played a significant role in the rise of the Rare Groove sound. For more information, check Terry Farley and Bill Brewster's London Warehouse Parties Pre-Acid House: An Oral History on Red Bull Music Academy Daily (https://daily.redbullmusicacademy.com/2017/06/london-warehouse-parties-oral-history)

In a 1990 interview with Yorkshire-based dance music journalist Vaughan Allen[4], Cargill reminisced about the importance of those Sunday night sessions at Rio: 'We started at a time when we couldn't really get hold of stuff we wanted to play in the clubs unless we made it ourselves.'

* * *

One day in the summer of 1988, David Bahar was hanging out with his school friend Patrick Cargill, the latter's musical partner in crime Ian Park and a mutual friend, Delroy Brown. He was another familiar face on Bradford's underground music scene like his brother, Derrick, and owned a formidable Reggae soundsystem that he'd built from scratch.

'It was a kick-ass system,' Bahar remembers. 'Derrick was very well known and was booked every weekend. He also had some great equipment - things like reverb boxes but also some music-making stuff.'

Brown suggested that Bahar should try making some music with Cargill and Park, who had already acquired a Roland TR-909 drum machine. 'Getting together made sense,' Bahar remembers. 'I was interested in making music, but all I had was a keyboard with a sampler function. They'd borrowed some things off Derrick and Delroy, but all they owned was that drum machine.'

Bahar was perhaps not the most likely of musical revolutionaries. For starters, he'd been raised within Bradford's sizeable South Asian community. He was married with a young child and had no interest in drink and drugs. Crucially, though, he was just as passionate about music as Park, Cargill and Collins.

'I was pure Rock & Roll at first until I heard Sugarhill Gang's "Rappers Delight",' he reveals. 'Then I heard "The Message" by Grandmaster Flash and the Furious Five. That was the biggest influence on me getting into black electronic music. I also had an auntie on my mum's side who was married to a Jamaican man. She was really a music head - most weekends they would be round at our house and my aunt would bring her Reggae music. I guess it was in my blood from an early age.'

Through his friendship with Cargill, Park and Kevin Harper, Bahar was already familiar with Chicago House and Detroit Techno. 'On Saturdays I used to drive Ian and Kevin over to Manchester with my then-pregnant wife,' he remembers. 'They'd go to Spin Inn and buy the latest tracks. I was hearing all this new music before 90% of other would-be House musicians as I was moving with the best DJs in the North of England.'

When Bahar followed up on Delroy Brown's suggestion and joined forces with Park and Cargill, the trio quickly found their groove. Park manned the TR-909 and focused on drum programming, with Bahar on keyboards and Cargill contributing riffs, chords and melodies here and there. 'The first

---

4   *I-D* magazine, April 1990.

track we did that night was called "Jazz Freak",' Bahar remembers. 'Pat said it was the best thing they'd done and I thought it was the best thing I'd been involved in, so we arranged to meet up again.'

Over the weeks and months that followed, sessions became more frequent. Cargill acquired a keyboard of his own, Park devoted more time to drum programming and Bahar added a Moog synthesizer to his small but growing collection of music-making machines. The trio borrowed additional equipment from Derrick Brown via his brother Delroy - himself an aspiring producer with a basic grasp of studio engineering - and the demo tracks began to stack up.

'We tried to get a record deal but we were turned down everywhere we went,' Bahar remembers. 'So we decided we had to put out our own track and booked some studio time.'

The trio clubbed together to pay for time in the studio, with Collins also chipping in after dipping into the funds he'd accrued from promoting the Soundyard. 'Edzy was a good DJ and a really good promoter,' Bahar remembers. 'The events he was promoting were selling out. He was also managing Unique 3 by this point.'

It was when the trio headed to the studio - a place owned by the brother-in-law of an old friend called Johnny Bell - that things really started to move. 'I was in music heaven being in a real studio for the first time,' Bahar says. 'When we first got there, Ian was talking to the engineer and I jumped on one of the synths they had, I think it was a Yamaha DX7. I started messing around and played this bassline. To fill in the spaces, I started playing this little melody with my right hand.'

The melody in question was sharp, high and rather lo-fi sounding, little more than a 'bleeping' refrain. 'Ian turned to me and said, "That's good",' Bahar remembers. 'So I just kept playing it.'

Park got to work on the TR-909, programming a complimentary rhythm track. It was at this point that Bahar remembered the bass-heavy feedback tone he'd recorded some weeks earlier. It was stuck into the sampler so that it could be used to replay the bassline that Bahar had come up with at the start of the session. Another lo-fi sounding synthesizer string part was added to give the track a more haunting quality. All three knew they'd created something rather special.

'We all knew it was going to kick off when Ian played it in the clubs off tape and Patrick popped some lyrics on it,' Bahar says. 'If we'd had more money at the time, we'd have probably booked another studio session and Patrick could have added some lyrics, but at the time it wasn't to be.'

During that day in the studio, they managed to complete two versions of this rough, raw and alien tune. Both were road-tested during Unique 3 DJ sets, usually to a rapturous response. Buoyed by the dancefloor feedback,

Collins paid for a small run of 500 records to be pressed up. It was credited to Unique 3 and the Mad Musician, the latter being the alias Bahar had selected for his productions[5].

Side A featured a track titled "Only The Beginning". In hindsight, it was a stunningly far-sighted title for a record that provided a blueprint for much of what followed in the years following its release. It began with sampled crowd noise and an announcer saying, "Ladies and gentlemen, live on stage here tonight we have Unique 3 and the Mad Musician. Check it out!" As the impressively sub-heavy bassline and loose, Electro-influenced House beat kicked in, another voice proclaimed, "you're in tune to Unique 3 and the Mad Musician, creators of the ultimate sound."

And what a sound! Driven forwards by Bahar's simple but devastating bassline, the kind of lo-fi bleeps and electronic blips usually found in cheap 1970s sci-fi flicks, footworker-friendly bursts of military-strength percussion and a ghostly synthesizer line, "Only The Beginning" was a sweaty rush: Bradford bass and Yorkshire jack that was every bit as alien and other-worldly as "Voodoo Ray". Crucially, though, it was nowhere near as polished or professionally produced; this was a combination of raw power, brilliant ideas and dancefloor-friendly elements that sounded like nothing that had come before.

It was accompanied on the B-side by an alternate version that was, if anything, even more potent. This was "The Theme", a revised take on the same basic track that began with Bahar's haunting synth line, Park's 909 drums, more alien bleeps and another booming vocal message: "We are the true underground Acid House creators, we hate the commercial House masturbators!"

When the bassline dropped, it somehow sounded even more raw, weighty and fuzzy: a headline-grabbing attraction that would go on to inspire an untold number of DJs in the months ahead. As a whole, "The Theme" was tighter, heavier and more refined than "Only The Beginning", distilling the essence of the track into seven minutes, 30 seconds of bassbin-bothering heaviness. Its two distinguishing features would provide the name of the musical movement that almost inevitably followed: Bleep & Bass.

• • •

---

5   'There was a lot of confusion about the name,' Bahar says. 'I wasn't in Unique 3 and in the studio on that first record there was only two of Unique 3 and me as the Mad Musician. Sometimes people would ask me who the Mad Musician was because they thought I was in Unique 3'.

As Unique 3 had financed and manufactured the record without the aid of a distributor, they had to get the records to shops themselves. Collins got lifts in friends' cars, took trains or hopped on coaches to sell directly to the dance buyers at the network of stores supporting the region's growing band of Acid House DJs.

'I remember when Edzy and the other lads came into Crash Records,' says Gez Varley, then a bedroom producer who had yet to start working with future LFO production partner Mark Bell. 'When they played it I stood there open-mouthed. I knew them from the breakdance scene and thought, "Fucking hell - I've got to do this. If they can make a record, so can I". It was local lads who had made this great record. Before that, I'd never believed that it was something one of us could do.'

As well as visiting Fourth Wave in Huddersfield and Manchester's Spin Inn and Eastern Bloc, Collins also headed south to Sheffield's FON Records. The latter's dance buyer was Jive Turkey's Winston Hazel, an important figure since he also hosted a weekly show on SCR (Sheffield Community Radio), a pirate radio station that could also be picked up by listeners in Bradford and Leeds.

'When Edzy brought it into the shop, it blew my mind,' Hazel says. 'It was so fitting for where we were going and for what we were doing. It was just next level. Unbeknownst to us, it dropped into our lap just at the right time.'

The same day, Hazel's DJ partner Richard Barratt swung by the shop. As he walked in, Hazel was playing this slice of mutant, jacking bass-funk over the shop's soundsystem.

'Straight away I said, "What the fuck is that?" When something like that comes in, you're blown away,' Barratt says. 'You don't know where you're going, but you know you're moving forwards. In hindsight, it's interesting that "Voodoo Ray" and "The Theme" landed around the same time. They fit with the Chicago and Detroit records we were playing, but they were different. They sounded like they had been made by people like us. You could hear that in the sonics and the way that they'd been put together.'

Both Barratt and Hazel quickly began hammering the record in their sets, turning the record into an anthem at Jive Turkey. 'When we put that record on, the footworkers would go mental,' Hazel says enthusiastically. 'Including me! To have something local to play was brilliant. I knew the power of playing local records, whether they were dance ones or Reggae ones, through the radio station. It also planted this desire to make music. When I first heard it I thought, "I wish I'd made that".'

The buzz around "The Theme" was palpable. It received heavy rotations in Leeds, Bradford, Sheffield and Manchester, with Mike Pickering and Graeme Park at The Haçienda being particularly supportive. 'When I heard it was a big tune at The Haçienda I went over there one night to see if I could hear it getting played,' David Bahar remembers. 'They wouldn't let me in. The same thing happened one night at the Warehouse in Leeds. I looked the doorman in the eyes and thought, "I don't belong here".'

Needing to increase his work shifts to support his wife and child, Bahar began stepping away from studio sessions. In his absence, Collins and Delroy Brown became more involved in the production side of Unique 3's work. 'The more DJing they did, the less time I spent with them,' Bahar sighs. 'It came to a point where we had nothing left in common. They had plans and I had plans. One day Edzy asked if I'd sell them the remainder of the tracks we'd been working on together. As I was spending more time working than making music I thought it was probably for the best. So one day they called by and took the tracks.'

Bahar didn't pack in music completely, though, and some of his solo tracks as the Mad Musician later appeared on Tribe Recordings, a short-lived label he founded with fellow Bradford producer and DJ John Khan. The imprint released two 12" singles, each featuring tracks from Bahar and the mysterious 'X-Plosion'.

Interestingly, some of Bahar's contributions to the EPs feature similarly bold basslines and synth sounds to "Only The Beginning" and "The Theme", alongside jazzier musical touches including Pat Metheny style guitars and keyboard solos. The EPs have become collectors' items, though very few outside of the Yorkshire scene have ever heard them.

Speaking for the first - and so far only - time about his little-known part in British dance music history, Bahar says he's proud of his achievements. 'It seems like another life, though I'm happy people are still interested in the track,' he says. 'I was just a kid really back then, but underground music was the place to be. My mum was old school and told me that as I had a family I had to stop going out all night and concentrate on them and my job. They were then my priority for 25 years.'

Eight years ago, Bahar returned to music and now regularly performs as a session musician. 'The kids are all grown up and I've gone through a divorce, so I'm now back to my first love: sweet music,' he says. 'If someone told me back then I'd be writing songs, playing music and recording it for a living, I would have said, "No way! I'm just a guy with a keyboard who loves basslines too much".'

* * *

As 1988 turned into 1989, Unique 3 were assessing their options. Thanks to the success of "The Theme" in clubs across the UK, they'd received several offers from labels looking to secure their signature. The first had come from Kool Kat's Neil Rushton, a former Soul all-dayer promoter who was in the process of setting up a new offshoot called Network Records. Collins turned this down but gave more serious consideration to two other offers: one from major label Virgin, who wanted to add Unique 3 to the roster of their dance-focused 10 Records sub-label, and another from Sheffield record shop owners Rob Mitchell and Steve Beckett.

'One day we visited FON Records to drop off some more copies of the record and Rob and Steve took us outside,' Collins remembers. 'They told us that they were thinking of starting their own label and wanted to sign us. They said that they had nowt, but they'd put everything they had into promoting us. If I'd known what I do now, I would have signed Unique 3 to their new label, rather than Virgin. What they created later that year with Warp Records would have been a far better vehicle for Unique 3 than a major label.'

Hindsight is a wonderful thing, but at the time Collins' decision to take up the offer from Virgin was understandable. Unique 3 were offered a big advance, the full backing of the label's promotional machine and funds to record a debut album. They would be the poster boys for the rapidly evolving Yorkshire Bleep & Bass sound - Northern heroes representing on a national and global stage rather than merely a regional one.

'Some people in their A&R department had heard that "The Theme" was a big record at The Haçienda[6] and had caught the buzz of what the record shops were saying about us,' Collins says. 'They'd also heard that we were DJing prolifically around the Northern circuit. They thought they were onto something. Back then, we didn't really have a lot of money - I had two kids to feed and holes in my shoes. In hindsight signing with them might have been the wrong decision, but at the time it was the only real choice.'

After they'd signed on the dotted line, Unique 3 were sent to FON Studios in Sheffield to work with one of the resident producers and co-owners, a fast-rising talent called Robert Gordon. The plan was simple: to re-make and remix "The Theme" ahead of its major label re-release. This time round, Cargill got to lay down the rhymes he'd been spitting over the record during the group's DJ sets, while Gordon helped the quartet to re-program the drums. Crucially, he also took up Unique 3's challenge of ensuring that the record had the weightiest sub-bass ever committed to wax.

'That remix of "The Theme" was my bass statement,' Gordon laughs. 'I got quite a lot more remix work from labels after that - people who wanted a version with extra bass.'

The reworked "Unique Mix" of "The Theme" is naturally far more polished than its rough and ready predecessor, with warm but weighty, Dub Reggae style sub-bass, drum machine beats that shuffle to the timing of UK Steppas style dancefloor Dub and synthesizer lead lines that sound crisp and high-tech. In other words, for all its sparseness, heaviness and

---

6   The other key DJ in spreading knowledge of "The Theme" west of the Pennines was Stu Allan, who regularly played the track on his radio show. He'd been given a copy by one of the staff in Spin Inn.

dancefloor power - the sub-bass wobble towards the end of the cut is almost rush inducing in its gut-punching intensity - the remix benefitted from being produced in a state-of-the-art studio.

It was, of course, the sheer weight of the bass that would cause the most commotion moving forwards. 'When we went to cut it in London, none of the mastering engineers wanted to take it on at first,' Collins says. 'We were given this guy called Geoff Pesche. I remember that one of the things he did to try and get more of the sub-bass on the record was to lie under the mixing desk and remove the glass valve limiters out of the back. He could have been sacked if he'd been caught doing that, but he thought it would help get more bass on the record. It just highlights that what we were doing at the time wasn't really understood.'

To make matters worse, when the record was released reports started emerging of blown speakers in clubs and bars across the UK. 'We did get banned from some clubs because of the bass on our records,' Collins laughs. 'At the time, we were really proud of that. When Virgin told us they were getting letters of complaint we saw that as a badge of honour. Clubs just weren't geared up for that kind of bass-heavy music at the time. They had to start getting proper soundsystems in.'

When it came to recording their debut album in the first few months of 1990, Unique 3 decided against making a bunch of sound-alike Bleep & Bass tunes. Instead, they raided the tapes from their bedroom sessions and produced a set that encapsulated many of their influences, from Hip-Hop and Electro to Dancehall, Dub, Breakbeat, Acid House and Soul. There were naturally a couple of radio-friendly cuts to appease their paymasters at Virgin - see the dancefloor-rocking club Hip-Hop single "Musical Melody"[7] and radio-friendly dance-pop cheeriness of "Rhythm Takes Control" - but for the most part it fairly accurately reflected the mix of musical influences heard on pirate radio in Yorkshire (particularly Unique 3's own station, Emergency 99.9 FM[8]).

'The things that turned us on musically we absolutely wanted to put into our music,' Collins says. 'That didn't just apply to us, but also producers elsewhere in the UK. New things don't come around that often, so there was a lot of excitement. Everyone wanted to get the biggest, dirtiest bassline on their tracks because that was something the press was talking about, and people were chatting about in clubs and record shops.'

---

7   This crept into to the top 30 of the UK singles chart in April 1990, leading to Unique 3 making their sole appearance on Top of the Pops.
8   Funded by Collins from his share of the Virgin advance, Emergency 99.9 FM was a Bradford-based pirate radio station that first crackled over the airwaves on 27 July 1990. It officially started broadcasting at lunchtime the following day, staying a feature of the local pirate radio scene for a number of years. Collins re-launched it as an Internet radio station in 2018.

There was certainly some press hype for the rapidly evolving, bass-heavy sound of UK dance music at the time. In the June 1990 edition of *i-D*, Matthew Collin confidently predicted that Reggae-influenced music from the UK would be the sound of the summer. 'Reggae's return to popularity has been the most insidious dancefloor revolution ever,' he wrote. 'It's gradually colonized the grooves, steered the rhythms, popularized the samples, donated its melodies, its entire culture... Reggae's emphasis on drum and bass and its passion for dubwise effects has now become the standard form in the dance industry.'

As they were trailblazers for the hard-edged sound of Bleep & Bass rather than the more comfy and laidback grooves pushed forwards by London's Soul II Soul and Bristol's Smith & Mighty and Massive Attack, many expected Unique 3's debut album "Jus Unique" to be similarly forthright. But as they told Vaughan Allen in an interview for *The Face*, they'd already become bored with the swathe of Bleep-heavy records that had appeared since they debuted "The Theme" in Bradford almost two years earlier.

'We're getting bored with that Bleep thing now,' Collins is quoted as saying. 'We're going to try something new. Problem is, we're getting out of it just as everyone else is getting into it.[9]'

Listening back almost three decades after it appeared in stores, "Jus Unique" has stood the test of time better than many similarly minded albums of the era. It begins with a reworked version of their most famous tune ("Theme III") then offers a sprint through down-low Hip-Hop ("Music Music", "Musical Melody"), bleeping, sub-heavy club cuts ('Pattern 12", "Code 274", "Phase 3" and the insanely weighty, largely overlooked "Digicality"), dancehall ("Reality") and Electro-rave fusion ("Weight From The Bass" and "7am", the latter made with Rob Gordon at FON). In hindsight, what Unique 3 delivered was not a purist Bleep & Bass album, but rather the only LP to mix the key elements of the style - the bleeps, the rumbling sub-bass and the skittish percussion programming - with the sounds and styles that influenced its creation. For that reason, it remains a landmark album.

Naturally, it never sold as many copies as Virgin was hoping, despite good reviews in the music press. They cut their losses and parted company with Unique 3 in 1991 after one final EP. By then, Bleep & Bass was far more associated with another Yorkshire city, Sheffield, and the phenomenally successful label Unique 3 had turned down the opportunity to join, Warp Records.

'First, it was "the sound of Bradford" and then "the sound of the industrial north",' Collins complains. 'Then finally it became "Sheffield Bleep". I suppose it's like any war: the victors re-write history.'

---

9   *The Face*, December 1990.

CHAPTER SEVEN

STATING A FACT

NIGHTMARES ON WAX AND THE ROLE OF RIVALRY

'All close friendships are marked with competition. Our earliest tests are against our siblings and playmates, and some of that rivalry endures amongst friends into adulthood. Like dogs play fighting, you learn not to bite hard.'

CHRISTOPHER BOLLEN [1]

Kevin Harper is stood on Merrion Street in Leeds, gesturing towards the entrance of what was once Ricky's, the sweaty basement space where Nightmares On Wax first made their name as DJs. Today is the inaugural edition of Ralph Lawson's Inner City Electronic festival and Harper has travelled over from Bradford to take a trip down memory lane.

Now in his early fifties, Harper is a gentle, smiling soul who tends not to say too much. Today he is dressed in his finest revivalist B-boy threads, with an Adidas tracksuit topped off by a peaked baseball cap, sizable sunglasses and a customized sports jacket. The jacket is a thing of rare beauty; on the reverse, it features an inspired graffiti style caricature of him as Boy Wonder, the scratch-happy Hip-Hop DJ turned House music evangelist and Bleep & Bass pioneer. Most people couldn't pull off the look, but Harper rocks it with the nonchalance of the breakdancing teenager he once was [2].

As Harper stands on the cramped side street, fat headphones slung around his neck, memories come flooding back. There's the time he was harassed at a bus stop by a posse of rivals from another city suburb for having the audacity to drop a Nightmares On Wax demo at Ricky's, numerous tales

---

1   Bollen, Christopher: Beyond This Point You May Encounter Nude Sunbathers, The Paris Review, 2017 (https://www.theparisreview.org/blog/2017/06/26/beyond-this-point-you-may-encounter-nude-sunbathers/)
2   Bollen, Christopher: Beyond This Point You May Encounter Nude Sunbathers, The Paris Review, 2017 (https://www.theparisreview.org/blog/2017/06/26/beyond-this-point-you-may-encounter-nude-sunbathers/)

^ **NIGHTMARES ON WAX** by Vanya Balogh

of impromptu breaking contests in the Merrion Centre, and a few chuckles about losing the DJ battle with Ital Rockers in Bradford. Yet I'm more interested in a story passed on by several sources that feels significant in the early Nightmares On Wax narrative. According to folklore, it occurred one Saturday night at Downbeat, the then DJ duo's weekly residency at Ricky's.

My sources remembered Unique 3 appearing on the dancefloor midway through the night and squeezing their way through the tightly packed crowd. As they approached the decks, one of the Bradford-based crew offered up a white label record, which Harper accepted. It was a copy of their debut single, the self-pressed double A-side containing "Only The Beginning" and "The Theme". According to folklore, Harper wasted no time in mixing the record in.

'Yes, that happened,' Harper responds with a smile. 'The reaction was so good that I ended up playing it three times in a row. The funny thing is, I put the wrong side on. Instead of putting on "The Theme", which was the one we'd heard before[3], I put on "Only The Beginning." It still went off though.'

As Harper confirms this important moment in Bleep history - this was quite possibly the first time Unique 3's Bleep & Bass blueprint had been played by a member of a rival crew - I remember a quote from an earlier interview with his then Nightmares On Wax partner, George Evelyn. 'Everything's responsive, right? We were representing Leeds. If the next man comes from Bradford, Manchester, Huddersfield and Sheffield with a tune that's his, you could guarantee someone from one of the crews in the neighbouring areas would be straight in the studio trying to create a rival tune.'

Evelyn seems acutely aware of his motivations, or at least those that drove him as a young man. Throughout the mid to late 1980s, he was driven by a desire to be a better DJ and producer than his local and regional rivals - people he'd encountered during his days as a battling breakdancer, then in the clubs of Bradford, Leeds and Sheffield. He'd grown up immersed in Hip-Hop and Reggae soundsystem culture, two musical movements where bettering your rivals took top priority.

While Harper was probably too laidback to let it worry him, Evelyn seems to have used rivalry to fire himself up. 'I'm not going to lie, all of us at some point didn't like each other,' he says of the small band of Yorkshire revolutionaries whose early musical moves resulted in the Bleep & Bass sound. 'I think it was mainly because we were young and had massive egos. We all loved what we did - it was just bravado. We were mates until it came to dropping our tunes to try and outdo each other.'

• • •

---

3   According to George Evelyn, the first time they heard "The Theme" was when Unique 3 played it off cassette at an event at Benson's in Bradford.

From the age of '13 or 14', Evelyn felt like an outsider. Not because he was the son of Caribbean immigrants, but because he was cruelly rejected by some of the boys he'd grown up with in Hyde Park, a student-heavy area to the west of Chapeltown, just off the road to Headingley. According to Evelyn, he was 'blanked' by a string of school friends after refusing to let them borrow a broken speaker he'd found at a jumble sale. He'd shown it to them at Teen Scene, a Monday night under-age disco at city centre club Tiffany's[4], but refused to hand it over. The next day at school, he was an outcast.

'Dennis Smith, who was the cockerel of the school, turned everyone against me over this speaker,' Evelyn remembers. 'It was really childish and stupid. There were a couple of my mates from school who stood by me - Wesley Armstrong and Clive Walker - but the rest blanked me. These were the guys I'd grown up with but we just sort of parted ways.'

When one door closes, another one opens. Now without an extended friendship group, Evelyn was a teenage breakdancer in need of a new crew. Happily, his sister had an idea. Her boyfriend of the time was from Bradford and his cousin, Darren Pascale, was a key member of the city's Solar City Rockers crew. 'Darren called me up and said, "I heard you break - do you want to join our crew?" We practice every Sunday," Evelyn says. 'So I went over the next Sunday to the sports hall they used to rent near Green Lane in Bradford.'

Breakdancing crews tended to include members who lived in one specific neighbourhood, town or city, and it was highly unusual for anyone to travel any kind of distance to join a rival collective. Ordinarily, Evelyn would have found a crew closer to home in Leeds, but thanks to local politics this wasn't an option. Thus, he hopped on a bus and headed across West Yorkshire to Bradford.

It was a life-changing moment. At his first practice session he met Kevin 'Boy Wonder' Harper, another Hip-Hop obsessive and aspiring DJ. After they'd finished popping and locking with the rest of the Solar City Rockers, Harper invited Evelyn back to his mum's house. He wanted to show off his latest skill: the ability to scratch like a New York DJ, albeit on a home hi-fi rather than a professional Technics turntable. Having bonded, the two teenagers began meeting up more regularly and spent hours making what Evelyn calls 'push button tapes'.

'You'd record a few seconds of a record, press pause, and then record a clip of another record and try to get it in time,' the talkative Evelyn says. 'We didn't know we were sampling, but that's basically what we were doing - pause and record sampling with a cassette deck. We used to do megamixes like that because neither of us had turntables [at the time]. I think it was the early stages of us trying to manipulate sound.'

---

4   This "Ritzy's" style commercial club hosted all-dayers during the Northern Soul era, as well as breakdancing sessions for teenagers in the early-to-mid 1980s.

Sometime in early 1986, Harper began DJing with fellow Bradfordians Patrick Cargill and Ian Park as Unique 3. Evelyn played with them a few times ('We were still Unique 3 even though there was four of us,' he laughs) but eventually decided that he required a DJ partner who was based closer to his Hyde Park home. 'I did a bit of stuff with this guy and we played as Nightmares On Wax,' he remembers. 'When Kevin stepped away from Unique 3, I asked him to come and join me in Leeds.'

'I think he was in need of a DJ partner,' Harper says as we loiter in the doorway of what was once Ricky's. 'By then he had turntables in his house[5] and I'd go over to jam. Eventually he asked me if I wanted to join him in Nightmares On Wax.'

It wasn't long before the pair were sharing a flat in Hyde Park. They were without regular work so spent much of their ample spare time mixing and sharpening their rapidly developing DJ skills. 'Me and Kevin used to do these DJ routines where we'd scratch, run round each other and throw the decks - all sorts of crazy shit,' Evelyn laughs. 'We didn't have much to do, so would spend time scratching and mixing. We also managed to blag a day in a recording studio through the local youth unemployment outreach centre. We used it to make a special megamix, which was then pressed up as a one-off acetate for us to play in our DJ sets.'

For now, any serious attempt at music production would have to wait: Evelyn and Harper were much more focused on hassling venue owners and club promoters in a bid to secure prized DJ slots. Surprisingly, their attempts were largely successful, something that didn't go down well with the rest of Leeds' young, aspiring DJs.

'When me and Kevin were coming up we were getting the gigs that nobody else was getting,' Evelyn says proudly. 'We were two 16-year-olds and we were DJing in town. All the other crews were like, "How come these guys are getting in there?" But our route was super-natural and super-organic. We'd befriended the local student community, and that's what led us to be invited to play in clubs. Most of the DJs from Chapeltown were approaching clubs at a time when they wouldn't touch anyone from the urban community.'

Like most neighbourhoods with a high student population, Hyde Park regularly played host to raucous house parties[6]. Evelyn and Harper regularly gatecrashed these to meet girls and grab free booze and drugs. 'There would often be bowls of mushrooms and piles of weed on the tables,' Evelyn remembers. 'You could just help yourselves. That was great. There were no after-parties really back then aside from the Blues, so it was a way of meeting people and having a good time.'

---

5   Evelyn bought the turntables through a grant from the Jubilee Trust, which the staff at a local unemployment centre had applied for on his behalf.
6   This tradition continues today. Well-regarded contemporary DJs such as Ben UFO and Midland cut their teeth in Hyde Park's house party circuit while studying in Leeds.

It was at one of these house parties on Chestnut Avenue - at the time known as "the most burgled street in Britain" - that they met a student DJ called Rob Wheeler. 'We just asked him if we could go and get our records and play a little set,' Evelyn says. 'He was like, "Yeah, sure thing!" So we went home, grabbed our records and rocked the spot.'

Wheeler was impressed and asked the pair if they fancied playing a set at Downbeat, his weekly student night at what Evelyn describes as, 'a function room within the Merrion Centre'. The following Saturday, Harper and Evelyn shared a 20-minute slot and got the dancefloor moving. As Wheeler was heading off for the summer a few weeks later, he asked them to stand in as resident DJs while he was away.

'From that point on we were involved in the night and it wasn't long before we were co-promoters,' Evelyn says. 'We just had a completely different route to getting into the club scene than anybody else from Hyde Park or Chapeltown. That sparked so much jealousy in Leeds. It was understandable but ridiculous, really.'

Nightmares On Wax were outsiders who had beaten their rivals to a plum gig. Having a weekly residency in a city centre club was a rarity back then, with only the cream of the crop locally - or those with good connections - being afforded this honour. Like Winston Hazel and Richard Barratt at Jive Turkey in Sheffield, Nightmares On Wax were given the opportunity to build a crowd through joining the dots between Hip-Hop, Soul, Funk, Jazz-Funk, Electro and House.

By the end of 1987, they were the sole residents and promoters of Downbeat, which had now moved to the cramped, sweaty basement space that was Ricky's. 'That became our shrine, our spot,' Evelyn enthuses. 'It was a blank canvas for us. Being record collectors, we had loads of different things we wanted to play. It started as being a predominantly student crowd, but soon it became a mishmash of students and the urban crowd, including the serious dancers from Chapeltown who were always at the best nights.'

When asked about the 18 months they spent as Downbeat's resident DJs, a broad smile breaks out across Harper's face. 'There was nowhere else like it,' he enthuses. 'We were always amazed at the response we got in that club. George would play all the top underground Hip-Hop tunes, and I'd play current and upfront House. We could play as raw as we wanted and get away with it. It was amazing! If you'd been there in those times, you would have loved it.'

• • •

By the time Unique 3 stepped onto the dancefloor at Downbeat with a copy of "The Theme" in October 1988, Nightmares On Wax had already started acquiring second-hand synthesizers and drum machines. One of their first investments was a Roland SH-101 synthesizer, a small but perfectly formed piece of equipment that played a key role in the making of A Guy Called Gerald's "Voodoo Ray". As a result, most wannabe first wave British House and Techno producers sought out a second-hand "101" in a bid to emulate the Manchester producer's peerless record.

The synthesizer's allure was partly down to the price (it was designed by its Japanese creators as an entry-level model) and it's easy-to-find nature, but the range of sounds you could create with it also played a part. As a monosynth, it was ideal for crafting top lines (simplistic, hooky melodies) and basslines. It featured a step sequencer with a basic save function, so you could program a bassline, press play and keep it going while you worked on the rest of the track. If you had the time and inclination, you could also utilize its features to mimic the wild acid sounds made famous by another Roland synthesizer, the TB-303 Bassline.

Roland's advertisements boasted that the SH-101 allowed users to quickly switch from "deepest rumbling bass, to screaming highs in a flash". Both of these elements came together on early Bleep & Bass records, with the synthesizer's square wave settings and sub-oscillator[7] providing the sounds heard on the genre's distinctive melody lines. Basically, by pitching notes down as much as possible, you could get booming, bassbin-shaking results. As Winston Hazel says, 'It was the deepest sound you could get.'

Alongside the cherished SH-101, Evelyn and Harper's ultra-basic home studio included a cheap four-track tape recorder and, from time to time, a TR-808 drum machine borrowed from Chapeltown Reggae musician and wannabe House producer Homer Harriott. Even by the lo-fi home studio standards of the time, Nightmares On Wax's set-up was a budget one.

'We recorded everything while sat on our living room floor,' Evelyn laughs. 'Everything was done on the spin. We'd have to record one section, then the next and try to keep it in time - it was very raw.'

The first finished track they were happy with was a Hip-Hop cut called "Stating A Fact", a chunky, dancefloor-friendly affair to which 18-year-old Evelyn later added rap vocals with the assistance of Age of Chance member Steve Eldrige[8]. Next was their first House track, "Let It Roll", a fuzzy and forthright affair that borrowed heavily from Big Daddy Kane's recently released "Set It Off" single and Doug Lazy's Hip-House jam of the same name. It boasted heavy but wayward drum breaks and a variety of crusty synthesizer sounds from the SH-101. It was a little messy but nevertheless had the makings of a dancefloor hit - at Downbeat at least.

---

7   For those interested in technical aspects of synthesizers, the SH-101's chipset allowed it to offer three sub-oscillator waveforms: square at -1 octave, square at -2 octaves, and 25% pulse at -2 octaves. A more detailed explanation can be found here: https://electricdruid. net/a-study-of-sub-oscillators/

8   Eldridge was a regular sight on the dancefloor at Downbeat and allowed Evelyn to record the vocals at his studio.

'When we played it for the first time off cassette at Ricky's the place went ballistic,' Evelyn says. 'I just remember me and Kevin hiding behind the DJ booth, scared with excitement, joy... all the emotions you can imagine running through your body. We must have rewound it and played it again about eight times - it was ridiculous.'

Their next demo was even more potent. Harper started working on it alone while Evelyn was out. Using the SH-101 and a copy of "Voodoo Ray", he spent hours trying to recreate the synth sounds that marked out Gerald Simpson's groundbreaking tune. 'I had the record on the turntable and the SH-101 on the go,' Harper remembers. 'I kept tweaking the sound of what I was playing so it sounded more like Gerald's track. When George came back, I played him what I'd recorded, which was this top line with no bassline underneath. George said, "You should put this underneath," and hummed the bassline. So, we got working, and the rest is history.'

The track in question was, in comparison to its predecessor, minimalistic in approach. Undeniably raw and loose with a percussive swing reminiscent of both Jazz-Funk and contemporary dancefloor Reggae, the cut came with not one but two ear-catching hooks. The first was a short sample of Nicola Collier's distinctive freestyle vocal from "Voodoo Ray", added towards the end of the process. The second was an addictive melody capable of worming its way into your subconscious and then staying there for weeks.

The cut's power, though, was derived from its crunchy, clattering drum hits and a rich, booming sub-bass part, which was designed to mimic the rhythmic feel and intonation of the catchy, rolling melody. Evelyn and Harper called the track "Dextrous" and quickly debuted it off cassette at Downbeat.

Once again, the response was rapturous. It became a staple of their sets in the weeks and months that followed, much to the irritation of many around Leeds. 'The amount of grief we got for dropping that demo at our own club night was ridiculous,' Evelyn complains. 'We even got threatened in a kebab shop. Some guy came up to us and said, 'That's not your fucking demo!' Me and Kevin just stood there quietly looking at this guy being all aggressive, but it was almost the biggest compliment he could give us.'

By this point, the issues caused by Leeds' local rivalries were only getting worse. While most of the DJs and music-makers enjoyed good relationships and a more friendly style of rivalry[9], the same couldn't be said for other young men in the city. Interestingly, it wasn't the tension between

---

9   The inner sleeve of Nightmares on Wax's 1991 debut album, "A Word of Science", contained thanks and shout-outs to many other DJs and producers from their home city, as well as regional rivals, fellow Bleep artists and the American House, Techno and Hip-Hop pioneers who had inspired them. John Peel, the first national radio DJ to support the Bleep sound, was also name-checked.

teenagers from Chapeltown and Hyde Park that boiled over, but rather their relationship with a crew of blazer-sporting young men from neighbouring suburb Meanwood.

'Most of the time it was just words, but it did occasionally get more serious,' says Tomas Stewart, then a member of Leeds Hip-Hop crew Breaking The Illusion (an act that brought together rappers, DJs and beat-makers from both Hyde Park and Chapeltown). 'One night it really kicked off at Downbeat. All these Meanwood lads were down there giving it large. I can't remember exactly what set it off, but within a few minutes it was like a scene from Gunfight at the OK Corral - it was this mass brawl that involved so many people on the dancefloor. It was one of the craziest things I've ever seen. The bouncers didn't know what to do, and the police didn't either.'

It was bad news for Downbeat, which was permanently cancelled a week or two later. After a short break, Nightmares On Wax re-emerged at the Warehouse, where they shared top billing as resident DJs with DJ Roy and his occasional fill-in, DJ Martin. This regular slot increased the pair's visibility further and really got under the skin of their most vociferous local rivals.

'I think there's loads of spin in Leeds on people who've done well,' Evelyn sighs. 'I think in any city you're going to get that 'small village' mentality - people who begrudge others success. Getting grief from other crews was just food and inspiration to keep doing what we were doing.'

● ● ●

On 1 July 1989, George Evelyn took delivery of 200 white label copies of an EP containing their first four demo tracks. It was a 12" single pressed partly out of necessity - record labels on both sides of the Atlantic had turned them down[10] - and partly in response to Unique 3's self-released success story, "The Theme". To pay for production, Evelyn borrowed £400 from his brother. Much of this went on manufacturing costs, but a significant chunk was also spent on mastering the record at Abbey Road Studios in London[11].

To sell the record, Evelyn borrowed a car and visited as many of the country's specialist record shops as possible. Within a week, the buzz around the record - and particularly "Dextrous" - was palpable. So much so, in fact, that more copies had to be pressed up to satisfy demand.

'Some shops would ask for 50 copies as soon as I walked in,' Evelyn says. 'I remember walking into Red Records in London, with Trevor Nelson working behind the counter, Dave Dorrell walking into the shop, and Paul

---

10   Evelyn and Harper travelled to New York in February 1989 to 'shop for records and sneakers' and see whether any local labels were interested in their tracks.
11   'I didn't realize it was Abbey Road at the time,' Evelyn says. 'All the way through the mastering session, I kept asking the engineer for more bass. He thought I was a jumped up little shit!'

'Trouble' Anderson swinging by. All of them said, "We've heard about this "Dextrous" tune, can we get a copy?' We had people like Mike Pickering hammering it at The Haçienda. The buzz was there, and in two weeks we'd sold 2,000 copies.'

One of Evelyn's first stops was FON Records in Sheffield, where his old breakdance rival Winston Hazel was manning the counter. He introduced Evelyn to one of the store's co-owners, Steve Beckett. 'Steve told me he'd heard about 'Dextrous' as Winston was playing it a lot at Occasions,' Evelyn remembers. 'He asked if we could exchange numbers because he was setting up a label[12].'

Beckett was as good as his word. After launching Warp Records at the tail end of the summer with Forgemasters' "Track With No Name", he needed new material. The imprint, which he'd founded with fellow FON Records co-owner Rob Mitchell and FON Studio engineer Robert Gordon, desperately needed more material. As all three men were keen to put something out by Nightmares On Wax, they decided that a remixed version of the rough-and-ready 'Dextrous' was the way forward.

Gordon cleaned up the duo's original version for the B-side, re-editing it to remove the unlicensed "Voodoo Ray" vocal samples, and then invited Evelyn and Harper to his home studio to do a 'high-tech' remake. 'That was the first time we'd been in or even near to proper studio,' Evelyn says. 'It was still a home studio, but Robert had some great kit. I remember he had an Atari computer and an M-1 keyboard... we didn't know what half of that shit was, but me and Kevin just took to it.'

Gordon claims that the Warp Records re-make of "Dextrous" was actually re-built from scratch after Evelyn and Harper went home. 'I re-programmed it all,' he says. 'That version is effectively a cover version by me, but I didn't want people to think it was a Rob Gordon record: It was a Nightmares On Wax record. I was trying to teach the artists on the label while fixing things here and there.'

Evelyn disputes this story, saying they'd already rejected a mix from Gordon before completing the final mix with Forgemasters' Sean Maher at Square Dance Studios in Nottingham[13]. Either way, the re-recorded version of "Dextrous", featuring the now familiar SH-101 melody and bassline combination but with some heavy new drums and spacey sounding synth sounds, was a triumph. It was notably weightier, with serious rhythmic swing and cute drum fills. 'It really did the business in the clubs,' Harper says. 'The reaction was amazing. I remember seeing a review in Mixmag at the time that said, "This tune kicks like a mule".'

---

12   Evelyn has told different versions of this story; in an interview with author Joe Muggs he claimed that Beckett said he'd heard DJ Martin play "Dextrous" at the Warehouse.
13   Gordon says that he sent Maher to Nottingham with specific instructions. In order to get the right result, he says he also phoned the studio's on-duty engineer and passed on the same technical remarks.

The record became a runaway success, selling enough copies to reach the lower reaches of the top 100 singles chart in the final week of 1989. 'It was crazy - we sold 30,000 copies of that record quite quickly,' Evelyn beams. 'It's phenomenal when you think about it.'

Keen to keep the ball rolling, Beckett, Mitchell and Gordon set them to work on a follow-up straight away. The success of "Dextrous" meant that Evelyn and Harper had enough spare money to expand their home set-up. Purchases included an Atari ST running Cubase (and later Creator Logic) and an AKAI sampler.

Despite their previous success and an expanded electronic armoury to call on, the recording process was littered with problems. First, they lost all of the samples that they'd saved in their new sampler. Frustrated, they headed to Sheffield to work in a temporary 'writing suite' set up by Warp Records in a dilapidated building behind Red Tape Studios. It was on one of these Steel City studio days that they were arrested.

'Unbeknownst to us, there'd been some complaints about kids hanging around in the building [we were using as a studio], smashing windows,' Evelyn remembers. 'The police had come just to have a look around and walked into this massive cloud of weed smoke. They arrested myself, Kevin and Andy [Jones], the engineer, and took us in a meat van down to the police station. I remember on the way them doing this good cop, bad cop thing. The copper sitting across from Kevin was hitting his hand with his other fist and said, "Don't you worry, when we get you down to the station you're gonna get it!" Kevin sat there and freaked out. I was really stoned so didn't give a shit!'

The problems didn't end there, either. It took "seven or eight mixes" to get the track right, and when it was finally sent off to the pressing plant, the lacquer cut got damaged on the way. The track's title, "Aftermath" was strangely fitting.

The single was, though, another rip-roaring success, reaching the dizzy heights of number 38 in the UK singles charts in October 1990. At the commercial zenith of the Bleep & Bass phenomenon, Evelyn and Harper had created a single that captured the zeitgeist.

It was notably different in feel to its predecessor, offering a looser, slightly more organic take on the Bleep blueprint. Its sweaty blasts of sampled breakbeats and twisted vocal samples were underpinned by a thunderously weighty kick-drum pattern and the kind of gargantuan, sub-heavy bassline capable of shaking venues to their foundations. This soundsystem wobbler also boasted a headline-grabbing vocal sample (lifted from Cuba Gooding Jr's early NYC House classic "Happiness Is Just Around The Bend") that added a decidedly human touch, something rarely seen previously in the sparse, heavy and musically militant world of Bleep & Bass. When heard rumbling from the Reggae soundsystems of Acid Blues such as Sonny's and Twilight, "Aftermath" must have sounded incredible.

Even today, nearly three decades after it was created, it remains an unashamedly heavy club record; a thrillingly bombastic rush of low-end power and mutant Yorkshire Funk[14] whose canny combination of sampled elements played well with London DJs raised on Rare Groove records and the emerging Breakbeat Hardcore sound. 'I was adamant when we did our beats that we sampled snares and breaks like we would in Hip-Hop,' Evelyn says. ' That's why our House tracks sounded the way they did. We brought this combination together, and that's what gave those early Nightmares tracks an edge.'

Curiously, Evelyn and Harper say that they never thought they were making a British brand of Techno, but rather bass-heavy House music influenced by Reggae, Soul and Hip-Hop. Getting the heaviest bass sound imaginable was fundamental though, as besting their Yorkshire rivals remained Evelyn's top priority. 'It was call and response,' he says sternly. 'When Gerald came with "Voodoo Ray" I felt like we had to respond. Then we came with a record, Forgemasters responded and then LFO. We just wanted to make the biggest, baddest record possible to represent our crew.'

Ironically, when Evelyn and Harper did deliberately move further towards Techno territory on 1991 EP "A Case of Funk" - a taster for their willfully eclectic debut album, "A Word of Science" - the reception from DJs and dancers was not what they expected. 'I think "A Case Of Funk" and "Bio-feedback" went over people's heads a bit,' Evelyn says. 'We weren't really up on the Techno thing, but that was the most Techno thing we did, without knowing it[15].'

The album that followed, "A Word of Science", was subtitled "The First and Final Chapter". The pair felt it was their only shot at glory and poured everything into it. Like Unique 3's "Jus' Unique", the album mixed typically weighty Yorkshire House and Techno sounds with Hip-Hop cuts and tracks shot through with audible nods to their Electro and Jazz-Funk heritage. Fittingly, the sprawling sleeve credits concluded with a verbal two-fingered salute to the duo's local rivals: 'This goes out to all of the people who said we would do and didn't mean it, and to all the people who said we wouldn't do it and knew we would.'

---

14   The sampled drum breaks and intricate fills offered a nod towards dancefloor Dub records. The influence of Dub was even more obvious in the drum programming, foreboding bassline and alien bleeps of the single's similarly heavy flipside, "I'm For Real".
15   Although overlooked in comparison to their earlier singles, the EP contains some killer cuts, not least the sub-powered wonkiness of "21st Kong" and the skittish Bleep & Bass purism of "Biofeedback".

In hindsight, "A Word of Science" was the beginning of the end for the first incarnation of Nightmares On Wax[16]. Both Evelyn and Harper admit to struggling to adapt to the rapidly changing nature of British dancefloors in the 18 months that followed the album's release. 1992 singles "Set Me Free" and "Happiness" are uncharacteristically breezy, upbeat and soulful. They borrowed heavily from both soulful US Garage and the piano-powered giddiness of Italian House, in the process losing much of the raw charm and industrial grunt that defined the duo's early Bleep-era material.

'I remember us being a bit of a loss at that time,' Evelyn says. 'There was some good stuff, but British dance music got really giddy for a period, then House music went super fluffy for a bit and certainly less raw. That kind of put us to one side for a little bit, but I think it's a good thing. Success to us wasn't getting in the charts or selling loads of records, it was seeing another DJ drop one of our tunes at a party and it going off. You know, being at a rave with 10,000 people and seeing people go crazy to your record. To us, that was the ultimate props.'

---

16   Kevin Harper decided to leave Nightmares on Wax in 1993, with Evelyn getting sole ownership of the project. 'I was just not feeling it,' Harper explains. 'I didn't want to make music any more. I never fell out with George, I just wanted to do something else with my life at that time.' The duo remain friends to this day and often meet up when Ibiza-based Evelyn visits West Yorkshire.

WARPED VISION

ROBERT GORDON, THE FORGEMASTERS AND THE DAWN OF 'SHEFFIELD BLEEP'

'There's talent seeping from the fingernails of Sheffield, but for a while, there was no release button for this new power. We had the ability to solve the problem, hence the birth of Warp Records. There's no hype, no scam, no gimmick. The talent was there, and now it has an outlet.'

ROBERT GORDON [1]

Perched at the top end of Hurlfield Road, a steady incline lined with inter-war council homes, ancient trees and high hedges, Sheffield Springs Academy is the epitome of a 21st-century secondary school. The red brick and steel-clad building is utilitarian but futuristic, a style seen so often in educational establishments built since the mid-2000s. Its ownership, too, is telling: while most Sheffield secondary schools were once run by the local education authority on behalf of the city council, Springs Academy is now one of 70 educational establishments across the UK owned by United Learning, a charitable company that specializes in taking over failing schools, many in down-at-heel inner city areas, in order to re-launch them as all-singing, all-dancing academies.

Springs Academy is the latest in a string of schools that have stood on the same spot since the Second World War. It came to life in 2006 following the demolition of the previous school, Myrtle Springs. That, too, had taken in pupils from some of Sheffield's most notorious sink estates; a sprawl of Brutalist tower blocks and post-war council houses that had started their slide towards serious poverty during the steel strikes of 1980 and '81.

---

1   Randall, Ronnie: Warp Factory Sheffield, City Beat Magazine, 1989

CHAPTER EIGHT

^ **FORGEMASTERS** by David Bocking

At the turn of the 1980s, the birth of Myrtle Springs was still some way off. On the site stood Hurlfield School, an ugly 1950s vision of civil architecture that could have come straight out of the Soviet Union. It took pupils from a relatively wide catchment area, but most notably two of the city's most famous social housing estates, Park Hill and Hyde Park.

Towering above the city centre skyline thanks to their position on steep hills, both Park Hill and Hyde Park were built on the sites of some of Sheffield's most impoverished post-war slums. The resultant developments were undoubtedly far-sighted, with blocks of maisonette style apartments accessed via high-rise "streets in the sky". When Park Hill opened to residents in 1961 (Hyde Park followed a few years later), its '996 ultra-modern flats'[2] and groundbreaking design were considered revolutionary, but by the 1980s were regarded as 'an eyesore looming over the city as a testament to broken dreams.'

As Sheffield suffered through recessions and a shrinking manufacturing sector, its angular, concrete-clad frontage and bleak Brutalist structure became associated with vandalism, crime and anti-social behaviour. What had once been a high-minded vision of communal living was now a handy metaphor for the Steel City's wider post-industrial decline.

As the go-to secondary school for Park Hill and Hyde Park residents in the late 1970s, Hurlfield had a reputation for being one of the toughest comprehensives in the city. Its staff members were undoubtedly dedicated, but poor behaviour amongst its multi-cultural pupil population was commonplace and recruiting new teachers was something of a struggle[3].

According to anecdotal evidence from former teachers, truancy was a big problem, too; at one point almost a third of the 900 or so pupils frequently didn't turn up, leading South Yorkshire Police to dispatch low ranking officers to the school permanently to track down truanting teenagers. Hurlfield, then, was the epitome of a troubled inner-city school, despite its location being relatively leafy and picturesque.

Like many state schools in the early 1980s, Hurlfield's pupil register contained a swathe of teenagers whose extra-curricular interests would eventually take them far beyond the cycle of youth unemployment and dead-end jobs that awaited their classmates. Variously obsessed by Reggae, Hip-Hop, Soul and Electro, these music-mad daydreamers mainly came from in and around the Park Hill and Hyde Park estates. Amongst them was a quintet of acquaintances who would go on to become Bleep & Bass pioneers:

---

2   Dabinett, Gordon: *Park Hill: Brave New Worlds?*, in *Standing at the Sky's Edge* official programme, Sheffield Theatres, 2019.
3   The same could be said of Firth Park School, whose pupils mostly came from the vast Shiregreen estate. Like Park Hill and Hyde Park, Shiregreen changed rapidly in the early 1980s following the collapse of the city's once mighty steel industry.

Winston Hazel, Sean Maher, Zye Hill, Glyn Andrews and, most significantly of all, a young soundsystem enthusiast, electronics builder, occasional DJ and drummer called Robert Gordon.

•••

On an overcast day in August 2018, Robert Gordon is sat in his dimly lit recording studio just around the corner from Sheffield United's Bramall Lane stadium. In front of him is a vast mixing desk, to the left a metal storage unit on which many of his vintage electronic instruments sit. Gordon gestures towards them, pointing out the samplers, synthesizers and drum machines he bought following a significant payday for work on Yazz's 1988 debut album, "Wanted".

Amongst the community of Techno fetishists and electronic music nerds scattered around the globe, Robert Gordon has always been an inspirational figure: a pioneer whose largely under-celebrated turn-of-the-'90s productions are solid sonic gold. In online messageboards, he's spoken of in hushed tones as a publicity-shy enigma who has all but vanished from view. There have been occasional glimpses of this near-mythical figure from time to time, but so little recently that some even wondered aloud whether he was even alive at all.

Happily, Robert Gordon is very much alive and well. On this particular August day, he's in fine form, laughing his way through anecdotes about his life and music career that have rarely been told before. He has previously agreed to occasional interviews in the past, but today's verbal probing - the first of several extended interviews we'd eventually complete for this book - is his first in almost a decade. For whatever reason, Gordon rarely goes on the record, but he's agreed to detail his remarkable role in the birth and spread of Bleep & Bass, a style he arguably did more than anyone else to popularize.

After taking a few tokes on a particularly pungent spliff, Gordon traces his love of sound to where it all began. 'The record player was my first toy when I was about two and a half,' he says. 'I learnt all the records in the box by the colours on the label. At about the age of four, I ended up having to play at my mum's parties because I knew the records and which side to put on to get the right songs. In a house of seven, I was in charge of the music.'

He laughs heartily before explaining how his mum's friends would ask him to set up their record players. 'That led on to later being asked to set up people's video recorders,' he chuckles. 'I was quite annoyed at that time. It was like, "Why don't you do it?" But my mum would say, "But you know how to do it, Robert." Actually, I didn't know how to do it; I just had the patience to read the instructions. They wouldn't and would bust stuff all the time.'

He starts giggling again at the memory. Although Gordon claims he was 'hardly Mr Technical', he did soon develop an interest in electronics, and more specifically the giant Reggae soundsystems he encountered at community events. With their giant racks of custom-built amplifiers, vocalists on the mic and DJs spinning 'funny 10" records with no labels', they were a dazzling sight.

Gordon's interest ramped up further as a '13 or 14-year-old' when a neighbour showed him his audiophile home hi-fi set-up. 'He had a Technics turntable, a Hitachi power amp with a silver front, and a JVC pre-amp with a brown front,' he recalls. 'There was this other little thing on top, so I asked him what it was. He said, "It's a little tone thing I made for myself - it does bass, midrange and treble." I was like, "You made that yourself?" He said yes and that it wasn't that difficult.'

A few weeks later, while browsing the Maplins catalogue, Gordon spotted the electronics kit in question. 'I built it, and then someone I knew came round the house, saw it and asked if they could buy it,' he says. 'So I sold it. I joke to people that I made more money as a kid by building little bits of sound equipment than I do now.'

During his time at Hurlfield secondary school, Gordon was known as the go-to guy for anything sound related. He built dub boxes, sirens, delay pedals and EQ units to order, using the money he made to buy records and instruments. At one point he even spent £280 - then a vast sum for a teenager from one of Sheffield's poorest neighbourhoods - on a bass guitar for the Roots Reggae band he'd just formed with his cousin Glenroy and classmate Glyn Andrews. Gordon also drummed in other local Reggae bands and alongside Andrews was part of the house band for the Hurlfield school production of *Bugsy Malone*. Also featured in a starring role was a popular teenager from the year above: Winston Hazel.

'Rob was on drums, I played the guitar, and Winnie played a main character,' Andrews remembers. 'The production was quite successful. We had a very encouraging music teacher called Mrs Wilson. Together the three of us were involved in a project she ran where we made a Funk tune. We called it "The Funky Frog" because it contained this frog type sound we made using an old EDP Wasp synthesizer. I'm sure Winnie did some scratching on the tune as well.'

The three friends were also regulars at Hurlfield's on-site youth club and community centre, an initiative paid for by Sheffield City Council's Youth Service in a bid to engage with teenagers and keep them out of trouble. Gordon remembers DJing there on numerous occasions, while Andrews says the youth club was, 'really good.'

By now, both Andrews and Gordon had started thinking about what they might do when they turned 16 in a couple of years. Gordon had graduated from merely playing in bands to manning the mixing desk at local Reggae gigs ('These were adult concerts, and I was only 14 or 15,' he says proudly), so a move into music production seemed like a good option.

'When the careers officer asked what I wanted to be when I grew up, I said that I liked records,' he says thoughtfully. 'Then I thought, "Should I be a DJ?" I could already do that. So I thought, "I should learn how to make records." I like records, so I should make records.'

When he left school, Gordon got involved with a 'black community cooperative' called Entertone. Funding was secured from Sheffield City Council's Youth Service, topped up by other local organizations that funded community projects, to buy musical equipment including a portastudio - a slimmed-down mixing desk with a built-in cassette recorder that could be used to record and produce local bands. The man in charge of the portastudio was, of course, Robert Gordon.

A year after leaving Hurlfield, Gordon, Andrews and the rest of Entertone's music-makers decided to spend some time recording away from Sheffield. The idea was to record a tape of all of their different projects, with Gordon handling production and mixing duties.

'Once a year we'd go to a stately home, take a load of equipment, stay up all night for two weeks and go mental,' Gordon laughs. 'I got a budget from the council to do it.'

The trip was a success, so the following summer Gordon and his Entertone collective - including Glyn Andrews, who by now was running music sessions two afternoons a week at a Youth Service drop-in centre near Sheffield bus station - headed to Unstone Grange near Chesterfield to record another tape. This one was arguably even better than the first, which had been doing the rounds amongst the Steel City's alternative musicians since the previous summer.

'One of the recordings ended up in the house that members of the band Chakk were sharing,' Gordon recalls. 'Mark Brydon heard one of his housemates playing and asked who had produced it. It was only little four-track portastudios I was using then - they were plugged into a big desk, but I was recording onto the four-track tape recorder. Mark reckoned the results I was getting sounded better than his brand new 24-track studio where they'd been working with Sly and Robbie. They needed an engineer, so I was introduced to them.'

* * *

Mark Brydon had initially come to the Steel City to study architecture at Sheffield University. Like many of the other students on his course, Brydon was an enthusiastic post-punk musician, concertgoer and occasional clubber.

'It was six years of not really doing architecture and messing around with music,' Brydon laughs. 'The architecture studio at the top of the Arts Tower[4] was full of music in those days. Everyone would play music, and that's how I got to know Alan Cross. He also lived next door to me on Brunswick Street. Our house was like a typical Young Ones student place - there would be junkies shooting up in the kitchen and God knows what else happening.'

When time permitted, the guitarist-turned-bassist would pop next door to record music with Cross on the latter's TASCAM four-track. They were hugely inspired by the experimental antics of local heroes Cabaret Voltaire and spent much of their time either making tape loops or recording themselves hitting things to create unique drum sounds.

In 1982 they recorded and self-released their first cassette as Chakk, alongside an extended cast of guest musicians and future bandmates. Titled "Clocks and Babies", the album was a non-stop patchwork or off-kilter Post-Punk grooves, skittish drums, reverb-laden freestyle Jazz horns, eccentric spoken-word snippets, lo-fi drum machine rhythms, snarling vocals and out-there electronics. It drew on a dizzying array of influences and ideas, reprocessing them via techniques populated by Cabaret Voltaire's Chris Watson, Richard H Kirk and Stephen Mallinder.

Naturally, both Kirk and Mallinder were fans[5] and in 1984 offered Brydon, Cross and company the opportunity to record free of charge in Western Works, a former industrial unit in the city centre they'd turned into a studio. The resultant single, a stuttering, heavily edited and rearranged chunk of low-slung Industrial Funk brilliance entitled "Out of the Flesh", was subsequently released on Cabaret Voltaire's Doublevision label. Thanks to widespread press hype - in part created by local NME journalist Amrik Rai - the single became one of the most talked about independent records of the year. As a result, Chakk was inundated with offers from the A&R teams at major labels. Eventually, they signed to MCA, but only after the label agreed to their one condition.

'We told them we'd only sign if they gave us the entire recording budget for the album to build a studio,' Brydon says. 'That's the way the Cabs had done it with Western Works. We wanted to have the means of production. It was absolutely right because our time with MCA was very short and messy.'

In hindsight, it was a brilliant move. Chakk quickly secured a space above a metalworking shop on the Whicker and set to work. 'It was like 80 or 90 degrees Celsius constantly - unbelievably hot,' Brydon remembers.

---

4   When it opened in 1966, the futuristic looking Arts Tower was the first skyscraper in Sheffield. It remained the tallest building in the city for almost 50 years. The building's other claim to fame is the presence of a Paternoster lift – a 'death trap' that was notoriously tricky to use. In fact, it is one of only a handful of working examples now remaining in Europe.
5   By this point, Watson had left the group to work as a location sound recordist for Tyne Tees Television. He's now one of the World's leading location sound engineers for film, contributing to many of the BBC's most famous nature documentaries.

'We then put in this rock wool as soundproofing, so it was totally tropical. We all worked on it, labouring and putting up the walls. We were up and running as soon as we could be.'

Chakk spent months recording an album at FON that was subsequently rejected by MCA. To try and get an LP produced that was acceptable to both parties, the label decided to hire an outside production team and asked the band for suggestions. 'We were listening to a lot of stuff like Gwen Guthrie's "Padlock" mini-album and Grace Jones' "Nightclubbing" - things that had been made at Compass Point studios in Barbados,' Brydon says. 'That's where we wanted to go [musically], so asked for Sly and Robbie. Getting them up to Sheffield was hilarious. Although they were very complimentary, it was never going to be right because the whole brief was so different to what we wanted to do. It was really fun to work with them though.'

The resultant album sank without trace, despite having some genuinely standout moments. Chakk's contract with MCA was torn up in mid-1986, but they got to keep the studio they'd built with the label's money. This was FON Studios[6], and over the following 18 months it would become a runaway success story. This was, in part, down to the contribution of their extremely talented new sound engineer, Robert Gordon.

'When I turned up for the interview I'd never worked in a professional studio,' Gordon says. 'It was the first 24-track studio in Sheffield - properly high-tech. They thought I'd have problems because some of the equipment is so sophisticated. One of the things they mentioned was the Yamaha CX5 music computer. I said, "It's all right - I have one of those at home and use it every day!" And I got the job.'

He didn't own one, of course, but Gordon did have an aptitude for getting the hang of quite complex electronic instruments quite quickly. 'When he started he was just this kid - 18 or 19 - but he wasn't intimidated by studios at all,' Brydon says. 'He knew how to line up a multi-track tape recorder and he barely ever had to look at instruction manuals. He'd say, "I've got this drum machine" and show you how it worked. He could mend stuff, build effects units - he just had this prodigious talent to understand studio engineering. In the early days, he was very patient and totally unflappable.'

It was only a few months after he started work at FON that Gordon was given a chance to produce his first track: a cut by Richard Hawley's teenage band, Treebound Story. The cut in question was called "Forever Green" and ended up on the B-side of the band's debut EP, "My Life's Example". It sounded great, with rich, warm bass underpinning glistening guitars, trippy

---

6   FON was reportedly short for "Fuck Off Nazis". The band and their manager Dave Taylor first used FON as the name of their record label, which was established in 1985 just prior to the band signing with MCA. FON Records released a number of Chakk singles before signing other bands from Yorkshire, most notably Leeds band Age of Chance. Confusingly, the record shop known as FON Records had no direct link with the studio, though at one point it was partially owned by Dave Taylor.

effects and typical mid-80s Indie-Rock vocals. The EP earned Treebound Story a live session on John Peel's radio show and more production work for both FON and Gordon.

All was not rosy in the FON garden though. At the time, the studio had barely any bookings and things weren't looking good for the future. 'We had a big meeting and they told me they were going to close the studio,' Gordon says. 'I said, "Why are you closing? You've got a studio and a record label. There are all these bands in Sheffield that John Peel plays - I don't know them, but if I walk down West Street I see Pulp, Hula, Artery. Why don't you record all those bands and put them out on your label? They took my advice, didn't close the studio and put out records from some of those bands.'

Brydon and Gordon quickly forged a partnership - later officially known as the FON Force - and were touted as producers on the rise. One of Gordon's productions for Age of Chance, a bustling Indie-Dance cover of Prince classic "Kiss", nudged the top 50 of the singles charts in December 1986. A year later, a track they'd made with two young House musicians from Nottingham, Mark Gamble and Cassius Campbell, surged to number three in the UK singles charts. This was Krush's 'House Arrest', one of the earliest UK House records to chart and a million-seller worldwide. It featured lead vocals from Gordon's then-girlfriend, Ruth Joy, and lyrics provided by his school friend Glyn Andrews.

'The lyrics had come to our friend John Bailey, another ex-Hurlfield pupil, in a dream,' Andrews says. 'I was at FON quite a lot hanging out and would play on some of the records at that time. Sometimes when Robert and Ruth were in the studio, I'd babysit their baby daughter.'

The runaway success of "House Arrest" made Gordon and Brydon in-demand producers and remixers. There were big-budget jobs for the likes of Pop Will Eat Itself, Erasure, Yazz and The Fall, as well as pet projects such as The Funky Worm, a trio whose members included Richard Barratt aka DJ Parrot. It was a funk-fuelled, sample-heavy fusion of Soul, Funk and House that became so successful in the clubs of the North on white label that Pete Tong licensed it to London Records.

That track, and the remixes they undertook for the likes of Test Department, Eric B & Rakim and Jakki Graham, proved that Brydon and Gordon knew how to make music for the clubs, even if at this point their clients wanted crossover hits rather than weighty underground anthems.

In 1989, Brydon and Gordon shared their studio secrets with Music Technology magazine, explaining their working methods and love of 'cheap equipment'. In perhaps the most telling segment, Gordon explained how the key to their productions was not shiny synths or strong choruses, but rather the electronic rhythm section.

'If we could find the same drum pattern and bass pattern to run all the way through a track non-stop we'd do it,' Gordon said. 'Everything is only there to make the groove feel better. It's true that for Pop you can't beat a strong chorus. If you're in a car listening to Radio 1 and a strong chorus comes on you can't beat it. But if a groove like one of ours was pumping out of Radio 1, you probably wouldn't hear it anyway because the bass was too deep[7].'

Although his FON work often involved creating club remixes that doffed a cap to the latest club sounds out of the United States, Robert Gordon hated House music. 'My friends Winston [Hazel] and Glyn [Andrews] liked House music, but I thought it was crap,' Gordon says bluntly. 'It sounded like somebody had made it in their house messing around. I was into studios, high-tech music - those Chicago House records sounded like things I'd done in the Portastudio when I'd just got my TB-303 and was messing about.'

For Gordon, everything related back to Reggae. Even if he was producing a sample-heavy cut for Pop Will Eat Itself, remixing Atmosfear's Brit-Funk classic "Dancing In Outer Space" or working with The Fall's notorious frontman Mark E Smith, the heaviness of the bass and the swing of the percussion always took priority.

'Robert once said to me that Reggae was the most important thing to happen to British Pop music,' Mark Brydon recalls. 'I thought that was interesting. He might disagree with me, but I think he approached all music with this Reggae soundsystem head on. Although he liked machines and machine music, what he made was just Reggae in a different package.'

Before landing a job at FON, Gordon had been considering making electronic Reggae music of his own - futuristic machine-led, sub-heavy workouts with the distinctive rhythm patterns associated with the popular "Steppers" style[8]. 'If I'd not got a job at FON I'd have been the first person to make electronic sequenced Reggae because that's the equipment I was building for myself at the time. By the time that Jammy came out with the "Under Me Sleng Teng"[9] rhythm, with the equipment I had, I could have made that record ten times over. I'd bought a drum machine and had remixed the sounds to sound like Reggae. I was going to set up a label and make Techno-Reggae.'

* * *

---

7   Bradwell, David: *Force Majeure*, Music Technology magazine, May 1989.
8   On 'Steppers' style Reggae, the bass drum plays every quarter beat of the bar. This helps give a driving, four-to-the-floor feel not dissimilar to Disco and House. However, most "Steppers"-driven Reggae music also contains intricate drum fills not often found in dance music derived from Disco. These fills, and the overall rhythmic arrangement of Steppers records, draw much influence from the polyrhymthic beats of African music.
9   "Under Me Sleng Teng" is widely considered to be the first digital Reggae rhythm. It was influential in ushering in an era of tough, machine-made Reggae, Dub and Dancehall, as well as the later "UK Steppers" style of heavy, club-focused digital Dub.

For someone who earned a living partially making dance music, Robert Gordon wasn't a regular clubber. He did make occasional visits to places where his good friend Winston Hazel was playing, despite his strong dislike for the developing House sound.

It was at one of these rare club outings to Steamer at the Leadmill, where Hazel and Richard 'Parrot' Barratt were playing alongside Graeme Park, that he heard a record that would change his musical outlook completely. 'I wasn't really into what was being played but, as a professional, I thought I should go and see what's going on,' Gordon admits. 'A track came on, and it caught my attention, so I went up to Parrot and said, "You know I don't like House?" He laughed and said, "I know Rob!" So I said, "What is this playing because it's not House?" He said, "Oh, I get it Rob, you don't like House, but you like Techno!" It was the first Techno I'd ever heard.'

The record in question was Rhythim Is Rhythim's "Nude Photo", a Derrick May produced chunk of mind-altering Motor City Techno full of clattering machine drums, twisted electronic motifs and fizzing, futuristic synth stabs. 'When I heard it, my jaw dropped,' Gordon enthuses. 'I thought, "Now we're talking!" I can deal with that - I can work with Techno.'

Gordon had just been paid a significant sum by Big Life Records for work on Yazz's debut album, "Wanted", so went out and bought £3,000 worth of new equipment for his home studio. This included an AKAI sampler, a DAT machine, a Korg M1 synthesizer and a '£100 mixer'. After opening the boxes, he spread the equipment out on his living room floor and connected it together.

A little later in the evening, Hazel paid him a visit. Gordon offered to show his friend how his prized AKAI sampler worked. 'I thought it was fantastic what you could do with it,' Hazel remembers. 'Without that lesson from Robert, I wouldn't have known where to start. He invited me to come round the next night. Now I knew what you could do with the sampler, I decided I'd take a record with me - the '85 remix of Manu Dibango's "Abele Dance" on Celluloid.'

When Hazel arrived the next day, Gordon had company: fellow soundsystem enthusiast Sean Maher, another former Hurlfield pupil who like Hazel had caught the House bug. 'Me and Rob were just chilling, having a smoke, listening to some tunes and playing around with his new equipment,' Maher remembers. 'Then Winston came over carrying this record.'

That Manu Dibango record had been a big favourite at Jive Turkey for some time. Crucially, it contained heavy Electro beats, a choice selection of killer drum breaks and some suitably trippy electronic noises. Hazel selected a passage to put into the sampler - a snappy break accompanied by a sliver of melody and a female vocal snippet - and the trio got to work.

'My idea was that we should make something like the Manu Dibango record, not sample it,' Hazel says. 'When Robert put it on the turntable and started to record it, because I didn't know how to make the track, that sample is what we ended up with, chopped off at the end. Then we worked out how to make it tight.'

Over the next four hours, the trio's first track took shape. 'We needed a Techno beat for it, and Robert already had this snare pattern that he liked to use on everything,' Hazel says. 'The bassline was a chopped down sine wave, and I picked out a melody on the synth that sounded quite alien and bit like it might have come from Detroit.'

Robert Gordon's drum programming has a distinctive trademark shuffle which while obviously influenced by Techno and Electro, boast percussive patterns that reflect the specific timing and intonation of electronic Reggae. 'There's a very particular drumbeat programming style on there,' Gordon admits. 'It's in the background, but it's Steppers. I did that drum programming to say, "I don't like House music, but if I heard these beats it would get me going." If I'm doing the drums, I'm going to do something I like. A straight four-to-the-floor like House wasn't for me - I needed something else.'

By the end of the evening, the track had been composed, produced, mixed and bounced down to a TDK metal cassette. 'One of the things that was a bit different was that when we came to mix it, we mixed it through that eight-track mixer, but we bounced it from the Atari ST [computer] to a little sequencing box,' Maher remembers. 'We transferred the tune from the Atari to the Roland MC-202 sequencer because it was tighter than MIDI. That gave it a different feel to how it was in the computer.'

They couldn't think of a title, so simply called it "Track With No Name". A little over three decades after it was produced, it still sounds astonishing. Put simply, "Track With No Name" turned Bleep & Bass into an artform and sounds every bit as futuristic and otherworldly as "Voodoo Ray".

While "The Theme" thrilled through its sheer weightiness, raw energy and the simplicity of its ideas, Hazel, Gordon and Maher's debut track drew together the emerging style's major influences - 808 Electro, Chicago Acid, Detroit Techno and Dub Reggae - while sounding every bit as polished, intergalactic and far-sighted as any record that had previously emerged from the Motor City. It was Sheffield's first contribution to the Bleep & Bass canon, and it couldn't have come from anywhere else.

'It's reactionary and catches a moment in time,' Hazel says. 'I think it reflects what we were experiencing at the time - experiences through music, the industrial devastation, the club scene and the climate of Sheffield at the time. It had the sound of the city we grew up in implanted through the track.'

Hazel wasted no opportunity in debuting "Track With No Name" on his next SCR radio show. The response from listeners was immediate. 'The phones went ballistic,' Hazel enthuses. 'All these people were ringing up saying how great it was. It sounded so solid. The next day when I went into work at the [FON] record shop, the other guys had heard it on the show. I told them about the response, and we all agreed that we should put it out.'

The following weekend, Gordon received a call from Hazel urging him to come down to Occasions. 'He said, "You've got to come to the club," but I wasn't that keen,' Gordon remembers. 'He said, "You have to come this time, there's something really good happening". So I went down there, and Winston called me over to the DJ booth. He said, "Watch this," and played the tape of "Track With No Name". It tore the place down.'

Quite what happened next is a matter of some debate. Gordon says he mixed the track at FON and pressed up 500 white labels with a track called "Shall We", a cut made largely by Maher at his home studio, on the other side. He claims that he took these down to FON Records to sell and that's when the idea of starting a record label was raised.

Other accounts state that the FON record store's owners, Steve Beckett and Rob Mitchell, were already thinking of launching a label, having previously failed to sell a sped-up, breakbeat-driven Hip-Hop track by local producer DJ Mink - produced under Gordon's supervision at the FON Studio - to record labels in London.

However it came about, the decision to launch Warp Records - and re-name the FON store in its honour - was taken sometime in early summer 1989. Beckett and Mitchell handled the business side of the label, taking out credit cards and an Enterprise Allowance Grant to help pay for the pressing and distribution of "Track With No Name", which by now had been credited to the Forgemasters[10].

Along with Hazel, Beckett and Mitchell worked tirelessly to promote the record, even asking friends to call record shops around the country and ask whether they had copies of the record in stock. 'We told them to ask for a few hot import things and hard to get hold of records, but also to make sure "Track With No Name" was one they mentioned,' Hazel says. 'That created massive interest, and the buyers in these shops started asking importers and distributors whether they knew anything about this mysterious track. Then word got out that it was from Sheffield, which got more people excited. The first 500 copies disappeared really quickly.'

Another pressing was immediately ordered, this time with the brand new - and now iconic - Warp Records logo designed by Ian Anderson of the Designers Republic, a rising star whose first job had been to design the cover to Chakk's "10 Days In An Elevator". The Forgemasters were now hot property, and it wasn't long before the remix requests started rolling in. Gordon and Maher would later tweak Inspiral Carpets "Commercial Rain",

---

10   Sheffield Forgemasters is the name of a leading steel-making firm founded in 1983 following the privatization of the British Steel Corporation. Its factories and forges still dominate the skyline in the Brightside area of the city.

but the first remixes completed were of Man Machine's self-titled debut on Outer Rhythm, an offshoot of Mute's pop-dance label Rhythm King that would soon handle pressing and distribution for Warp.

Surprisingly, it was not Gordon but Maher who provided the two sparse and weighty revisions of the Man Machine record - bass-heavy beasts that are every bit as heavy as the few Bleep & Bass records that had come before. 'Steve Beckett took me down to Square Dance Studios to do that one,' Maher reveals. 'What I did was very basic, bass-heavy and stripped back. One of the mixes was meant as a dub, which is why it has a trippy feel. I knew my way around the studio a bit, but I was thrown in the deep end. You'd always get an engineer at a studio session, so you couldn't fail really.'

As the hype around the Forgemasters grew, Beckett and Mitchell called on favours from FON's Dave Taylor to connect them with friendly journalists in the music press. They also began to think seriously about how Warp Records might develop and how they could turn it into a viable enterprise. In the office they'd set up in the back room of the record shop they ran, the pair started thinking seriously about where their new label might lead.

'Rob Mitchell, in particular, wanted it to be a proper business,' Richard Barratt says. 'Plenty of other people in the scene who started labels were just pissing around. Winston and myself just wanted new tunes and didn't see this as a potentially massive thing, but Rob and Steve did.'

Although decisions on what to release and when were taken by committee - Gordon, Mitchell and Beckett jointly owned the label, but Hazel was also asked for his input given his impeccable dancefloor credentials - there was only one de-facto 'musical director'.

'Rob and Steve were great business people and very smart, but I don't think they really understood black music at all,' Glyn Andrews sighs. 'Robert [Gordon] was so important to how the early records on Warp sounded.'

It's certainly true that Gordon had something of a Midas touch when it came to mixing and mastering. Listen to any of the first ten or so releases on the label - pretty much all of which Gordon contributed to in one way or another - and you'll notice how sonically precise they all are, especially when compared to many other leading British House and Techno records of the time: all warm, deep, weighty bass, crystal clear beats, stargazing synthesiser sounds and tough, tightly programmed percussion with just the right amount of looseness. Robert Gordon took sound seriously, attended record cutting sessions at the Townhouse in London and handpicked the mastering engineer he believed would guarantee the best possible results.

While we sit in his studio chatting about the early Warp Records story, I remark that the sound of Gordon's records makes me think of two things: exceptionally well produced "high-tech" Dub - high-tech sound being one of his sonic obsessions - and the kind of sci-fi futurism most associated with Detroit.

'My music, and Techno at the time, was a decadent form of Afro-Carib-bean music,' he responds. 'I call it ultraviolet neon planet. There's a light in a specific place, which few people have seen, and we're all trying to get to it independent of each other. We were using the same voice with no words.'

He pauses to take another long drag on an industrial-strength spliff before continuing. 'Sometimes when you go into a studio, look around and switch everything on, it lights up like you're in a spaceship. Then you look at the speakers and think, "I wonder what they can put out? How would the music sound if the equipment could make it itself?" So make some music that fits in with what it looks like, right? It's tomorrow's equipment - make tomorrow's music.'

Gordon says he also had other motivations for launching a record label. For Beckett and Mitchell, Warp may have been both a business opportunity and a chance to represent their local scene; for Gordon, releasing music that would unite his friends on the dancefloor was of utmost importance.

'From my experience, the Warp experiment was a success because I did get both my white and black friends dancing to the same records,' he says. 'Some of my black friends still said, "House music is shit", but I told them to trust me because it was different. It was House or Techno, whatever you want to call it, made by a Jamaican guy. The weight of the bass was there to appeal to them.'

● ● ●

One Monday night in the summer of 1989, Robert Gordon decided to accompany Winston Hazel to one of his regular out of town gigs - a weekly shindig at a club in Huddersfield called Sunset Boulevard. Hazel was by now a regular up there thanks to his friendship with resident DJ John Charles.

'John was from Sheffield originally, and he always got me to do Soul sec-tions at his various nights,' Hazel explains. 'It really began to kick off and you started getting dancers coming from all over Yorkshire - minibuses full from Sheffield, Leeds and Bradford. That was very helpful in terms of being able to break new music. It was the first place I played the tape of "Track With No Name" outside of Sheffield.'

Hazel wasn't the only Yorkshire DJ that John Charles got to play at those Sunset Boulevard sessions; in that year, the weekly night also boasted appearances from Bradford's Unique 3 and Leeds' DJ Martin and Night-mares On Wax. As a result, the night became a focal point for the develop-ing "Yorkshire Bass" and "Sheffield Bleep" sound - a kind of neutral meeting ground for musical rivals from across the county.

'It was really important,' Gordon asserts. 'I don't know how it came about originally - maybe it was the only club in Yorkshire that would tolerate a bunch of black guys blasting the system every week - but they let us all do what we wanted to musically. Although it was on a traditionally dead night, it was always packed out. Everybody came from all over for the progressive music and especially the cassettes and dubplates. I knew it was a scene that needed harnessing.'

In front of a crowd that contained footworkers, Hip-Hop heads, ravers and Jazz dancers, DJs from rival crews could take it in turns to show off their latest bedroom productions and one-off "specials". All dreamed of getting the best reaction. To achieve that, you needed some serious bass-weight.

'For us, it was all about the bass drop,' says Leeds' Tomas Stewart, whose "Mindsong EP" was released by Warp in early 1991. 'We responded to weighty bass and drums that were tight and heavy, like Electro. When we started hearing records from London with breakbeats in, we thought they sounded too messy and loose. They just weren't tight and heavy enough for us.'

Many of the earliest Yorkshire-made Bleep & Bass cuts were aired at Sunset Boulevard before they'd appeared on vinyl. This offered an opportunity to Warp's Robert Gordon, Steve Beckett and Rob Mitchell. 'The DJs would stroke their own egos by playing tapes of tunes they'd made, or their mates had made the night before,' Gordon says. 'Then I'd be there in the car park outside asking if I could sign the tune they'd just played.'

It was on one trip to Sunset Boulevard that Gordon and Winston Hazel heard DJ Martin play a track he'd recently made in his attic with two shy teenagers. It was incredible: sparse, futuristic and rush inducing, with lower sub-bass frequencies than any record either had heard before. Afterwards, Gordon asked if he could get a copy of the cassette. Scribbled on the tape's thin white label were three letters: LFO.

THE TRUE CREATORS

THE RAPID RISE OF LFO

'Normally when you played some huge record, four or five people would come up and ask what it was. When I dropped "LFO" for the first time in 1990, 25% of the people in the club rushed up to the decks to ask about it. When it broke down to the 'L...F...O' vocal and the bass, people were literally shrieking - they'd never heard bass like it. Even for people who had been in Dub Reggae sound systems, this was so far beyond anything.'

JD TWITCH

One evening in 1987, Paul Edmeade was ambling his way across Chapeltown, minding his own business. As he strolled down one typical side street - think rows of tightly packed back-to-back terraced houses - a sporty Ford Escort with a noticeably loud exhaust pulled up beside him. The driver, a young black man with a beaming smile, wound down the window and called out towards him. 'You're that kid who DJs and can scratch aren't you?'

Edmeade, an enthusiastic teenage breakdancer turned wannabe Hip-Hop DJ, replied, 'Yeah, why?' The driver beckoned him towards the car. 'Get in'. 'No, no,' Edmeade responded, rightly questioning the motives of a stranger who was several years his senior. 'Come on,' the driver said, 'I want to talk to you.'

Reluctantly, Edmeade got in the car and was driven to the gentleman's house on Bayswater Mount, a lengthy suburban street that sloped upwards from Harehills Road towards the sprawl of Chapeltown. 'I saw that he had two Technics turntables and a mixer,' Edmeade remembers. 'I was like, "Wow!" Very few people had two decks and a mixer back then. He told me to show him what I could do. I was a bit cocky. So, I was doing all my scratches,

CHAPTER NINE

^ **LFO** by Vanya Balogh

and he said, "You've got to show me how to do that." So I said, "What do I get out of it? Can I come and use your decks when I want?" He said, "Of course, and I'll show you how to mix." So I taught him to scratch, and he taught me to mix records together.'

The stranger in question was Martin Williams, better known around Chapeltown as DJ Martin. At the time, he was one of the few local Soul boys with decks, which he'd acquired with money from his first job. 'My dad nearly killed me,' Williams laughs. 'When you've been using inferior decks, that's what you do! I was addicted to buying records and DJing.'

Williams had been turned on to Jazz-Funk by his older brother, who was not only a regular dancer on the all-dayer circuit but also a keen hi-fi enthusiast. Under his watchful eye, Williams fell in love with Soul and Funk music. By the time he met Edmeade, he'd also fallen for the new House sounds coming out of Chicago.

'When the original House records started coming in, I was all over that because I just thought it was a breath of fresh air. That was like Electro to me - as fresh as that sounded, my head was just exploding with the sounds coming out of the early House scene.'

It was perhaps inevitable that Williams got into DJing. Although he played his first gig at the Ritz where Leeds Arena now stands, it was his regular Friday night sessions at the West Indian Centre on Chapeltown Road - years before SubDub made it one of Leeds most talked-about venues - that first drew him to the attention of dancers.

He also featured regularly behind the turntables of other popular Chapeltown venues including the International Club (soon to become the Phoenix club when it reopened following a fire) and the Trades Club. Crucially he was also close to another local DJ hero, Warehouse resident Roy Archer. 'I used to help DJ Roy out at the Warehouse sometimes,' Williams remembers. 'I used to love standing in the DJ booth and watching him.'

It wasn't long before Williams was being touted as not only one of the stars of the Chapeltown scene, but also one of Leeds finest DJs. Crucially, he always had time to nurture the talents of fellow Soul boys, Hip-Hop heads and House freaks from the local area. 'Martin had the records,' Edmeade says. 'He was like a real, live DJ who was at a higher level to everyone else. He provided a great outlet for people to get things done.'

Williams' friend Homer Harriott, then a part-time Reggae musician, is keen to stress what a pivotal role he played in the local scene. 'Even guys like Kevin [Harper] and a few others, would go and dance when he DJed,' Harriott says. 'He was like the person right at the centre of what was happening.'

Williams was naturally a regular on the all-dayer circuit, where he'd turn up at events alongside friends such as Paul Edmeade and Edward Irish, a dedicated "driller" from the Elite crew of competitive dancers based out of the Northern School of Contemporary Dance on Chapeltown Road. While Williams claims he was never much of a dancer, Harriott remembers differently. 'He'd come down to the Checkpoint West Indian Centre some-times and dance with the real dancers - the crews,' he says. 'At Check-point [in Bradford] myself and Mark [Millington] used to chat with Martin when he was there.'

The passion and enthusiasm Williams had for House music, in particu-lar, was infectious. Both Harriott and Edmeade say that they were turned on to the style through his DJ sets. In Harriott's case, it quickly led to buying an Atari ST on Williams' suggestion, so that he could make House tracks of his own.

By then, Williams had already set up a small studio of his own, based in the attic of the terraced house he shared with his girlfriend (and a little later, their baby daughter). His other passion, outside of music, was computers. By the standards of the time, Williams was incredibly computer literate, so it didn't take him long to master the ins and outs of a cracked copy of Cubase. 'I had a really strong computer background and knew exactly what sounds I wanted to hear,' he says. 'Most people who say they do this or that, it's really just a fluke, but you need to be on the platform to catch a train. If you're on it, then sooner or later then you'll stumble on something that's different.'

●●●

Sometime in 1988, unemployed 18-year-old Bramley boy Gez Varley was offered the opportunity to enrol on a photography and graphic design course at the Side Step youth training centre on Sweet Street, just down the road from the "dark arches" complex of tunnels beneath Leeds railway station.

Varley, like many of his peers, had spent much of his teenage years as a committed breakdancer. He knew many members of rival Leeds and Brad-ford crews - Chapeltown's Connect Four and Bradford's Solar City Rockers, in particular - by name, having battled with them at competitions during the height of the Electro craze. When he turned up for his first day at Side Step, he was surprised to see quite a few familiar faces milling around.

'One of my school mates, Lee Kenny, was there, as was the rapper Toz, who later did some stuff with Nightmares On Wax,' Varley remembers. 'Because we were all into Electro and Hip-Hop, everybody knew each other. Side Step was like a little hub.'

Varley, like some others in his Side Step peer group, had already begun tinkering around with electronic instruments. 'My older brother had this cheap Boss drum machine, like a little toy with a microphone out port,' he says. 'My brother was programming all this stuff because he was into New Order.'

By this point, Varley had already fallen in love with House and Techno, which he saw as a natural evolution from his beloved Electro. One day in the autumn of 1988, he was flicking through the racks at Crash Records on the Headrow in Leeds City Centre, when his old breakdance rivals Unique 3 walked in carrying a box of white label records.

'There were two, three kids like me in there, so I said to Edzy, Pat and Ian, "I haven't seen you in a while, what have you been up to?",' Varley fondly remembers. 'So they said, "Well, check this." They stuck on "The Theme", and the hairs on the back of my neck and arms went up.'

When Varley was left some money in his grandfather's will, he spent it on music-making equipment. 'I bought a Casio FZ-10 sampler, a TR-808 drum machine and a TB-303. It was all easy to use except the sampler, which had a manual that was this thick,' he says, placing his hands six inches apart for emphasis. 'Bit by bit I got into making music, and then I met up with Mark Bell.'

A shy and softly spoken fellow member of Side Step's photography and graphic design course, Mark Bell had first come to Varley's attention during the Electro era. 'We first faced off as rivals on a Saturday afternoon in the Merrion Centre,' Varley laughs. 'We reconnected at Side Step. He'd been in this little group with some other lads from Lofthouse, like Richard Brook, who later went on to be in Wildplanet and release records on Warp. By the time we met up again at Side Step, Mark had stopped working with them.'

Bell and Varley had yet to work together when they started on a computer skills module at Side Step. On their first day, they were surprised by the identity of their course tutor: Martin Williams. 'We knew him because he was a pretty well-known DJ, but I'm not sure he knew us,' Varley remembers. 'When we did that course and Martin turned up to teach us it was like, 'I know that guy!' At that point, everybody on the scene knew him because he'd had a few spots at the Warehouse and played in Chapeltown a lot.'

Through their shared love of cutting-edge electronic music, the three men started talking before and after lessons. 'Mark was very quiet,' Williams remembers. 'We talked about music and Mark buying some old analogue stuff. He really knew his keyboards. He was really into synthesizers.'

It wasn't long before Williams, who had previous when it came to nurturing the talents of would-be local DJs and producers, invited Bell and Varley to come and work on some music in his home studio, locally known as 'the Attic'. Over the next 18 months, a strong working partnership developed, resulting in some 20 to 30 completed demos according to Varley and Williams.

'Going up into Martin's attic was like entering an Aladdin's Cave - he had thousands of records and all stuff that we'd missed,' Varley says. 'We were like, 'How did you get that?' For quite a while we were there like, four or five days a week. Martin gave us a set of keys to his house so we could let ourselves in because he was still working. At one time we were pretty much living on fried chicken - there was this bin bag in the studio full of KFC boxes and Coca-Cola cans. I remember looking at Mark and saying, "We should probably go home now - we've been here for days!" It was kind of weird but great at the same time.'

Studio sessions regularly went on late into the night, with Williams giving Varley and Bell lifts home in his sporty Escort. 'My dad just thought I was a dosser because Martin would drop me off at two in the morning,' Varley laughs. 'He'd be blazing up the road in this racy car with the music blaring. I'd be like, "Martin, turn it down, you'll wake my dad up!" My dad would be leaning out of the window, shaking his head. It's quite funny when I look back on it.'

Although his attic was cramped, Williams had a tendency to invite friends and acquaintances from the area to come and hang out in the studio. He'd then blast out the latest demos he'd made with Bell and Varley over his weighty studio sound system. 'Pretty much everyone would go and hang out or make music up there[1],' Homer Harriott says. 'It probably wasn't ideal for a guy with a girlfriend and a new baby. There wasn't much privacy - it was straight up the stairs past the bedrooms and the bathroom. The set-up was simple - Atari-ST, Juno 106, Casio sampler.'

While working with Bell and Varley, the Attic's minimal set-up was boosted by the few bits of equipment that the duo already owned. 'We didn't have much money at the time, so we were pooling our resources,' Varley remembers. 'Martin had an Atari and the soundsystem in the attic. Mark had a Jen Electronics SX1000 keyboard that we did the little bleepy melody lines on. I had a sampler and a couple of other bits.'

When the opportunity arose, all three would add to the set-up by acquiring keyboards or drum machines cheap from pawnshops, second-hand stores and - on one famous occasion - from some local lads. 'They said they had these keyboards so we said we'd take a look,' Varley says. 'One of them was this Kawai K1. I asked them how much they wanted and they said they couldn't let it go for anything less than £60. I looked at Mark, and it was like, "How much have you got?" I think we had about £50 between us, so we got it for that."

It was a smart move. The K1, which was blessed with some deliciously futuristic pre-sets, would play a role in the track that would later propel them towards super-stardom and provide the critical and commercial high point of the entire Bleep & Bass movement: "LFO".

Exactly when the track was conceived has been lost in the mists of time, but it reportedly only took a few hours to lay down the first demo version. With Williams at the controls and Bell and Varley suggesting samples or

---

1   Student dance music journalist Vaughan Allen, future Leeds DJ hero Ralph Lawson and Blues DJ Drew Hemment all remember heading up to the attic and hearing what would become "LFO" in various stages of development.

playing in potential lead lines, it all came together quickly. One of the first elements laid down was plucked straight from the presets of the recently acquired K1 synthesizer.

'It had this amazing preset, and I thought we had to use it," Varley says. 'I played around with that preset to see what I could come up with and, you know what? I couldn't get it to sound any better than the original preset. That's why we didn't change it, because it was just perfect.'

The preset in question turned up in the famous sweeping, spacey chord sequence that kicks the track off and provides a dreamy, futuristic focus throughout. "You could have got a load of monkeys from Leeds University, given them some beers and it wouldn't have taken them long to find that preset,' Williams laughs. 'There were some other flukes in the production process as well. When you're putting a sequence into that rack-mounted Casio sampler and stick in more than eight notes, something drops out, so the latter part takes priority. There was a lot more stuff that was meant to be in the track but fell out, because of the limitations of the equipment.'

The track's eventual power did not derive from the preset's far-sighted, Motor City Techno vibe, but rather the intense heaviness of its bassline; or, to be more precise, a bassline that alternated between a "high" motif - inspired by Rhythim is Rhythim's Detroit Techno slammer "Wiggin", which featured on the B-side of the 1988 UK reissue of "Nude Photo" - and the lowest, weightiest sub-bass tone they could find.

To add a finishing touch, Varley suggested utilising the Texas Instruments "speak and spell" machine that Williams had recently bought for his six-month-old daughter. The trio had already decided that they wanted to be known as LFO after the Low Frequency Oscillation control that featured on almost all the synthesizers they owned, so Varley suggested spelling out the letters using the popular child's toy.

'Martin and Mark both thought it was a great idea,' Varley says. 'I thought that it would help people remember the track in clubs and who we were. It totally worked, because when the track started being played out more people would go into record shops in Leeds and ask for that track that goes, "L-F-O". It was all about recognition.'

It's hard to argue against the theory that "LFO" became the purest distillation of the Bleep & Bass sound. It's as timeless and futuristic as any Motor City Techno classic, as loose and punchy as the snappiest '80s Electro roller and as weighty as any redlined Dub Reggae anthem. It boasts ear-catching bleeps, glassy-eyed chords and low-end that kicks you in the guts. Listen to it over a Reggae sound system or a sizeable club rig and its sub-bass frequencies will rattle your ribcage and send your mind spinning.

'We had a small, limited desk that was pretty crap,' Williams remembers. 'It was about getting the sounds right at source and then using the gains - a bit like using the EQs on a DJ mixer. We'd fill the sound spectrum with the bass. When they recorded the bass sound on "LFO" it took a long time to get it right because it kept dropping out of the mix[2].'

There's some disagreement on where the trio's sub-bass obsession came from, but it's likely a mixture of the influence of the raw and fuzzy bassline on Unique 3's "The Theme", Williams' determination to ensure that the record sounded good at the Warehouse, and a desire to create records that resonated over the Reggae systems installed in local Blues clubs.

'I remember we did some early demos and one night Martin was due to play at this Blues in Chapeltown,' Varley says. 'So we finished this track, got in his car and went up to this place that was in a terraced house. Martin was playing to a packed crowd, dropped this tune, and the place went mental. The atmosphere in those Blues was great and we got to test out a lot of tunes on heavy Reggae soundsystems.'

Before his surprise death in 2014 after a short illness, Bell frequently played down Williams' role in early LFO productions, stating in interviews that he was never a member of the group and that his contribution was limited to arrangement and mixing[3]. By all accounts, this is incorrect; Williams was not only the group's engineer and mixer, but also their link to the dancefloor.

'Without Martin, I doubt those early LFO records would have sounded and been finished off the way they were,' Varley says. 'That's why I always mention Martin in interviews, but for some reason, Mark never did. He was always trying to change history.'

Bell is sadly no longer around to refute the charge, but others around Chapeltown at the time agree with Varley's assessment. 'People often knew what they wanted to do but didn't know to make it - that's what Martin could do,' says Homer Harriott. 'He could turn their ideas into an end product, which is why a lot of things revolved around him. He was also a DJ, so knew how to arrange things for maximum dancefloor impact. At the time Gez and Mark weren't DJs. Without Martin, "LFO" wouldn't have turned out the way it did[4].'

---

2   According to both Gez Varley and Homer Harriott, Williams bounced down around ten different mixes of "LFO" before settling on what became the "Leeds Warehouse Mix". Amongst these was a particularly sparse and heavy "Dub". Somewhere there exists a cassette of these alternate versions, though Williams and Varley have yet to find it.

3   In an unpublished interview shared online in 2003 and later quoted on Wikipedia, Bell said the following of their relationship with Williams: 'We gave a tape of our recordings to DJ Martin who helped loads with arranging our tracks so it would work on the dancefloor. We'd been messing around with drum machines since we were 13.'

4   Aside from playing a key role in the making of the track, Harriott says that Williams also came up with the "LFO" band name.

Robert Gordon agrees with Harriott's assessment. 'You can tell that Mark and Gez had been influenced by Martin,' he asserts. 'Eventually, they could do it themselves, but when they were starting out he was a big help.'

* * *

The fact that Williams was a popular and hard-working DJ meant plenty of opportunities to play "LFO", as well as the other tracks they'd completed and compiled on a demo cassette. Quite where "LFO" was played for the first time remains a matter of debate - Williams remembers a gob-smacked crowd at the Warehouse when he spun it there soon after completion, while Varley seems to think it was first dropped at a Blues - but all three members of LFO knew from the start that they had a famously heavy club hit on their hands.

'Oh, we definitely knew it was big - the reaction in the clubs was always mental,' Varley says. 'We did the track pretty quickly, and Martin said if we couldn't get a record deal then we'd find a way to get it out ourselves, either by getting a bank loan or credit card. We asked him how many he thought we could sell, and Martin said we'd easily shift 5,000.'

In the end, they didn't need to plunge themselves into debt to get the track into stores. Salvation arrived during a trip to Sunset Boulevard in Huddersfield, where Martin was playing a guest slot. In the crowd was Robert Gordon, who had accompanied Winston Hazel on the journey north. Gordon was on the lookout for material to sign to Warp Records. Bell, Varley and Williams were aware of Gordon, having previously met him during their frequent trips to check out Winston Hazel DJing at Kiki's and Occasions in Sheffield.

Later that night, all four men made their way outside, got inside Williams' car and stuck on the LFO demo cassette. 'We sat in the car outside the club going through the tracks one by one,' Varley remembers. 'As we went through, Robert was like, "We'll sign this one, and we'll have that one as well, but it's more like a B-side." He said he'd definitely sign us but that he couldn't offer us much money.'

Gordon was as good as his word. He sent Warp business partners Rob Mitchell and Steve Beckett up to Leeds to visit LFO at the Attic. Since none involved knew all that much about contracts, they signed the inlay of the demo cassette to mark their agreement.

When it came to mastering the track for release, Gordon headed down to the Townhouse in London with Williams, Bell and Varley to make sure that the record sounded as heavy as it could possibly be. 'I recently spoke to the engineer that did the cut of "LFO", Kevin Metcalfe. He said it was his first introduction to heavy bass,' Varley says. 'Without Robert Gordon's input, they couldn't have cut it. They just weren't used to that kind of sub-bass.'

When asked about the validity of this story, Gordon nods. 'The cutting engineer had never come across anything like it,' he recalls. 'I remember that we blew the fuses on his cutting system. It's the only time anything I've been involved in has ever done that. We had to stop, put a new fuse in and start again. I still think I have the lacquer of the cut that blew the fuse somewhere.'

It was a taste of things to come. Like Unique 3's "The Theme", LFO's masterpiece soon became famous for blowing speakers in clubs across the UK. When Warp finally began to send out promo copies to DJs in early 1990, it was patently obvious that it was far more powerful than almost any other record that had come before.

'I remember my friend Neil Macey ringing me up to tell me that there was this track coming out with ridiculous bass,' Altern8's Mark Archer recalls. 'The next time I went over to the Network Records office, where Neil worked, I asked him to stick it on. When the sub-bass kicked in, the whole building shook. The following weekend Neil played it in his set at this wine bar in Burntwood. The sub-bass absolutely annihilated the bar's glass collection.'

It wasn't just club DJs who went crazy for "LFO", either. 'I remember John Peel playing it on Radio 1,' Varley says. 'I grew up listening to his show - it was appointment listening for the whole family. I remember one night my dad shouting up to me: "Gerard, get down here - John Peel is playing your song on Radio 1!" It was ace, man.'

After what seemed like 'an eternity' waiting for "LFO" to be released, it finally landed in record stores on 8 July 1990. Backed by the similarly heavyweight "Track 4" and "Probe (Cuba Edit)", the record simply flew off the shelves. The following Sunday, it entered the singles charts at number 43. Three weeks later, it was sitting pretty at number 12. By the time it finally slipped out of the top 100 in the middle of August, "LFO" had sold over 120,000 copies, and become one of the biggest club records of the summer. Suddenly, Bleep & Bass was the toast of British dance music.

The impact of "LFO" was also felt much further afield than British clubs and illegal raves. It was the first Warp record to be licensed for release in other territories - France, Belgium, Greece and Australasia to begin with - and also led to a US deal with leading New York label Tommy Boy (who had, fittingly, previously released many of the killer Electro tracks that had been such a formative influence on Bell, Varley and Williams).

The record's influence could also be heard in a spate of records that, one way or another, bit its style. There was Mind of Kane's "Out of Control", a record so similar that LFO could arguably have gone after them for copyright infringement, Fantasy UFO's "Fantasy Rushour", and a spate of cuts that used similarly sparse and robotic "speak and spell" vocals in some way (see T.T.O's "T.T.O" and D-M-S's "Brand New World", for starters).

Even more featured booming sub-basslines and sci-fi chords courtesy of the Kawai K1, such as "The Attic" by Belgian producer Lhasa. It's unlikely the latter knew that "LFO" had been recorded in a converted loft space but, in hindsight, the track's title is especially fitting.

'When "LFO" came out I told them that what they'd done would last for years,' Robert Gordon says. 'I knew that everyone was going to try and beat it, particularly the heaviness of the bass, but that they wouldn't be able to. I never tried to beat it - I knew it was the ultimate.'

It would be the start of great things for LFO, and specifically Mark Bell and Gez Varley. While they simmered away about the increasing number of rip-offs and copycat Bleep records clogging up record shop shelves, Martin Williams' mind was elsewhere. 'I wasn't bothered about those records at all,' he says matter-of-factly. 'I'd already moved on to other things.'

CHAPTER TEN

ITAL ANTHEMS AND BASSIC BEATS

THE FURTHER ADVENTURES OF DJ MARTIN AND THE CHAPELTOWN CREW

'Firmly underground, Bassic are the latest addition to a collection of northern labels that try to give people what they want to hear and dance to. "Dance music is just going to grow and grow," says [label co-owner] Steve, "but major record labels have lost contact... Things are moving back to the street again".'

VAUGHAN ALLEN i-D magazine, December 1990 [1]

The runaway success of Warp's first few releases did not go unnoticed in Leeds. In Nightmares On Wax's 'Dextrous" and LFO's "LFO", the West York-shire city had provided the Sheffield label with two of their biggest hits to date; records that had transcended their admirably underground roots and scaled the dizzy heights of the UK singles charts. The sales figures involved were staggering, suggesting that Bleep & Bass - a sound first pioneered in West, rather than South Yorkshire - had captured the imagination of a whole generation of dancers. When articles emerged hailing the sound of "Shef-field Bleep", many in Leeds bristled.

---

1   Allen, Vaughan: Bleep Generation, i-D, issue 87, December 1990.

'It really used to piss us off,' Gez Varley says. 'Honestly, it genuinely annoyed us. People would come up to us all the time and ask where we lived in Sheffield. I would say, "I've never lived in Sheffield," and they'd reply, "But you're LFO!" We just couldn't shake the stereotype.'

Some in Leeds were desperate to put the record straight. To do that, they would need an outlet of their own - a label that could not only rival Warp for the signatures of local artists but also offer a similar level of studio support. After all, Warp could call on the immense talents of Robert Gordon. When he wasn't around, aspiring artists could work in the label's small city centre studio with the assistance of professional engineers Phil and Andy Jones. Crucially, the label was also based in a record shop, with staff plugged into the mains of Britain's rapidly changing dance music landscape.

At the time, Leeds had two record stores that may have been able to replicate the success of their Sheffield rivals, Jumbo and Crash. The latter was based on the Headrow, slap bang in the city centre. The shop's owners, Steve Mulhaire and Jerry Gallagher, had become enthusiastic supporters of the growing dance scene and, like Steve Beckett and Rob Mitchell, had employed a leading local DJ to be their import buyer: Martin Williams.

Having quit his job at Side Step, Williams was now dividing his time between DJing, working in his home studio and manning the counter at Crash. He was a popular figure locally, not only because of his reputation as a DJ but also his willingness to help and encourage others. Williams' production credentials were now sky-high, too, having played a pivotal role in the city's most celebrated record of recent times, "LFO".

Williams was not basking in the success of "LFO", though. For reasons that remain opaque, he'd parted company with Mark Bell and Gez Varley and was now looking for a new musical challenge. Exactly what happened between the three men is shrouded in mystery, though it appears that Bell and Varley - with or without the encouragement of Warp's Steve Beckett and Rob Mitchell - decided they'd prefer to move forward without Williams.

'I don't know what happened other than they cut contact with Martin with no real explanation,' Homer Harriott says. 'I guess they just wanted to stop working with him. I would imagine they thought that they didn't need him. At the time, I told him that he needed to get his head together. Martin just wanted to leave it and move on, but I thought it was important that he got credit for the work he'd done and the part he played in it. He got that, but he really didn't want to cause a fuss.'

Gez Varley has not gone into detail about the episode, though he does 'deeply regret' the way that Williams was treated. The two have remained friends, though, and even after his departure from the group Williams was happy to offer Varley advice when they bumped into each other in Leeds.

'Martin told me to be careful when we were dealing with Warp,' Varley reveals. 'He said, "You only have their word". I said, "But why would they rip us off?" Martin said, "It's not that, just that you don't know the ins and outs of their deals and how they run their business." He was, and remains, a very nice guy.'

Understandably, Williams has no desire to rake over this particular portion of his past. 'I just don't talk about anything negative - I'm a positive guy,' he says with a smile. 'I'm not going to slag anyone off. We just went in different directions. I thought they wanted to be Pop stars, but that didn't interest me. I just wanted to keep making underground records.'

* * *

In the weeks following his surprise departure from LFO, Martin Williams redoubled his efforts to record more music. He quickly found a willing studio sparring partner in Homer Harriott, a slightly older friend from the Chapeltown scene he'd been working with for some time.

'I originally met Martin because I lived next door to his girlfriend in Chapeltown,' Harriott remembers. 'He was a computer technician, so when it came to move from an analogue to a digital set-up, Martin came and helped me out. He had the links and the knowledge. At the time I was going to Martin's house quite regularly, so we got close - at that point in time, we were best friends.'

The pair began regularly getting together to make music. With very different skill sets, they formed a formidable partnership. 'I was in bands and could play guitar and keyboards, whereas Martin could really only play the odd bassline or a basic melody,' Harriott says. 'Martin was an engineer and gave his perspective from the DJ side of things. He could tell what needed to be done to make it right for the clubs.'

To illustrate his point, Harriott talks in detail about the way the pair worked together on tracks. 'I could put together a track - drums, melodies, and so on - then Martin would deconstruct it to make it more DJ friendly,' he explains. 'He'd say, "We don't need this," or, "We need to start this element later." He'd always start with the drums, then a noise, and then suggest where the bassline should come in. Then we'd build the track up from there. That's the way Martin thought - he was very clear about how you'd structure a track to get a crowd excited.'

Williams describes himself as a 'problem solver' - a lateral thinker adept at finding a solution to whatever problem arises - and insists that those he worked with, and Harriott in particular, were the real talents. 'Homer is exceptionally talented,' he says. 'I wouldn't class myself as a real talent, certainly not compared to Homer and even the guys in LFO. I had a really strong computer background and knew exactly what I wanted to hear.'

Many in Leeds will say otherwise[2]. To those who came through the Chapeltown scene at the time, Williams and Harriott are unsung heroes. 'Martin was a great guy and very important, but Homer's contribution sometimes gets overlooked,' Tomas Stewart says. 'Homer was a great musician, and he was happy to lend his equipment to all of us - for example, it was his TR-808 that we used on the first Breaking The Illusion record. He was a bit older than us, so we all looked up to him.'

When Crash Records owners Steve Mulhaire and Jerry Gallagher decided that they wanted to launch a record label to rival Warp Records, it made perfect sense to turn to Martin Williams and Homer Harriott. Not only did they work together well, but they were also friends with every significant DJ, dancer, rapper and wannabe producer in Chapeltown, Harehills and Hyde Park.

'Because Martin worked in the shop, Steve and Jerry knew him well and what a big part he played in the success of "LFO",' Harriot says. 'One or both of them thought it was a good idea to start a label[3]. They knew that Martin being a well-known local DJ and having production and engineering skills would be a great place to start.'

In their first meeting with Mulhaire and Gallagher, Harriott and Williams mentioned a string of talented local youngsters they could work with: Breaking The Illusion (whose members included both Tomas Stewart and Paul Edmeade), Lee Kenny aka rapper/vocalist LSK and Ital Rockers man Mark Millington. Mulhaire and Gallagher liked what they heard, so offered to rent studio space and finance the acquisition of some key pieces of music-making equipment.

Situated above the Kickflip skateboarding shop on the street corner where Merrion Place meets New Briggate, the Bassic studio was up and running within weeks. 'Steve and Jerry gave Martin and myself sets of keys and just said, "Keep us posted",' Harriott remembers. 'With Martin's gear and the new equipment - an SH-101, Juno 106 [synthesizer] and a new Atari ST - we had some good stuff in the studio. We went to see the guys we were hanging out with, because they were always round my house or Martin's, and invited them to get involved. Most of them had already started getting some kit, but their home studio set-ups were very basic.'

While Mulhaire and Gallagher got ready to release the first 12" on Bassic Records - Unit 93's melodious Acid House cut "Trust No One", which the pair had signed to get the ball rolling - Williams and Harriott set to work on re-making a sparse but heavy demo recording offered up by Mark Millington. He'd made it in his bedroom the previous year.

---

2   Drew Hemment, who briefly DJed alongside Williams at a Blues, ended our interview by proclaiming, 'If you write Martin Williams back into history, you'll be doing the world a great service.'
3   It was reportedly Gallagher who put up the money to fund Bassic Records, though Mulhaire was also actively involved in running the label.

'I used to make tracks with my brother, Kevin, with this little kiddie drum machine, a Roland SH-101, a small keyboard and a four-track,' Millington remembers. 'We had a few fallings out, and one was over that tune. So it just sat there for a while. Then one day I played it and everyone's ears pricked up.'

Millington copied the track onto another cassette and gave it an airing at his next DJ set. 'It just took off - people went mad in the place,' he enthuses. 'Later that night, I went to the Warehouse where Martin was playing and gave him the tape to play. To hear your track getting played and see the reaction from the DJ booth in the Warehouse was amazing.'

Millington also took the tape down to Sheffield and across to Sunset Boulevard in Huddersfield to test it out; on every occasion, the dancefloor went ballistic. 'That first version of "Ital's Anthem" was so good,' Gez Varley says. 'It was incredibly raw and bass-heavy. A lot of people in Leeds will tell you that they prefer that to the version that eventually came out.'

Winston Hazel and Robert Gordon were keen to sign it to Warp, but Millington turned down their offer. 'At the time, Warp were caught up in "LFO" getting into the charts, so they had a lot on their hands,' he says. 'I just wanted to get my track out, and the guys behind Bassic loved it so much that they got me in the studio as soon as they launched the label.'

The demo itself was skeletal at best, featuring a raw, sharp, high-register bleep melody, a shuffling drum track and a suitably sub-heavy bassline that mirrored the melody of Millington's main hook. 'The demo was mainly the melody and bassline with some drums,' Harriot remembers. 'The melody and the bassline being the same was very strange from a musician's perspective. But it worked, and it was all about how the arrangement went - it was all about the drums and the bass.'

The bass was, of course, hugely important to Millington, a man who had been one of the first dub-heads in Leeds to embrace House and Techno. 'For me, it was all about bass - a rhythmic bassline that had a vibe to it,' he says. 'It used dub elements in the tune, like the Mikey Dread samples, to make it "rockers to rockers". The sound of Bleep & Bass was very sparse, so you had to have something to carry it. When the bass drops in, it lifts you up.'

Williams, too, was by now warming to the speaker-rattling pleasures of Dub-influenced basslines and production, despite being a self-confessed Soul boy at heart. 'Normally I wouldn't listen to Dub, but play it through a proper soundsystem and I could listen to it all day,' he remarks. 'Because I'm like that, I think that the music I made with people like Homer and Mark was influenced by what I wanted to hear over a great soundsystem. We wanted to get that sound at source, rather than going to the expense of buying a soundsystem and waking everyone up. It's artificial in a way, but it worked in clubs.'

This attention to bass-weight is evident on all of the Bassic Records releases Williams and Harriott were involved in, especially the re-made version of "Ital's Anthem", subtitled "The Trebledown Bassup Mix". It's as pure an expression of the early Yorkshire Bleep & Bass sound than anything that came out of Sheffield or Bradford.

Its construction was similar in many ways to "The Theme" and "Dextrous" - think bass and bleeps that play the same melody at the top and bottom of the synthesizer keyboard - with steppers-style drums that doff a cap to both the programming style of Robert Gordon and the sweaty, all-action percussive build-ups of Chicago "jack tracks". There was a sparse bass break a-la "LFO" - a build-and-release trick later used in many other Bleep cuts - and some suitably spacey chords. It remains a fine chunk of low-end science and British dancefloor futurism.

Like eventual B-side "Science (First Mix)" - a similarly weighty but slightly more spacey affair driven forwards by more Afrofuturist Steppers drums and ragged TB-303 style acid lines - "Ital's Anthem" was mixed live by Millington on the Bassic studio's mid-range mixing desk. 'There was no arrangement,' Millington states in a matter-of-fact way. 'I still do my mixes like that, in the old Dub manner. The mix that appeared on the record was a one-off, you'll never get that again.'

With the first Ital Rockers record in the bag, Martin Williams and Homer Harriott turned their attention to the rest of their Chapeltown connections. The first to take up their offer of studio time were Alan Payne and Mark Millington's brother Kevin. Others would drop in and out of sessions, offering a germ of an idea or a vocal line before slipping away to go dancing and DJing. It was all very loose.

'People would come in and knock ideas around,' Williams says. 'I'd do programming and some arrangement, but it was always a group effort. The simplest ideas usually ended up with the most raw records.'

The track that Payne and Kevin Millington made with Harriott and Williams was raw even by Bleep & Bass standards. "Soul Thunder" did, of course, boast the by now obligatory melodic bleeps, and once again they mimicked the bassline. This bassline was a little different from those that had come before, though, being as razor-sharp as it was weighty and sub-heavy. The drums, too, showed a bit more influence from original Detroit Techno, while the track's main breakdown also included some dreamy and loved-up chords courtesy of the Juno-106.

The most revolutionary thing about the track, though, was the presence of vocals. On the incredible A-side "Drillers Mix", these are stripped back to a single, often-repeated phrase - "Can you feel the rhythm, can you feel the rhythm, Juno's playing in tune" - but on the flipside "Vocal Mix" there are verses, choruses and even a rap section from Lee Kenny aka LSK.

The man behind the lead vocal was Edward Irish, a local "driller" who had recently graduated from the Northern School of Contemporary Dance on Chapeltown Road.

Alongside his good friend Marvin Ottley, Irish was a member of the Elite team of dancers who battled footworkers from Manchester, Nottingham and Sheffield at every opportunity. A year or so earlier he and his Northern School of Contemporary Dance colleagues had been the focus of a lengthy article in *The Face*. The piece was about the rebirth of the Jazz dance scene in Leeds, where dancers trained in balletic moves threw shapes to House and Techno as well as heavily percussive Latin records and Chick Correa style Jazz-Funk. This was going on elsewhere in Yorkshire and Lancashire, too, though *The Face* hadn't noticed.

The piece is a fascinating time capsule, detailing the various key club nights that both attended; in most cases, these were venues and Blues (euphemistically referred to as "weekly house parties") that featured regular sets from Martin Williams. It was he who got Irish into the studio, believing him to be another potential musical talent to be nurtured. Although Irish's contribution to Juno's "Soul Thunder" was limited to vocals, he and Williams recorded a swathe of tracks at the Bassic studio that never saw the light of day. 'Edward was very talented,' Williams reflects. 'I actually found some of those tracks we worked on together recently. I was surprised at how good they sounded[4].'

● ● ●

Edward Irish was not the only student at the Northern School of Contemporary Dance with musical ambitions and a passion for throwing shapes to contemporary House and Techno cuts. In one of the years below was a student from Leicester called David Duncan.

Unlike Irish, Duncan had been making music since his early teens. 'I studied micro-electronics and got a diploma in that, so wanting to make electronic music was just a progression from that,' Duncan explains down the phone from his Copenhagen home. 'My set-up was pretty simple - I had one of the Yamaha DX series synthesizers, a sequencer and a four-track. When I came to Leeds, I'd make music when I came back from the Blues. I'd bang through track after track that way such was the inspiration of the Blues. It gave me so many ideas.'

---

4   I can confirm that this is certainly the case. Most of the tracks are Deep House cuts with occasional Bleep & Bass flourishes, with Irish's slick, soulful vocals rising above cuts that doff a cap to Larry Heard and Dream 2 Science. If they had been released at the time, they would now be spoken of as early British Deep House classics.

Through going out dancing in Leeds, Duncan eventually became friends with many members of the extended Bassic family. 'Being at the dance school probably pushed me towards going out in certain places, which also happened to be where they were hanging out,' he says. 'Dancers always went to where the real party was. That's how the two scenes were linked together and how I ended up meeting DJ Martin, Mark [Millington] and the others.'

When they first met, Williams had no idea that Duncan made music; in fact, he only twigged when a mutual friend played him some of the dance student's demo recordings. 'Martin liked my stuff, played it to the rest of the Bassic crew and then asked if I wanted to make a record,' he says. 'I was never going to say no! As I'd been making electronic music for quite a few years, I wanted there to be quite a bit of artistry behind it. I wanted to make a piece of music that would last the test of time.'

With the help of Williams and Harriott, Duncan did just that. Over six months, countless all-night studio sessions[5] and numerous revisions, the three men turned Duncan's "Pressure" demo into a stunning work of audio art. 'What I had when I got in the studio is maybe what you'd call a blueprint, but what we ended up with was a completely different track,' Duncan says. 'It evolved a lot as we worked on it in the studio. We stripped it apart completely and then developed each of the elements individually. We did things like sampling bass parts from other Bassic releases then tweak those to make them sound as deep and dubby as we could. We kept doing things until we ended up with sounds we liked.'

It was a labour-intensive process, but one that all three men enjoyed. 'I think Martin really enjoyed being in that situation,' Homer Harriott says. 'He could forget about himself and work with the two of us all night if he wanted to. David had more experience of making music than anyone else we worked with and a singer that he wanted to work with. Even so, we still spent hours with him just working on the drum track.'

The resultant track, "Pressure", was pretty special. It was deeper, more Dub-fuelled and spacey than anything that had come before in House or Techno, not just in the UK but also around the world. Its bassline was earth-shatteringly heavy, raw and hypnotic, while the rolling rhythm fused digital Dub style percussive fills with the titanium-clad beats of Roland's TR-808 drum machine. There was a whisper of a female vocal, too, as well as Juno-106 chords that soothed and seduced the senses. It was, and remains, an exceptional record.

Even better though is the trio's extended flipside revision, "Pressure Dub". It's a triumph of rumbling sub-bass, echoing vocal snippets, elongated dub trails, locked-in late night drums and deep space bleeps that

---

5   Williams still worked during the day and preferred to lock himself in the studio with his friends and collaborators for a longer period of time. Mark Millington remembers 'many nights' spent jamming in the studio with Williams, while Homer Harriott recalls him cutting down DJ commitments in order to devote more time to studio work.

flit back and forth across the full stereo spectrum. It may well be the most artful, detailed and well-made Bleep & Bass track ever committed to vinyl; a staggeringly good fusion of early morning Techno nous and bassbin-rattling future Dub. Put simply, it's sonic perfection.

Although "Ital's Anthem" and "Soul Thunder" proved popular, it was "Pressure Dub" that really put Bassic Records on the map. Support for the single within the DJ community was significant, with the cut playing particularly well amongst those who would later go on to play a starring role in the development of Jungle - the likes of Jumpin' Jack Frost, Bryan Gee and Rage residents Fabio and Grooverider.

The hype was real, with Rhythm King co-founder Martin Heath keen to get in on the Bassic sound. He already knew Williams through his work on "LFO"[6], which was one of the Warp Records singles pressed and distributed by his label's Outer Rhythm offshoot. Heath not only licensed "Pressure Dub" for a wider UK and European release but also dragged Williams and Harriott down to London to discuss remix work. When they got to the label's offices, Bassic's in-house production team was rather surprised to see a familiar face.

'Mark [Millington] was in the room next door to us - he'd come down on the same train but hadn't told us he was heading down,' Harriott remembers. 'Outer Rhythm had offered him a record deal. I was a bit pissed off at the time because he could have told us what he was up to and we could have been involved.'

Millington subsequently signed on the dotted line, later releasing the fine - but largely overlooked - "One Day EP". "Dreams", the EP's standout moment, was a cultured chunk of Bleep & Bass heaviness: a dark, mind-altering affair full of layered basslines, heady electronic bleeps and glassy-eyed female vocal samples. It was one of the last Bleep & Bass cuts Millington produced before re-emerging as Iration Steppas in 1994.

As for Williams and Harriott, they took up Heath's offer of providing remixes for an Outer Rhythm release. The track chosen was Man Machine's "Animal". 'We didn't really like the track, so the only thing we took from the original was the animal noises,' Harriott remembers. 'We just thought, "Let's do a really raw version and see how it goes". It was fun, and we did it in a night, experimenting with a lot of MIDI patches and changes. There was minimal equipment involved - I think it was just a sampler, a Juno 106 and a Kawai K1 synthesizer.'

Two of the three mixes they completed were released, with the "Primordial Jungle" mix being a surging version of what Fabio and Grooverider called "Jungle Techno" - all humid rainforest noises, haunting, delay-laden

---

6   Martin Williams says that Heath once told him that Outer Rhythm's decision to fund the manufacture and release of Warp's first eight or ten releases came after he heard "LFO" for the first time in the autumn of 1989.

vocal samples, booming bass, intergalactic chords and polyrhythmic, African-influenced drums. It was electronic Afrofuturism, Yorkshire style, and remains the only release on which Harriott (as DJ Homes) and Williams (as DJ Martin) were credited.

'We just focused on making Bassic successful rather than producing our own tracks,' Harriott says. 'It's a shame, really, because we should have been the primary artists as we were bringing so many people to the label. We were producing artists and couldn't find time to work on our own stuff. But as we got more into it, we never really established what we should be doing from a legal position and in terms of getting recognition for our work.'

The two men worked tirelessly during the brief period that the Bassic Records studio was active, though as the tracks they co-produced got more popular the label's problems began to mount. At the heart of the issue was an almighty row between some of the label's artists, who felt - unfairly - that Mulhaire and Gallagher were taking advantage of them.

'Things went a bit weird,' Harriott sighs. 'Some of the artists thought that by selling 10,000 records, or whatever, that they would receive £10,000. But it doesn't work like that, because costs have to come out of sales which can leave a relatively small amount - a couple of grand maybe. Me and Martin knew this, but some of the artists didn't understand.'

One of the artists was so outraged by what he saw as being ripped off that he grabbed a set of keys to the studio from Harriott's car, let himself in and made off with some of the equipment. After much arguing, Harriott and Williams successfully persuaded the person involved to return the equipment and take his grievances directly to the label's owners. 'They did, and it was cool,' Harriott says. 'I don't think Jerry was too happy. As a crew we just sort of drifted apart after that.'

Mark Millington refers to the episode as 'the feud': If that hadn't taken place, who knows what might have happened? Martin was a great producer in those days - a real genius in the studio. If that feud hadn't happened, I'm sure big things would have followed. The tracks that came out of Leeds at that time still sound raw.'

The trio of singles Harriott and Williams engineered and co-produced for Bassic Records still rank amongst the top echelon of Bleep & Bass tunes. Their significance lies in the obvious links with Chapeltown's soundsystem culture, the tracks' toughness and the inspiration they gave to producers elsewhere in the UK, especially within the nascent Breakbeat Hardcore scene in London. They may not be as widely known as those released by Warp Records, but they're every bit as mind-blowing.

It's likely that the messy end to the Bassic Records saga had a profound effect on Martin Williams. An honest, kind and conscientious man with a record of helping others achieve their dreams, Williams spent little more time pursuing his own musical ambitions. He parted company with Crash

Records, bowed out of DJing and took up a job in IT. Later down the line, he got involved with boxing, eventually becoming a professional trainer specializing in mentoring boxers from troubled backgrounds.

Today, he looks back fondly on his brief but successful DJing and production career, which forms just a small part of an impressively varied CV. ' If I died tomorrow, I can't say I haven't done owt[7],' he says proudly. 'I've done a lot, and it's more good than bad. If I was doing it all again, I would have done it with the same mindset, but I might have tried to make some money in order to make something even more underground. Now I enjoy finding boxers with talent to take on fighters managed by moneymen, so we can knock them off their perch. I watch a lot of films where the little guy takes on the big guy. That was my mentality with music.'

● ● ●

As Bassic Records was imploding, Mark Bell and Gez Varley were getting ready to release their first record without Martin Williams. They'd enjoyed a busy few months since "LFO" rocketed into the higher reaches of the singles charts, completing countless interviews and remixes for Leeds favourites the Bridewell Taxis - West Yorkshire's answer to the Stone Roses - and Virgin-signed Scottish band Botany 5.

When Warp Records began mailing out copies of the duo's hotly awaited new single, "We Are Back", the accompanying press release bristled with attitude. 'Irked by several patchy imitations by people who have jumped on to the bass bandwagon over the past nine months, LFO return with their second single,' it stated. 'A mammoth effort in their quest for originality, LFO prove once again with this track of thunderous proportions that frequencies below 20hz belong to them.'

Described by music weekly *Melody Maker* as 'sheer unadulterated lunacy'[8], "We Are Back" was another colossal slab of industrial-strength Yorkshire dance music. There were no bleeps, though, but rather a mixture of raw, redlined Electro drums, metallic melodies that sounded like they'd been crafted by smashing steel beams into each other, and another fearlessly sub-heavy bassline. Perhaps the most notable feature though was a Kraftwerk style vocoder vocal taking aim at those who followed in their footsteps. 'There are many imitators,' it thundered, 'but we are the true creators.'

At the time, many thought it was a sideswipe at British synthesizer legend Paul Hardcastle, who had been locked in a bitter row with Warp Records over the band's name. He'd first recorded as LFO in 1988, recording a track

---

7   For those not from Yorkshire, "owt" means "anything",with "nowt" being its natural opposite.
8   *Melody Maker*, Singles reviews, 15 June 1991.

called "Brainstorm" for a compilation of new Acid House tracks. When he cheekily remixed and reissued the track in the aftermath of Bell, Varley and Williams' chart success, all hell broke loose.

'He did use the name first, but Warp checked it with a lawyer and we were covered because the law states the name belongs to whoever made it famous first,' Gez Varley explains. 'He was jumping on our bandwagon. Warp sent him a letter saying that if he did it again, he'd be sued. In interviews he still says he's LFO though. It doesn't make any sense.'

Yet "We Are Back" was not a response to Paul Hardcastle or the many other tracks made in tribute to "LFO". In fact, the pair's inspiration was much closer to home. 'We did it because loads of people in Leeds slagged us off for getting in the charts, saying that we'd sold out,' Varley complains. 'It was the Chapeltown lot, mainly. Some of them might have known Martin, but he definitely didn't slag us off. We thought, "fuck 'em". "We Are Back" was another statement - a sort of two-fingered salute.'

Given that Williams was a popular figure and that many thought he was hard done by - not a statement he agrees with, for the record - it's perhaps unsurprising that feelings ran high within the Blues parties and home studios of Chapeltown. LFO were now operating in different circles to their former contemporaries and collaborators, with a freshly signed US deal with New York label Tommy Boy - an imprint that saw them fit seamlessly into the vibrant Miami Bass scene - and a string of live dates in the diary.

For Warp, LFO was an act that they could market and promote to those raised on Indie music as well as Techno aficionados. They were two young white lads from Leeds who talked in interviews about taking on the music establishment, a trait that later saw them appear on the front cover of the *NME* smashing up guitars. With their Indie background, Steve Beckett and Rob Mitchell dreamed not of releasing singles that rocked clubs, but rather putting out albums for artists who performed live.

'Having had the background of the record shop, we'd really seen the difference between the Rock labels and dance labels,' Steve Beckett explained to DJ Benji B during a 2007 Red Bull Music Academy lecture[9]. 'Dance labels would come along and be very trendy for a year, and then no one would be interested. But with the Rock labels we looked up to from the Indie side, like Mute and Factory, they had a whole look and really developed the artists, recording albums, sending them out on tour. We took that model and applied it to dance music, so LFO were the first people we worked with where we were, "Come on, guys! You've got to make an album".'

---

9   *Steve Beckett: The Warp Factor*, Red Bull Music Academy, 2007 (https://www.redbullmusicacademy.com/lectures/steve-beckett-the-warp-factor)

According to Beckett's account[10], Bell and Varley were hesitant at first but eventually got the idea. To assist them, they offered the duo a chance to regularly record at Warp's rented studio space above Red Tape Studios in Sheffield. 'The FON studio and Human League's studio were on the same floor,' Varley remembers. 'We used to go and ask Phil Oakey what different bits of recording equipment did. We used to just hang out there[11].'

'It was really about getting that [idea of making albums] into their heads, then them going into the studio and making albums they realized could work electronically, like Kraftwerk, Pink Floyd or Tangerine Dream,' Beckett told the RBMA lecture audience. 'It was about making electronic albums people could appreciate from start to finish, rather than just making one-off dance records.'

Released on 22 July 1991, LFO's debut album "Frequencies" was a triumph. It arrived in stores at a time when many music journalists still mistakenly believed that dance music acts couldn't produce great albums. More importantly, it showed Bell and Varley to be producers with a distinctive vision. While "We Are Back" and "LFO" were naturally present - Warp finally crediting Martin Williams as producer on the sleeve - the rest of the set was notably less raw and frenetic than their colossal club cuts.

Largely melodic and ear-pleasing with greater reliance on Electro-influenced beats, "Frequencies" was a mature and hugely entertaining set that marked a significant departure from their Bleep & Bass roots, despite the presence of some seriously heavy low-end pressure. In fact, it was more akin to what would become Warp's staple sound in the years ahead, the "intelligent dance music" style Electronica ushered in by the label's 1992 compilation "Artificial Intelligence". Warp's dalliance with Bleep & Bass, a style it had done so much to promote, was almost at an end.

---

10   Steve Beckett was asked on at least five different occasions to do an interview for this book, both through Warp Records PR team and old friends such as Winston Hazel. He turned down every request.
11   This ties in with what Graham Massey has said about encountering Bell and Varley in Sheffield during trips to record at FON. Massey also says they regularly had drinking competitions with the pair, which the Yorkshiremen won hands down. Yorkshire 1, Lancashire 0.

PLAY THE FIVE TONES

THE BLEEPS AND CLONKS OF CABARET VOLTAIRE AND SWEET EXORCIST

'Sweet Exorcist was the right music at the right time. It was kind of liberating.'

RICHARD H KIRK FACT magazine, 2017 [1]

Like it was most Wednesday nights, Occasions was packed to the rafters when i-D magazine held the Sheffield leg of its grandly titled "World Tour" on 25 April 1990. The reason this particular venue and date was picked was simple: Cuba, Occasions' infamous midweek party, was one of the hottest weekly events in the North of England.

The importance of the party was first outlined six months earlier in Jocks magazine, when Warp Records founders Steve Beckett, Rob Mitchell and Robert Gordon explained the role Cuba played in shaping the Yorkshire Bleep & Bass sound. 'About 30% of the stuff played at Cuba is Sheffield originated,' Gordon explained. 'A lot of demo tapes are tried out, it's total hardcore dance.'[2]

Winston Hazel, one of Cuba's resident DJs, echoed Gordon's points in an interview with Rob Young for his 2005 history of Warp Records. 'The first breed of bedroom producers started bringing recordings into Cuba to hear their tracks played on a club soundsystem and to gauge a dancefloor

1 Dylan Wray, Daniel: Richard H Kirk on Thatcherite Pop and why Cabaret Voltaire were like The Velvet Underground, FACT magazine, February 2017.
2 Randall, Ronnie: *City Beat – Warp Factory Sheffield*, Jocks, 1989

CHAPTER ELEVEN

^ **CABARET VOLTAIRE** by Vanya Balogh

response,' he said. 'Nearly all the Warp tracks were first given dancefloor air and tested on a well-versed crowd. LFO, the Step, Tomas and Tuff Little Unit were all given maximum rotation.'

Despite being on a Wednesday night, Cuba was a pull not only for serious dancers from across Yorkshire and the Midlands, but also signed and unsigned producers from elsewhere. Mark Millington, Martin Williams, Paul Edmeade, Tomas Stewart and David Duncan all recall semi-regular visits, while Hazel and DJ partner Richard Barratt remember testing out some early LFO cuts in the presence of Mark Bell and Gez Varley. 'I remember playing one particular demo they brought down - maybe "Track 4" or "Mentok 1" - and the crowd going mental,' Barratt says. 'I looked at Mark Bell, and he was stood there stony-faced. There was no reaction to what was going on at all[3].'

Cuba was popping off even more than usual when *i-D* magazine rolled into town. It was a heaving mass of sweaty bodies, with almost every significant figure from the local scene present amongst the packed crowd of Occasions regulars, glassy-eyed students, football lads and fashion-conscious girls. Most were wearing brass dog tags embossed with the *i-D* logo and the date and location of the party - a novel replacement for tickets that was reportedly the work of Cuba and Jive Turkey co-promoter Matt Swift.

'It was a really big deal at the time,' Sheffield DJ Pipes remembers. 'I remember it being over-capacity and that there were some live sets. That guy Man Machine played, probably because he was on Outer Rhythm which at that point had a deal with Warp.'

Man Machine was the recording alias of Ed Stretton, a London-based radio-producer-turned Acid House evangelist who first rose to prominence as one half of Jack 'N' Chill, whose 1987 cut "The Jack That House Built" was one of Britain's first crossover House tracks. He'd re-emerged as Man Machine the previous autumn with a self-titled track that boasted ludicrously bass-heavy remixes by the Forgemasters.

'I did about eight or so live dates and that party in Sheffield was one of the better ones,' he remembers. 'I used to dress up in this robot-inspired outfit with loads of lights on it - a really hot and heavy costume. I'm not sure what the crowd thought but, from memory, my set went down well.'

There was another live act on the line-up, too, though their involvement wasn't advertised beforehand: local industrial funk heroes Cabaret Voltaire, fresh from the release of their new album on Parlophone, "Laidback, Groovy & Nasty". It had landed to mixed reviews two months earlier and saw Richard H Kirk and Stephen Mallinder joining the dots between Industrial Funk, Chicago House (via collaborations with Windy City originals Marshall Jefferson and Ten City), and the 'Sheffield House sound' (as *i-D* put it) of Bleep & Bass.

---

3   The importance of Cuba in shaping some of the early Bleep & Bass cuts can be spotted in the name of one of the B-sides to "LFO": "Track 4 (Cuba Edit)"

'Performing live and playing "godfathers" for the night, Cabaret Voltaire were treated as highly as they are regarded,' wrote Simon Dudfield in his later *i-D* magazine report. 'But the most fuss was caused by DJs Parrot and Winston, with a following any band would envy, proving that the House sound of Sheffield has the potential to be massive.'

With the help of Barratt and Hazel, Dudfield was able to distill the essence of the 'Sheffield sound' better than any writer had done before, putting the now-familiar Bleep blueprint into print for all to absorb, admire and act upon. 'Hard underground tracks with heavy Reggae basslines is a sound unique to Sheffield,' Hazel told Dudfield. 'The black scene, with its emphasis on hardcore and its emphasis on bass, has put ideas into whites and it has rubbed off onto whites into a heavier sound.'

Dudfield remarked that the combination of 'sparse electronic bleeps' and 'heavy bass pulse' typified 'the Sheffield sound': 'Emphasizing the black/white crossover, Winston celebrates the fact that Reggae bass is meeting white electronics and producing something that is exclusive to the city.'

While you could argue that it wasn't unique to the city - Leeds and Bradford had produced the earliest records in the style, and the cut that kicked it all off was made in Manchester - Dudfield was certainly correct in making a link to the "white electronics" that had dominated Sheffield's recent musical heritage.

A decade earlier, Sheffield had been one of the few British outposts of experimental electronic music with a small scene of dedicated pioneers who obsessed over synthesizers rather than guitars. Some of these had gone on to great commercial success with a more pop-leaning sound - think Human League, Heaven 17 and ABC - while others had stuck to their guns and produced futuristic, industrial-strength experiments inspired by the growing bleakness of their poverty-strewn, concrete-clad city. In truth, it was a small collection of like-minded "futurists" who turned Sheffield on to electronic music, with Cabaret Voltaire, who began experimenting with tapes and synthesizers way back in 1973, being the first and arguably greatest of the lot.

Initially founded by bored school friends Kirk, Mallinder and Chris Watson, the "Cabs" Punk-era work was decidedly noisy, bleak and cutting edge, with the band blending Musique Concrète style sound collage, grumpy guitars and morose, stylized vocals. Alongside Throbbing Gristle, they later became flag-bearers for the Industrial sound of electronic music, before embracing other influences - most notably Electrofunk and the bass-heavy sound of Dub Reggae.

Their records became hugely influential, inspiring black teenagers in Detroit, New York and Chicago as much as the tracks they loved by Kraftwerk, Yellow Magic Orchestra, Depeche Mode and fellow Sheffielders the Human League. In fact, the three founding fathers of the Motor City Techno movement - Juan Atkins, Derrick May and Kevin Saunderson - were primarily inspired by European electronic music, with the sounds of the Steel City towards the top of their list of influences.

When Sheffield began to find its own dance music sound in the late 1980s, it could be said that Techno had come home. 'All these industrial places influence the music you make,' Warp co-founder Rob Mitchell told journalist Jon Savage in 1993. 'Electronic music is relevant because of the subliminal influence of industrial sounds. You go around Sheffield, and it's full of crap concrete architecture built in the 1960s; you go down to an area called the Canyon, and you have these massive black factories belching out smoke, banging away. They don't sound a lot different from the music[4].'

In Simon Dudfield's *i-D* report, Richard H Kirk was a bit blunter. 'Everything people make here is very hard,' he said. 'Perhaps it does have something to do with the heritage.' Barratt, too, was typically forthright when asked about the links between the dance sounds of Chicago, Detroit and Sheffield: 'Detroit and Chicago are both Northern American towns. Chicago is a steel town. Sheffield is a Northern steel city in England. Work it out for yourself.'

● ● ●

When it came to commenting on Sheffield's electronic music pedigree and unspoken trans-Atlantic connections, Richard Barratt probably felt like he was stating the obvious. A year before *i-D* waxed lyrical about the sparse, bass-heavy sound of his home city, he'd already spotted a correlation between the homegrown records his friends were making and the clanking Industrial Funk of Cabaret Voltaire.

Barratt had been playing their records since he started DJing - especially the more floor-friendly cuts such as "Sensoria", "Sex, Money, Freaks" and "Crackdown" - and had already developed friendships with both Richard H Kirk and Stephen Mallinder. In fact, he'd even spent some time with Kirk in the pair's legendary Western Works studio, a former cutlery workshop that had previously hosted studio sessions from the likes of 23 Skidoo, Joy Division and Chakk. 'Richard and Mal were very welcoming, especially to non-musicians like me who were interested in making music,' Barratt says. 'They were great - very encouraging.'

It's certainly true that both members of Cabaret Voltaire believed in offering opportunities to people from within the Sheffield scene, especially those with interesting ideas or who shared their militant socialist beliefs (which, in Sheffield at the time, was pretty much everyone on the alternative

---

4   Savage, Jon: *Machine Soul – A History of Techno*, The Village Voice (Rock & Roll Quarterly insert), 1993

music scene). Fittingly, prior to Richard H Kirk moving in - quite literally, as he lived there for a period - Western Works had been the local headquarters of the Socialist Workers Party.

'It still had posters on the wall from that movement when we arrived,' Kirk told me during a 2013 interview. 'That was all interesting, so we left it on the walls. Quite a few bands came through there, some of them well known like The Fall and New Order, some just local bands who came and went. As we had a studio and rehearsal space we weren't using all the time, we just thought we'd get other people in. It was also somewhere to go after the pubs closed. I always used to describe it as Andy Warhol's Factory on a small budget. It was a meeting place and somewhere to hang out.'

Crucially, Kirk and Mallinder were also regular club-goers and could often be seen hanging out at Jive Turkey after it launched in November 1985. 'Jive Turkey had kind of grown up with us,' Mallinder says. 'We were involved from the moment it started. We did our performance for the [Old Grey] Whistle Test there, even though what we were doing was quite different to what they were playing in the club. We took Winston and Parrot with us on tour as our DJs - we were all mates and part of the same Sheffield scene.'

Barratt's sessions in Western Works were initially limited, and by the middle of 1988 he had other things on his mind, specifically the surprise success of "Hustle To The Music" by The Funky Worm, a record he'd made with Mark Brydon and friends Julie Stewart and Carl Munsen. Brydon had invited the others into the studio after orchestrating the making of Krush's big-selling "House Arrest" single with Robert Gordon the previous year.

"Hustle To The Music" was a suitably funky affair that mixed classic Disco and Soul samples with sweaty blasts of Rare Groove-friendly break-beats, a Chicago House-influenced acid bassline, jazzy keys and occasional blasts of saxophone provided by Chakk member Sim Lister. Brydon and Barratt had no expectancy that it would be a hit anywhere other than on the dancefloor at Jive Turkey. In fact, its initial limited FON Records release sold out, and the track became popular in clubs throughout the UK.

Predictably, major labels soon came calling. They'd seen the success of FON's previous in-house dance production for Krush and wanted a piece of the action. WEA won the bidding war, ordered new remixes from T-Coy and Graeme Park, and made a video in which Barratt and Munsen pranced around giant plant pots in ridiculous outfits. Despite this abomination - or perhaps because of it - the record rose to number 13 in the UK singles chart, was licensed for release in other territories (most notably the United States) and left WEA hungry for more Funky Worm records.

'It was great that it was a half-arsed hit, but it was a double-edged sword,' Barratt sighs. 'We had no idea what to do next and the follow-up records were terrible. We ended up being pulled every each way to try and make a Pop record. None of us had a clue - not us, not the people at FON, and definitely not WEA. We just ended up with some bland shit. By the end of the process I was screaming to get away.'

By the time the record ascended the charts, Barratt's frustration was about to boil over. "Voodoo Ray" and "The Theme" had blown him away, while the heavy, minimalist tracks being produced by his Yorkshire contemporaries - and particularly Forgemasters' "Track With No Name" - excited him much more than the Pop-dance records that WEA was ordering the Funky Worm to make.

'Stuck in a deal with a major label making insipid Pop crap and hearing the emerging Bleep sound made me want to weep,' Barratt admits. 'It was like someone had captured the heartbeat of our scene and pressed it onto plastic.'

Looking for an escape, Barratt popped round to visit Richard H Kirk at Western Works with the idea of collaborating on some underground Techno tracks. Kirk was receptive, not least because he was getting increasingly frustrated with the demands of Cabaret Voltaire's own major label masters, the EMI-owned Parlophone Records.

The Cabs previous album, 1987's "Code", had not been a rip-roaring commercial success. Although it was co-produced by Adrian Sherwood, a producer with impeccable underground credentials, the set was far more influenced by American Electrofunk and dancefloor-focused Synth-Pop than the band's more experimental early work. It came accompanied by glossy videos and an extensive marketing campaign, both of which rubbed Kirk up the wrong way. Mallinder, a more laidback, outgoing and cheerful character than his intense, forthright and occasionally paranoid bandmate, fitted the role of 'Pop star' more than Kirk ever would.

'I interviewed Cabaret Voltaire a number of times, and Richard could be hard work,' sometime *i-D* and *The Face* journalist Vaughan Allen remembers. 'He spent most of the interviews talking about pornography. He was a very different character from Mal [Stephen Mallinder], who was lovely. I can forgive Richard though because it was partly that aspect of his character that made him one of the true geniuses of electronic music.'

When it came to recording a follow-up to "Code", Parlophone urged Cabaret Voltaire to think big. As a result, Kirk and Mallinder decided to explore their love of black American dance music further by decamping to Chicago to work with one of the city's most successful House producers, Marshall Jefferson.

'The world had changed a little bit with what happened in 1988, both down in London and up north, so quite naturally we shifted with it,' Mallinder muses. 'We wanted to retain our connection with black American music. We'd worked with American producers before, like Afrika Bambaataa and John 'Tokes' Potoker, so it wasn't alien to us. We were breathing the air of the club scene, like a lot of people, and that's why the album developed as it did.'

The original idea had been to disrupt their usual routine of recording at Western Works and then mixing the subsequent tracks elsewhere, hence writing and producing a chunk of the album in Chicago. It wasn't quite as successful a process as they'd hoped, despite getting roughly half of the album in the can, and on their return to the UK Kirk was more frustrated than he had been for some time.

'I wasn't very happy where Cabaret Voltaire was going at that point,' Kirk explained in a 2017 interview with Daniel Dylan Wray. 'I thought that the "Groovy, Laidback and Nasty" album was a really watered down version of Cabaret Voltaire. EMI were chucking all this money at us and getting it totally wrong[5].'

The album had yet to be completed when Richard Barratt turned up at Kirk's door inviting him to collaborate on some Techno tracks. 'Listening to the early Bleep tracks, I thought that although the obvious influences were Reggae, House and Techno, I thought it would be interesting to do something with Richard,' Barratt explains. 'In Sheffield, there were these older electronic musicians who'd inspired a lot of that early American House and Techno stuff so to me it made sense.'

Despite the duo's longstanding deals with WEA and EMI respectively, they pressed ahead with regular studio sessions at Western Works, creating music with Warp Records in mind. Kirk was a past master at making clanking electronic music that sounded like it was roughly forged from pure Sheffield steel, while Barratt - a hero to Sheffield dancers as DJ Parrot - had an instinctive grasp of hooks, basslines, and the very specific demands of contemporary dancefloors.

They began by jamming out a Detroit and Chicago influenced Techno cut that placed sampled electronics from Yellow Magic Orchestra's "Computer Games" and spacey synth sounds atop a squelchy bassline and a sweaty drum machine rhythm track rich in handclap-heavy fills[6]. The track was introduced by a spoken word sample from *Close Encounters of the Third Kind*: 'Everything's ready, you're on the dark side of the moon: play the five tones.'

---

5   Wray, Daniel Dylan: *Richard H Kirk on Thatcherite Pop and Why Cabaret Voltaire Were Like The Velvet Underground*, Fact, February 2017 (https://www.factmag.com/2017/02/05/richard-h-kirk-interview-cabaret-voltaire-sandoz/)
6   This "early version" of "Testone' can be heard on Warp's 2011 Sweet Exorcist retrospective, "Retroactivity".

Over the next few weeks, the track was developed further with the addition of a whole new bleeping melody line that would soon become one of the most iconic lead lines in dance music history[7]. The pair added a fatter, weightier bassline[8], and the kind of ghostly chords that made the record sound like it had been beamed down from some far-off planet.

They called the cut "Testone", and by autumn 1989 it was already causing a commotion on the dancefloors of Cuba and Jive Turkey. Warp's co-founders mentioned it in interviews as a forthcoming attraction but declined to reveal the identities of the producers behind it, aside from saying that the artist was known as Sweet Exorcist (a name borrowed from the title of a Curtis Mayfield record that Barratt and Kirk both loved).

'Before and at the time it came out, Kirky was signed to EMI, and I was still signed to Warners as part of the Funky Worm deal, so we had to keep quiet,' Barratt says. 'There could have been some trouble if the labels had found out straight away. If we'd taken it to either company, they wouldn't have understood it and would have put a stop to it coming out. We were pretty sneaky originally.'

While they initially remained in the shadows, it didn't take long for word to get out about the record. Accompanied by a pair of ghostly, mind-altering reworks ("Testtwo" and "Testthree"), "Testone" first appeared in stores in early 1990, spending seven weeks in the lower reaches of the top 100 singles chart. It became as ubiquitous as "Dextrous", "The Theme" and "Track With No Name" and was quickly followed by a remix 12" featuring superb remixes from Robert Gordon. These featured Gordon's trademark Steppers-influenced rhythmic shuffle, even heavier bass and an arrangement capable of doing even more dancefloor damage than Kirk and Barratt's original versions. 'That remix is a Techno nerd's wet dream,' Robert Gordon laughs. 'I did it at FON with all the best equipment. It's the most high-tech mix I ever did.'

Kirk and Gordon were, in some regards, kindred spirits. 'I learned so much from Robert,' Kirk told me in 2013. 'He taught me a lot in terms of sonics and programming on the Atari. He knows so much about bass.'

The two later got together at Western Works to record what would become "The Mood Set EP" on Network Records. Credited to XON, the EP contains a trio of weird, psychedelic and off-kilter Techno tracks that are noticeably deeper than any of the other Bleep & Bass-era Techno cuts that emerged from the Steel City.

---

7   The famous bleeps from "Testone" popped up in sample form on numerous records in the months following the record's release, most notably the KLF's chart-topping "Live at SSL" version of "3AM Eternal", much to Barratt and Kirk's irritation.

8   The bass-weight may have been influenced by Robert Gordon, who – without credit – did some additional Atari-ST programming on "Testone"

'We did that record over about three days at Western Works,' Kirk explained. 'Rob brought over all of his analogue stuff - he had some great old synthesizers and sequencers. We just set everything up and did it. We did a track a day, producing and mixing everything within three days. Later we tried to do some other stuff, but it never came out as well. We actually signed a deal with Network to do another 12" and an album, but sadly it never happened.'

To help get "Laidback, Groovy & Nasty" across the finish line, Robert Gordon and Mark Brydon were enlisted to help co-produce and mix some tracks that would more accurately reflect the heavyweight club sound that was rapidly developing in the Cabs' home city. 'I was very comfortable working with the Cabs because I'd played some bass on "Code", but the sessions were weird,' Brydon remembers. 'When they came into the studio, Richard would be hovering around saying, "You can't change that!" We did think it was odd the Cabs having us help them make dance music. At that point, Mal [Stephen Mallinder] was singing more and they were both fed up of not having hit records. I think they saw it as an opportunity to still be cool but have hits.'

The involvement of the FON Force boys resulted in the undisputed highlight of "Laidback, Groovy & Nasty" - lead single "Easy Life". While still a Cabaret Voltaire record, it boasted warm and weighty bass, Bleep style lead lines and enough energy to make sure it moved the crowd at Occasions. Fittingly, it came with a trio of remixes from Robert Gordon - a vocal-free "Vocal Mix" and two decidedly strange dubs - and a "Jive Turkey Mix" that was overseen by Richard Barratt under his DJ Parrot alias.

'I didn't do the remix, but I did contribute the African style drum break that's sampled on it,' he remembers. 'I remember that during the session I had to lie down on the floor because somebody was smoking this really evil marijuana.' Robert Gordon remembers Barratt requesting a drag before it all went wrong. 'It killed me,' Barratt says. 'I was lying down between the speakers, underneath the mixing desk for at least an hour. I'm not a dope smoker anyway, but that experience certainly didn't help.'

* * *

"Laidback, Groovy & Nasty" was the beginning of the end for Cabaret Voltaire's strained relationship with EMI Records. In the years that followed, they produced a string of records that showcased their particular take on contemporary Techno and Electro, most notably the "Body & Soul" album on Belgian imprint Les Disques de Crepsicule (the lead single, "What Is Real", is basically Bleep & Bass with vocals). Kirk and Mallinder's relationship was beginning to fray around the edges, with the former spending more time at Western Works working on solo projects and Sweet Exorcist tracks.

By the time they got round to making a follow-up to "Testone", Richard Barratt and Richard H Kirk were getting bored of Bleep & Bass, or at least the sparse, simplistic melodies that were now starting to appear on every second UK-made club cut. 'The Bleeps bandwagon is rolling,' wrote Matthew Collin in a December 1990 piece on Sweet Exorcist in i-D magazine. 'Even London acts are getting in on it, for Christ's sake. The sound is becoming a millstone around its creators' necks.'

Barratt seemed to agree with Collin's concerns. 'People just think that you can put some bleeps and heavy bass on anything and make loads of money,' he was quoted as saying. 'There will be a flood of records like that - there has been already.'

Sweet Exorcist's response was to coin a new term for the sound of the records they were now making: Clonk. The track that gave their new micro-genre its name was certainly not lowest common denominator Bleep & Bass. Both of the 12" versions - subtitled "Freebass" and "Homebass" respectively - were mixed by Robert Gordon, who once again ensured that the sub-bass was deep, heavy and capable of coursing through the bodies of dancers at Cuba and Jive Turkey.

Rich in off-kilter, African-influenced drum machine polyrhythms, modem style electronic pulses and alien-sounding minor key motifs, Clonk was the most underground and leftfield club cuts yet to emerge from Yorkshire. For the most part, it sounded like someone had dropped an ecstasy tablet, gone wild in a steel mill and committed the ensuing metallic cacophony to wax.

It was followed shortly after by "Per Clonk", a low-slung chunk of bass-heavy Techno-Funk which played around with some of the same elements as its predecessor, and the deliciously clanking and percussive insanity of "Samba", where off-kilter synthesized marimba melodies danced above quirky vocal samples, mind-mangling electronics and a typically rumbling bassline. Both were brilliant but bonkers, offering rhythms that appealed to Jazz-dancers but left many DJs confused.

Before parting company with Warp Records, there was one final blast of polyrhythmic, dancefloor-focused insanity from Sweet Exorcist: the "CC EP", a suite of tracks based around re-using and re-processing the same basic set of percussion and vocal samples. There were still bleeps present - especially on the wild "Testone" sequel "Trick Jack", whose name may have doffed a cap to another Warp-signed act, Tricky Disco - but, by and large, the vibe was far funkier, with samples lifted from Latin-tinged Post-Punk records and rubbery Jazz-Funk cuts. This was not Bleep & Bass or even Clonk, but rather some form of mutant industrial Techno-Funk.

The duo had trailed this sound in the i-D magazine interview. 'What we're making is modern electronic Funk music,' Barratt said. 'I hate it when people call it rave music - it's not. Rave music is just rehashed and re-sampled music - lowest common denominator[9].'

By the time that the "CC EP" was repackaged as the first album on Warp Records, the label's co-founders were already thinking about where to go next. While Bleep & Bass as a sound had not yet run its course - and Warp would release another handful of industrial-strength Yorkshire Techno records before the spring of 1992 - the style was changing rapidly thanks to the input of others outside of Sheffield, Leeds and Bradford. What had started as records made for a very specific audience had captured the imagination of a whole generation of DJs, dancers and producers across the UK and beyond. It was now they, not the sound's pioneers, who would shape the future sound of British "Bass music".

---

9   Collin, Matthew: *Sweet Exorcist, i-D* magazine, December 1990.

PART THREE

LOW FREQUENCY OVERLOAD

'Before you know it, it's a whole movement.
I don't even know how that happens.'

FABIO [1]

---

1   Fintoni, Laurent: Nightclubbing – Rage, Red Bull Music Academy Daily, 2015

HARDBEAT & BASSLINE

OZONE RECORDINGS AND THE RUSH OF RAPID MUSICAL CHANGE

'There was definitely a period where everything had a bleep on it. Some of the records were really, really good, but some were a bit too giddy - almost a kind of kiddie-friendly version.'

RICHARD BARRATT

It didn't take long for Bleep & Bass to capture the imagination of DJs, dancers and electronic musicians throughout the UK. It had started life as a sound created to cater for the very specific tastes of dancers in the North of England, and Yorkshire in particular, but by the summer of 1990 it was almost impossible to escape the distinctive sounds of lo-fi electronic bleeps and earth-shaking low frequency basslines.

Bleep was far from the only show in town for those dedicated to the escapist rush of dancing all night in dimly lit basements, crumbling former factories and illicit open air raves, but it did offer something markedly different to what had come before. To varying degrees it had reprocessed and re-imagined elements of Chicago House, Detroit Techno, Electro and electronic Reggae, channelling them into a form that not only stood apart from the American-made records that had kick-started the UK's Acid House revolution but also struck a chord with listeners from a wide range of social and ethnic backgrounds.

The commercial success of some of the style's formative records was little less than staggering. While it came at a time when almost all forms of contemporary dance music were racking up significant sales, it's still remarkable that such unashamedly underground and, by the standards of the times, hard-edged records could gatecrash the UK singles charts. Once upon a time, a record couldn't chart without extensive daytime radio play; now, strong support in the clubs and on pirate radio could be enough for a record to sneak into the top 50 or prick the ears of the A&R men and women in the dance departments of major labels.

Yet except for "The Theme", the earliest Bleep hits were not backed by the marketing and promotional power of large record labels. Warp and Bassic were not big organizations, but rather tiny independent record labels from unfashionable northern cities. It was proof, were any needed, that runaway success was possible if you broke the mould, even if you were running an underground Techno label out of a storeroom behind a record shop. In November 1990, the *Sheffield Star* reported that Warp, 'now claims 1.4 per cent of all record sales in Britain, only a slight way behind long-established labels like Chrysalis, Sire and Mercury, and above others with a higher media profile[1].'

For dance music mad entrepreneurs with drive and ambition, Warp's success - and that of other independent dance imprints elsewhere in the UK and continental Europe, most notably Belgian stable R&S Records - proved that it was possible to indulge your passion and start a viable business in the process. It's perhaps unsurprising then that between 1989 and 1991 there was a huge upsurge in the number of dedicated dance labels operating in the UK. Not many of these specifically modelled themselves on Warp, though plenty embraced the new UK Techno sound of Bleep & Bass, offering up records that mixed crucial elements of the sound with their own influences and inspirations.

Inevitably, one of the first labels to do just this and launch in the wake of Warp's runaway success was based not in London, Leeds or Manchester, but rather a short stroll across Sheffield city centre from Rob Mitchell and Steve Beckett's Division Street store. This was Ozone Recordings, an imprint founded almost by accident by a distributor of low-key Indie-Rock records. For a brief period in the early 1990s, its releases became as ubiquitous - on record shop shelves at least - as those of its cross-city rival. Not as wedded to a distinctive sound aesthetic as Warp, Ozone would continue to offer-up energy-packed club cuts well into the 1990s.

● ● ●

Listening back to the Ozone Recordings catalogue today, you'll struggle to find many tracks that are quite as timeless, inspired and groundbreaking as "LFO", "Pressure Dub", "The Theme", "Ital's Anthem" or "Track With No Name". That's not to say that it doesn't contain some genuine gems or that its releases were poor, but rather that it's a mixed bag - both in terms of quality and content. This is something that can be said for many dance

1   Quoted in Young, Rob: *Labels Unlimited – Warp*, Black Dog Publishing, 2005

labels active before and since; after all, dance music is by its very nature functional, created with particular environments in mind, and arguably more influenced by current trends than almost any other form of popular music.

It would be fair to say that Ozone Records was possibly a little scatter-gun in its approach, particularly in its formative years between 1989 and 1991. It was never a purist Bleep & Bass imprint, despite regular missives that referenced the sound. Up until the point that it ceased trading in 1995, Ozone built up a wide-ranging catalogue that included Hip-Hop influenced cut-up jams, bombastic Acid House, UK takes on Detroit futurism, US and Italian influenced House, and even the kind of surging, breakbeat-heavy cuts that would become the staple sound of raves in muddy fields off the M25 and former airfields in Essex. In hindsight, it was reflective of the many different directions British dance music was pulling in during its formative years. While some labels had a unique voice, Ozone focused on offering up excitable club tracks made by a young and enthusiastic bunch of producers who were just beginning their careers.

The label's dancefloor eclecticism stemmed, in part at least, from the background of the label's founder and owner, Kevin Donoghue. A former employee of RCA Records and sound engineer at Rotherham's Music Factory studios (most famous for spawning the short-lived Jive Bunny mega-mix phenomenon), Donoghue established his first label, Native Records, in 1985. The imprint put out a mix of Indie-Rock, Punk and Metal, with Donoghue also building up a successful record distribution business called Strike Force.

In general, record distributors tend to be more acutely aware of sales trends than almost anyone else in the music business. Like many of his distribution colleagues, Donoghue had noted the jaw-dropping growth in sales of club-friendly 12" singles. He could see, too, how Techno and Acid House were becoming musical forces to be reckoned with within the city in which he lived. Rob Mitchell and Steve Beckett's Warp Records store was packed with customers on Fridays and Saturdays, with local DJs eager to hand over their hard-earned wages for copies of the latest must-have club cuts.

Through Native and Strike Force, Donoghue not only had useful contacts within the Sheffield music scene but also access to many of the same demo cassettes that local producers had been passing to the freshly launched Warp Records. He knew, too, that dance offshoots of indie labels could be a success, with Skysaw Records sub-label Rham! enjoying a string of hits with A Guy Called Gerald before he was snapped up by CBS/Columbia Records.

By his own admission, Donoghue was not a dance music specialist. Even so, he managed to secure several decent releases with which to launch the label. These included a pair of singles from long-time Native Records artists Mark Swanncott and Sean Maloney (previously known as Screaming Trees, and now operating as both Success and Countzero), and Panic, an early alias of Allen Saei, later to become a legendary figure in UK Techno under the now-familiar Aubrey pseudonym.

The Success and Countzero records were especially potent. Both had been made at Western Works with Richard H Kirk, who delivered a range of exceedingly raw and bass-heavy mixes. The "Strip Down Acid" mix of "Trip-wire" is particularly raw and wild - all booming bass, mangled TB-303 acid lines, crunchy machine beats and sampled drum solos - while Countzero's sparse but tough "Positive Nuisance #2" is the epitome of the hard and heavy sound popular in key Sheffield clubs at the time.

For reasons that are far too complex to explain, Donoghue also ended up with another big local record: DJ Mink's sweaty and excitable "Hey! Hey! Can U Relate?", a Robert Gordon production that put Sheffield's premier Hip-Hop DJ front and centre. It had initially been pressed up and sent to club DJs by FON Records, but the label collapsed before it could get a full release. Eventually, it would re-emerge on Warp with new mixes by Mark Brydon and Richard Barratt (under his then DJ alias, Parrot), but not before Donoghue had thrown it out on Ozone.

It's worth reflecting a little on the Mink record. It has been almost crim-inally overlooked in recent times, with its bustling and full-throttle, House tempo Hip-Hop sound being at odds with almost everything else released by Ozone and Warp at that time. Yet it's an important record as well as a great one. It was an anthem at Occasions and other key Sheffield clubs, of course, but it also proved influential within the London scene, where Rare Groove and Hip-Hop were far more popular.

'Some people have said that "Hey! Hey! Can You Relate?" may be the first Jungle record, because of the drum programming and the way it switches between breaks quickly at a House tempo,' co-producer Robert Gordon says. 'It's definitely Jungle style programming - you know, where you snip up breaks and stitch them together in time with a beat underneath it.'

Ozone owner Kevin Donoghue was undoubtedly fortunate to receive "Hey! Hey! Can U Relate?" and those other Sheffield-made singles, but he was acutely aware that he needed to find someone more in tune with con-temporary club culture to take on the role of finding and signing tracks. A solution presented itself when Pat Scott and Tim Garbutt, two out-of-town DJs with a rising reputation on the Yorkshire scene, decided to pay him a visit.

'Myself and Tim went over to Sheffield one day with some tracks we'd made to see if we could get a deal,' Scott says. 'We visited Warp first. They said that they liked them but wanted more work done. On the same day, we went to see Kevin at Strike Force. Straight away, he said, "I'll take them". Money was tight for us at that point, so we were happy to get signed. Kevin also asked us if we could bring him some other tunes, so I started getting involved with the label's A&R.'

Although fresh to this kind of role - neither had worked for a label before - Garbutt and Scott were no newcomers to dance music and club culture. They'd yet to reach their twenties but were already scene veterans. Like so many others in the Midlands and the North, they initially bonded in their hometown of Woodhall Spa in Lincolnshire over a shared love of graffiti, Electro and breakdancing.

By the age of 13 or 14, they'd become regular attendees of Jonathan Woodliffe's Sunday afternoon Electro sessions at Rock City in Nottingham. They travelled to Lincoln to breakdance, too, alongside their good friend Jason Bradbury (later to become a recognizable face on British television as host of *The Gadget Show*).

'In 1985 we bought Technics turntables in order to cut up the breaks and play Hip-Hop records,' Scott reminisces. 'The two of us were very much into the DMC battle competitions. They were predominantly Hip-Hop, but later on, people did start using a bit of House in their routines[2].'

The duo made their public DJ debuts a couple of years later. Scott broke cover first, landing himself regular sets in Lincoln, while Garbutt, who was a year older, moved to Harrogate and secured a Saturday night residency.

Over the next two years, they began to land more regular slots across Yorkshire, with Garbutt eventually securing a residency at The Warehouse in Leeds to complement his regular sessions in Harrogate. 'I eventually started doing the Friday night at the same place in Harrogate with Tim,' Scott says. 'We added this Monday night, and we'd get DJs from all over Yorkshire and the Midlands to come and play for us - people like Parrot, Winston and Allistair Whitehead. If you had the time and a night off, you'd go and visit other people's nights.'

Scott was just as busy as Garbutt, making semi-regular appearances in Nottingham's clubs. He also frequently travelled to London to buy and sell records. Between them, Garbutt and Scott were well aware of the subtle differences between the various club scenes up and down the M1.

"Everybody had their own thing going on,' Scott says. 'In London, Acid Jazz, Rare Groove and Hip-Hop were massive, and then later the early Breakbeat Hardcore stuff. The Italian House sound became huge in Leeds - it was the same in Manchester and Nottingham, partly through Graeme Park playing in both cities. Sheffield was different - it was clearly the most 'industrial' in terms of the club sound out of all of the major cities.'

---

2   One of the chief instigators of this fusion of Hip-Hop and House in DMC battle competitions was North West DJ Chad Jackson. He moved to DJing after being a regular "under-age" clubber at nights run by Greg Wilson in Warrington, Wigan and Manchester. He won the DMC World Championship in 1987 and spent the next year travelling the world playing to packed audiences. By 1988 he was a resident DJ at The Haçienda and an in-demand remixer. In 1990 he had a top ten hit with "Hear The Drummer Get Wicked", a heavyweight, breakbeat-driven single that made use of a dizzying number of samples.

Given their dedication to the club scene, it was almost inevitable that Scott and Garbutt would at some point turn their hand to music production. They first dipped their toes in the water in 1988, booking a day at Square Dance studios in Nottingham. "My mum gave me some money for my 18th birthday, and Tim had been given some by his folks a year earlier as well, so we put that together and booked out a day in the studio,' Scott says proudly. 'Those tracks never came out - we ditched them afterwards. To be honest, it was probably more a case that we didn't have the money to finish them off properly - it was about a grand a day to hire the main studio at Square Dance.'

The duo returned to the studio sporadically over the next six months when money allowed, saving up bits and pieces of their DJ fees to afford studio time. They finished the tracks that made up their first Ozone release in early 1989, and it was these Detroit Techno influenced workouts - "Motion" and "Diffusion" - that got them a deal with Ozone Recordings as Trak 1.

Despite signing with Ozone in mid-1989, they had to wait what felt like an eternity for the record to appear in stores. This naturally left them very frustrated. 'Ozone had a distribution deal with Polygram, which was great for export and ensuring lots of copies were out there, but also meant that we had all these releases stacking up,' Scott sighs. 'By the time they came out, they didn't always reflect what was happening in the clubs. Everything was a year behind, which was ridiculous.'

While waiting for the record to be released, they headed back to Square Dance to make more music. This time they didn't have to dip into their savings, as Kevin Donoghue had paid them an advance against future sales royalties that could be used to pay the studio bills. Even so, with Square Dance costing up to £1,000 a day for a studio and an engineer, Scott and Garbutt had to work fast.

'We made three of our 12" singles - that's all six sides of the records - within two and a half days,' Scott laughs.' Some of the tracks were made and finished within six hours. Kevin just said to us, "All right lads, get in the studio and get it done". We didn't think about it, we just got on with it. I think we'd have liked to have worked on them a bit more, but the fact that they were quite raw was appealing to some people.'

These three singles, plus their other solo and collaborative projects that appeared throughout 1990 and '91, displayed an astute ability to tune-in to contemporary dancefloor trends. On their second and third Trak 1 EPs ("For This" and "Street Violence"), Scott and Garbutt variously fused elements of Brooklyn Breakbeat, Detroit Techno and Chicago Acid. Their first single as Ionic, "Global World", also cleverly joined the dots between Bleep, early Orbital and Belgian Techno.

Arguably best of all, though, were their collaborations under the New Age Technology guise. These were unashamedly inspired by the Bleep & Bass style emerging around them in Sheffield and Leeds, where both now lived. Their first missive under the guise, also called "New Age Technology", boasted the kind of heavyweight bass, post-industrial percussion and alien melody lines that were Bleep's aural trademarks. Their subsequent follow-up 12", "You Say", sounded like it could have been produced by Richard H Kirk and Robert Gordon during their short-lived XON collaboration.

'When we went into the studio, the tracks we made represented what we were playing in the clubs: Piano House, Bleep and Techno with breakbeats, which was more a mixture of everything,' Scott remarks. 'That summed up everything that was going in on the clubs and the records that we were playing at the time. We could have just made three Bleep tunes, but it wasn't us - we had influences from all over the place.'

This hotchpotch of contrasting styles and influences would become a feature of the wider Bleep & Bass movement throughout late 1990 and '91. It also remained a trademark of Scott's other productions throughout the period. Check, for example, the pianos, breakbeats, bleeps and druggy bass of 1703's "Hypnotize", and the throbbing sub-bass, New York Deep House flourishes and Disco vocal samples of Zone's "Don't You Want Some More".

Both of these tracks were co-produced by Matt Elliss, an emerging producer from Doncaster. Scott had started working with him when Tim Garbutt decided that he wanted to work more with Jez Willis, a friend from the Leeds scene. In hindsight, it was a good move by Garbutt: together with Willis, he had a string of colossal hits as Utah Saints, developing a full-throttle, sample-heavy brand of House that became hugely popular around the world.

'The three of us - Tim, Jez and me - used to DJ together a lot at that time,' Scott says. 'When they did Utah Saints, I went on to do other things with different people. We had a few things still waiting to be released by Ozone, which were kind of finished, but not finished in our eyes. I just left them with Kevin, and I parted company with the label midway through 1991.'

Scott continued to produce but began devoting more time to both DJing and selling records to stores from the back of a van (unlike some within the scene, he'd fully embraced the entrepreneurial brand of capitalism promoted by the Conservative government). Before he left, Scott oversaw the production of Ozone Recordings' first compilation, a double-vinyl retrospective titled "Hardbeat & Bassline". It offered a neat snapshot of the imprint's most significant period - a time when it rivalled Warp in prominence, if not in sales.

'In all fairness, Ozone was always the poor relation of Warp,' Scott says. 'I think you'll probably find that a number of the label's early releases from Sheffield artists had been taken to Warp first and turned down. But they launched the label well and after that Ozone was on the map. The thing is, Kevin is not a dance music head - he's a straight-up Rock & Roll guy. He'd signed all sorts of different things before I turned up and it was a really crazy mixture of tunes.'

When Scott departed, the responsibility for sourcing releases reverted to Kevin Donoghue. As a result, Ozone Recordings' output became increasingly hit-and-miss over the years that followed[3]. 'Things changed so quickly,' Scott sighs. 'From late '90 to '93, things just started going in all sorts of directions. If you weren't really tuned into it, you suffered. Kevin admits that he got desperate after I left - he was just putting stuff out and hoping it would be a success. There were definitely some bad releases on Ozone, but there were bad releases on a lot of labels at that time.'

---

3   Pat Scott later bought the rights to the Ozone catalogue and began releasing new material in 2016.

BIO RYTHYMS

NETWORK RECORDS AND THE MIDLANDS CONNECTION

'These are the 1990s and it's time for the poll tax. Why should you care about these things? Because this is the sound Salvador Dali would have made had he bought an 808 drum machine instead of a paintbrush. This sequenced surrealism is new music for an old age, the kind of sonic art created when human beings fall in love with machines and computers. This is special.'

JOHN McCREADY "Bio Rhythm" compilation liner notes, 1990 [1]

On a steamy hot night in July 2019, two music industry veterans are addressing a room full of mostly middle-aged House and Techno enthusiasts at Café Artum, a record shop, bar and event space in Birmingham city centre. Stood behind a pair of Technics turntables and an oversized DJ mixer, the two swap eyebrow-raising anecdotes in between short snatches of records they were involved in signing, licensing, promoting and releasing during the '80s and early '90s.

Both are enjoying themselves immensely, offering up anecdotes that have the assembled crowd in stitches. Both men are on home territory; not only do they live locally, but they've also been associated with music in the Midlands since the 1970s. The most high profile of the pair is John Mostyn, a slender, smiling figure with sweeping silver hair. He first rose to prominence in the late 1970s as manager of 2 Tone signed Ska revivalists The Beat, before going on to manage countless other acts during the 1980s.

---

1   Various Artists: Biorthythm – Dance Music With Bleeps, Network Records, BIOLP1, 1990

CHAPTER THIRTEEN

^ NEXUS 21

By the time he met the man standing to his left, Neil Rushton, Mostyn was managing one of the bands that came out of the collapse of The Beat, Fine Young Cannibals.

During the late 1980s Mostyn and Rushton, who was once one of the UK's leading Northern Soul promoters, worked together a lot. Between them, the duo were responsible for turning a handful of Detroit musicians into global dance music stars. Through their work with Derrick May and Kevin Saunderson, two of the founding fathers of Techno, the duo helped change British dance music forever.

At the dawn of the 1990s, Neil Rushton was one of the most significant figures in the UK's rapidly expanding dance music industry. He was the first to see the potential of licensing and reissuing Detroit Techno at a time when most of his contemporaries were still focusing on the House sound of Chicago, and then helped introduce the sound to a wider audience thanks to a pair of now-legendary compilations on Virgin Records' dance subsidiary 10 Records. Equally significantly, Rushton was also the co-founder of a label that would become one of the leading dance independents of the era, Network Records.

Based in Birmingham and intrinsically linked to the Midlands scene surrounding it - as well as post-industrial cities in America's Midwest - Network was a tireless promoter of contemporary Techno music from both sides of the Atlantic. Its tried-and-tested releases championed both Bleep & Bass-inspired anthems informed by records on Warp and Bassic, and mutations of the breakbeat-driven, all-action Hardcore rave records more readily associated with Reinforced, Shut Up & Dance and XL Recordings.

Like the latter label (and Warp for that matter), Network eventually tasted chart success. Impressively, Rushton and his motley crew of label employees - co-founder Dave Barker, wordsmith John McCready and local DJ turned unofficial A&R man Neil Macey included - achieved all this while creating their own myths and challenging the status quo.

'We'd come from nowhere, were managing Detroit techno's biggest acts, had our own label and were based in Birmingham,' Rushton proudly tells the assembled audience at Café Artum. 'The fact that we weren't part of the London [music industry] establishment was great. We actually played up to that to make out that we were more anti-establishment than we actually were.'

Although a serious business sometimes involving eye-watering amounts of money, Network and its predecessor, Kool Kat Records, were part of what Mostyn and Rushton make sound like a Techno Boy's Own adventure. On this muggy evening in Britain's second city, the pair offers up a succession of entertaining and eye-opening stories.

They explain what happened when Derrick May met Herbie Hancock for the first time in the dressing rooms at Heaven (spoiler: May ran round the walls before exiting the club and was subsequently not seen for days); reveal how Kevin Saunderson had to be persuaded to release Inner City's "Big Fun" ('I told him it was brilliant and that it would change his life,' Rushton enthuses); and offer up shaggy dog stories about meetings with music industry executives in which Rushton and McCready deliberately acted outrageously to earn more money for the acts Network were managing.

'Before we went to the meeting I said to John, "Let's just be outrageous - I'll be Malcolm McLaren and you be Paul Morley",' Rushton says, referencing two of the most infamous characters in British Pop music during the 1980s. 'So when these executives from Virgin America asked us how much money we were after for Altern8 to sign for them I said, "£250,000", which is a crazy amount. They said, "That's ridiculous". We knew we were never going to get that much as an advance, we were just playing up. To cut a long story short, the advance ended up being £160,000, which was unheard of for a dance act at that time.'

* * *

Neil Rushton was exactly the kind of can-do individual that would have delighted Margaret Thatcher and Norman Tebbit. He started his career as a newspaper reporter but then quit his job in the early 1970s to become a full-time event promoter. In 1979, he launched his first record label, Inferno, in order to license and reissue rare and in-demand records that were popular on the thriving all-dayer scene.

When he decided to turn his back on event promotion in 1980, Rushton continued running the label as a hobby and managed to shift 30,000 copies of Gloria Jones' "Tainted Love", a stomping Soul anthem that pricked the public consciousness following the release of Soft Cell's celebrated Synth-Pop cover in 1981.

'Inferno was very Punk in ethos, but we knew the basics,' Rushton explains while sat nursing a beer at Café Artum. 'We were putting out things by the Carstairs, Freda Payne, Barbara Mills and the Showstoppers. I learned a lot about running a label, particularly about publishing and licensing.'

Some of these lessons were harsh - by the time the imprint collapsed in 1985, Rushton owed £10,000 to the bank - and he admits that mistakes were made along the way. 'Six months before the Soft Cell record came out I'd been offered the publishing rights to "Tainted Love",' he sighs. 'Gloria Jones' producer Ray Harris rang me up one night and told me he was coming over to the UK and wanted some money to spend in the casino. He said that for $1,000 I could have the publishing for the song to go with the pressing rights. I said "no". Biggest mistake of my life.'

Following the demise of Inferno, Rushton returned to work as a newspaper reporter, first as a staffer on local newspapers and later as a freelancer on Sunday newspapers including the News of the World. 'Music was my obsession, my passion, but I had no intention of going back into music full time,' he says. 'I didn't think I'd ever have the opportunity.'

But Rushton was blessed with the entrepreneurial spirit so beloved of the Conservative government. When an opportunity finally arose for him to re-enter the music industry in 1987, he naturally grabbed it with both hands. 'One night I went out for a drink with my friend Pat Ward,' he says. 'That night, he introduced me to a guy called Dave Barker, who was a DJ with an office in Bishopsgate in Birmingham. For some bizarre reason - and there was no masterplan - we just decided to start a new record label called Kool Kat.'

Rushton was well aware of how popular House music was becoming, particularly in the Midlands and the North of England. He believed that there was room in the market for a new label serving up DJ-friendly 12" singles of US and UK-made House tracks. It was still a considerable risk, though, but one he was willing to take.

'It was a big step because I had three kids, and one was only six months old at the time,' he admits. 'I had to promise Jane, my then-wife, that I would make it work. But when we came to try and license records from Chicago, we were getting the crumbs because people like Damon D'Cruz at Jack Trax and Pete Tong at London Records had already signed up the best stuff.'

Although Kool Kat did snap up some gems from across the pond - Denise Motto's delightfully sleazy "I M N X T C" being the most celebrated - Rushton and Barker soon realized they'd have to pick up British productions to keep the label going. One of their first releases was an audacious compilation album titled "House Masters - USA v UK Showdown".

While it would be hard to argue now that many of the showcased artists were genuine "House masters", the format was genuinely unique. One side featured tracks from American artists, while the other showcased five British House tracks, most of which were produced by Midlands-based artists. The standout cut was "House Reaction" by T-Cut-F, a Nottingham-based duo comprised of vocalist Delroy St Joseph and producer Mark Gamble.

'From leaving school I was obsessed with synthesizers, drum machines and samplers,' Gamble says while sitting in the home studio he built in the late 1980s. 'I remember hearing some early House from the US and thinking, "I've got the same synthesizers and drum machines so I could make similar records". Those records were so exciting and very inspirational.'

By his own admission, Gamble was never a DJ and hardly an enthusiastic clubber. He was a musician and producer who obsessed over electronic instruments and dreamed of making a living out of his passion for dance music. He rarely worked alone and surrounded himself with friends who were DJs, singers and rappers.

In 1987 he had multiple projects on the go; as well as T-Cut-F he was collaborating with Cassius Campbell (AKA Nottingham DJ Cassrock) as Krush. With the assistance of Sheffield vocalist Ruth Joy and producers Mark Brydon and Robert Gordon, Gamble produced "House Arrest", a single that became an enormous Pop hit around the world.

'Looking back now, "House Arrest" wasn't really proper House,' Gamble says. 'The B-side ["Jack's Back"] was a much more credible House track[2]. We didn't set out to make a Pop record though - that was just how it developed in the studio with Mark [Brydon] and Rob [Gordon]. It did get us on Top of the Pops, though, which was an amazing experience.'

While "House Arrest" was beginning to make its way up the charts, interest was also growing in the Gamble-produced T-Cut-F track on Kool Kat. Through a music reporter of one of the newspapers he still worked for part-time, Neil Rushton found out that Mick Clark at 10 Records was interested in licensing it for re-release. It was a chance to put all he'd learned so far about licensing to the test.

'I knew Mick's name because he was involved with the Jazz-Funk scene down south in the early '80s, so I went down to see him,' Rushton says. 'Lo and behold I licensed "House Reaction" to him. I did a deal whereby Kool Kat got more money for overseas releases as well as the UK ones. I'm pretty sure Mark [Gamble] earned more out of that deal than he ever did out of "House Arrest" on FON Records.'

The T-Cut-F deal was just the beginning. While that may have confirmed that his A&R credentials were sharp, Kool Kat still needed to make more signings. With the best Chicago House cuts off-limits, Rushton turned his attention to the new electronic records coming out of his beloved Detroit, and particularly those released by Metroplex, KMS and Transmat.

'I was drawn to them to begin with because they were from Detroit,' Rushton enthuses. 'Because of my Soul background, I'd been to the city to buy records. I collected records from there, so I loved these new electronic records that were coming over.'

He was particularly excited by Rhythim Is Rhythim's "Nude Photo", a popular seller on import amongst the dedicated DJ community in the Midlands and North. Having wondered aloud whether licensing it for a UK re-release would be a good idea, Rushton bit the bullet and called Transmat Records - a label he was convinced was some kind of lucrative, big money operation. In reality, it was a bedroom operation helmed by the man behind the Rhythim Is Rhythim project, Motor City Techno pioneer Derrick May. Rushton was naturally rather surprised when May answered his call.

---

2   He's right: "Jack's Back" has held up remarkably well. It was a luscious chunk of British Deep House that sounds like the missing link between Mr Fingers and the Pet Shop Boys. Listen carefully, and you'll spot some proto-Bleep melodies amongst the gorgeous synthesizer chords, acid bass and sweaty machine drums.

'I told him how I couldn't believe how good his tracks were, particularly "Nude Photo" and "The Dance",' Rushton says. 'I told him we had no money but loved the music and had boundless enthusiasm. It was a bit of a gamble, but I invited him to come over and stay with me over Christmas. We somehow rustled to get enough money together to pay the airfare.'

During May's subsequent trip to the UK, Rushton managed to get John Mostyn to pull some strings and set up a meeting for him with Julian Palmer at Island Records' usually on-point dance offshoot 4th & Broadway. He gave Palmer the big sell, explaining that May's music was the next big thing. 'Myself and Derrick played him "Nude Photo" and "Strings of Life" and Julian just said, "I don't get it",' Rushton recalls. 'I thought, "This is not good!" Derrick was a genius and Palmer was an A&R legend. 4th & Broadway was one of the coolest dance labels around and, to me, it was the perfect fit for Derrick.'

Despite this setback, Rushton was still able to get May some remix work during his trip. There was a session in Square Dance Studios in Nottingham with Mark Gamble reworking "House Reaction", plus a day spent revising Bang The Party's "Release Your Body" for important early London House (and later Techno) imprint Warriors Dance. May also sprinkled some of his Motor City magic over "Tired of Being Pushed Around" by Fine Young Cannibals side project Two Men, A Drum Machine and a Trumpet.

Having earned money on his trip - and not only from flogging the 50 or so copies of "Strings of Life" he'd brought with him - Derrick May was naturally impressed with Rushton and how he operated. 'Before he went back, Derrick said to me, "You've got to manage my friend Kevin [Saunderson]",' Rushton says. 'So once he'd left I went to see Mick Clark at Virgin to deliver Derrick's remix of "House Reaction". That's when I told him I had a great idea.'

The idea in question was a compilation showcasing the work of May, Kevin Saunderson, Juan Atkins and the new generation of Detroit producers that were following in their footsteps. 'I told him that there was this whole new thing going on in Detroit, which was different to Chicago House but running parallel to it,' he says. 'I suggested that I license the tracks to Kool Kat, put together the compilation and license the whole thing to Virgin.'

Much to Rushton's surprise, Clark agreed. He was dispatched to Detroit to sign the tracks and work on production, taking with him two music journalists who would pen articles for *NME* and *The Face* respectively, Stuart Cosgrove and John McCready. When those articles appeared some months later, the pair's flowing prose introduced a wider UK audience to the new sound of Detroit Techno, a genre tag that had yet to be fully applied to the music by its creators. There are contrasting stories of exactly who came up with it, though Rushton says he was inspired by a complaint from one Detroiter that the music was not 'the new House sound of Detroit' - the compilation's working title - but rather 'Techno music'.

Either way, the name stuck, with the subsequent compilation - "Techno! The New Dance Sound of Detroit" - introducing this new wave of Motor City dancefloor futurism to Britain's growing community of bedroom dance music enthusiasts and wannabe DJs. Thanks to the way it was promoted and presented, it also offered a clear narrative for listeners to buy into.

'Think of Detroit and you automatically think of Motown, but be careful not to think too loud because the new grandmasters of Detroit Techno hate history,' Stuart Cosgrove wrote in his now-legendary sleeve notes. 'Techno music is unashamedly modern in its outlook. It is a mesmerizing underground of new music that looks to the future, breaks with the past and blends European Industrial Pop with black American Garage Funk. It is not simply dance music but a series of sound experiments that often deny the logic of more uncomplicated dance sounds like Chicago House.'

It wasn't just DJs and dancers who were enthused by the hot new sounds coming from the Motor City, but also those who stumbled across the tracks while listening to the radio. 'Hearing Detroit Techno on the radio for the first time changed my life,' says Edward Upton aka DMX Krew, then an electronic music-mad teenager from the sleepy town of Bedford. 'The radio show I was listening to played four or five tracks from "Techno! The Dance Sound of Detroit", saying that Techno was a new form of House music. Those tracks really struck a chord with me. Most of them were very melodic and melancholic - "It Is What It Is" by Rhythim Is Rhythim and "Sequence 10" by Anthony Shakir are very definitely bittersweet.'

The impact made by the compilation and its swift follow-up was tangible, and Neil Rushton was in the perfect position to take advantage. With assistance from John Mostyn he began managing Derrick May and Kevin Saunderson, while also becoming the go-to man for Detroit artists looking for deals in the UK. Kool Kat snapped up the overseas rights to a string of brilliant Motor City Techno records, sometimes doing secondary licensing deals with Pete Tong at London Records or Mick Clark at 10 Records.

May and Saunderson were delighted by the life-changing sums of money Rushton was able to make for them through publishing, licensing and remix deals. In fact, Saunderson was so delighted that he not only bought Rushton a copy of the rarest Northern Soul record of all, Frank Wilson's "Do I Love You (I Really Do)"[3], but also gifted him the publishing rights to "Rock To The Beat".

'The track started getting big in Europe, and there were cover versions done, including one that went top ten in France and one that went top ten in Holland,' Rushton remembers. 'Because we had the publishing on the track

---

3   This was only the second copy of the record ever discovered. A Detroit record dealer unearthed it while Rushton was over visiting the Motor City on business. He mentioned this to Saunderson, complaining about the high price, and was surprised when his young charge presented him with the legendary record. The copy Rushton owned was later sold for over $30,000, a record amount at the time.

we kept getting all these phone calls. In the end, we had a Dutch auction for the European rights to Kevin's original version. We told Kevin to rip up the paperwork and we'd give him 80% of whatever we got. In the end, the winning bid was close to $120,000, which is crazy.'

There were further deals, too, including an agreement for Inner City's "Big Life" to be used on a beer commercial in the US. 'In the middle of all of this, Kevin called me up and said, "I have $250,000 credit on my first publishing statement",' Rushton says proudly in his distinctive West Midlands accent. 'From where we were when I first went over to Detroit eight or ten months earlier, the landscape had changed completely.'

● ● ●

When Network Records launched in early 1990, the British dance music landscape had changed from what it had been when Rushton made his life-changing trip to Detroit with Stuart Cosgrove and John McCready. Thanks to Bleep & Bass and the first stirrings of Hardcore, the UK was beginning to find a united voice that was decidedly different from the American records that had originally inspired it.

It made sense, then, that Neil Rushton and Dave Barker's new venture[4] should join the dots between authentic American Techno and the new wave of British productions that put heavy sub-bass and alien bleeps front and centre. The pair already had a string of great new tracks from Chicago and Detroit to release, including Neal Howard's "Indulge" (a track Rushton believed was almost as good as Inner City's "Big Fun"), Mark Kinchen's "Somebody New" and "Mood" by Symbols and Instruments, a young Windy City trio whose members included future Deep House heavyweights Derrick Carter and Mark Farina.

In addition, Rushton had also snapped up more tracks from Midlands-based producers. Chief amongst this new intake was Nexus 21, a Stafford-based duo comprised of Mark Archer and Chris Peat. Along with school friends Dean Meredith and Andrew Meecham, Peat and Archer had been releasing Acid House and Detroit Techno-influenced tracks since 1988. These appeared under a wide variety of aliases on Blue Chip Records, an offshoot of a local recording studio owned by Neil Rushton's old Northern Soul scene colleague Kev Roberts. Archer and Peat had been working at the studio, dividing their time between basic engineering and recording hot new tracks for Roberts to release.

---

4   Kool Kat survived the collapse of its distributor, PRT, a year or so earlier, by doing joint ventures with Jaz Summers' Big Life label. However, Rushton and Barker decided to kill off Kool Kat and launch a new imprint in order to have total creative and financial freedom.

By the time Nexus 21 signed to Network, Blue Chip had gone out of business, though the pair had already released a rather good debut album, "The Rhythm of Life", a very Motor City sounding single, "Still Life (Keeps Moving)" and an 'Italian House style tune' under the alternative alias C&M Connection ("Another Night"). The latter 12" included a "Techno Dreams" re-make on the flipside that brilliantly fused the bittersweet bliss of Detroit futurism with the alien bleeps and heavy bass that were rapidly becoming a cornerstone of the UK sound.

'It's all about the idea of having the same ingredients, but in different levels,' Mark Archer muses. 'Our first influence for the Nexus 21 tracks and that "Another Night" remix, which was meant to be a Nexus 21 mix, was a big pile of Detroit records. We were influenced by what was happening in Leeds and Sheffield, but the producers in those cities had slightly different inspirations. They had Detroit, their Dub soundsystem backgrounds and Hip-Hop as their influences.'

Under a new name, the "Techno Dreams" mix of "Another Night" became the title track of Network Records most significant early release: "Bio Rhythm", a self-styled compilation of "dance music with bleeps". The sleeve artwork included a short essay from John McCready that claimed that the compilation was inspired by a series of tiny raves that took place a year earlier in a Midlands-based chain of launderettes.

'Biorhythms is the name of a revolutionary idea which remains unknown outside of the Birmingham area,' McCready wrote. 'Local rave promoter Sueno de Niro came up with the idea of turning his launderette shops into small scale legal raves. His shops were fitted with 5k rigs [soundsystems]. The city's ravers would queue up outside the shops with bags full of soiled Naf Naf sweatshirts. The local constabulary was outraged. They couldn't do anything to stop the dancers while the washing machines were spinning round.'

McCready went on to explain that the soundtrack to these micro-raves was provided by, 'upfront local DJs like Neil Macey and DJ Persil'. Macey was a genuinely important figure in the Network story. He DJed in various venues around the Midlands, though it was his weekly events at the No. 7 wine bar in Burntwood, Neil Rushton's home town, that would become the testing ground for future Network releases as well as the white-hot promos he received from Warp. It was Macey who introduced Mark Archer to Neil Rushton, and the Network co-owner would regularly consult him before signing tracks.

The reference to Macey aside, the rest of McCready's liner notes were creative, to say the least. It goes without saying that there were no Biorhythms micro-raves. It was myth-making pure and simple: a trend that would continue throughout the Network Records story. 'Because there was a slight element of truthfulness behind it - there was a club in Leicester that Neil Macey played at called Bliss, which inspired Cyclone's "A Place Called

Bliss" that later came out on Network - people couldn't work out whether it was true or not,' Mark Archer remembers. 'It would have been mental if it had actually happened, but it wasn't so far out that it couldn't have happened. Neil [Rushton] and John [McCready] just made up these great urban legends.'

Both men had an inherent sense of how to get headlines in the music press. They'd previously caused a commotion during the promotion for one of Kevin Saunderson's Inner City releases by getting the Detroit producer to slag off UK-made techno. 'I got into trouble over that,' Rushton laughs. 'It was a complete scam. Mick Clark wasn't happy - he rang me up and said, "You can't do this! It's outrageous!" He was getting grief from their press department. I just told him that we were effectively slagging off some of our own artists to get publicity. When he came to see us a few weeks later, Mick said, "Why am I telling you off? What you're doing is great!"'

* * *

With its tight track listing and mischievous sleeve notes, "Bio Rhythm" was a commercial success, leading to an inevitable - and arguably even stronger - sequel in the autumn of 1990. Both volumes cashed in on the growing hype around Techno, and Bleep & Bass in particular, by offering up a mixture of authentic American cuts from the likes of Juan Atkins, Derrick May, MK and Neal Howard, and fresh UK Techno numbers from Nexus 21, Energize (an early alternate alias for Dave Lee aka Joey Negro), Robert Gordon and Richard H Kirk as XON, one-hit-wonder Heychild (whose "Heychild's Theme" was a bright and melodious take on UK-Detroit Techno fusion) and Network stalwarts Rhythmatic.

The latter was a brand new project from Mark Gamble and Leroy Crawford. Since "House Reaction" and "House Arrest" became big successes, Gamble had spent much of his time in Sheffield working on a Krush album that would eventually be abandoned. Being surrounded by some of the architects of the Bleep & Bass sound undoubtedly inspired him, though it was hearing Unique 3's "The Theme" for the first time in a London club that really changed his outlook.

'When I heard "The Theme", I just thought, "Wow",' Gamble says enthusiastically. 'It was the hook and the bass that got me. I heard it and thought, "That's the future". The simplicity, the raw sound... it was great. When we came back from London, that was the kind of record I wanted to make.'

The first Rhythmatic single, "Take Me Back", was as raw and heavy a Bleep & Bass cut as you're likely to hear. Its sparse, ear-catching Bleeps in the vein of "Testone" or "The Theme" came accompanied by raw, skittish drums, warehouse-ready synth stabs and sub-bass so heavy it was liable to blow speakers.

'Myself and Neil Macey kept asking Mark to go back to the studio and tweak the bass on "Take Me Back",' Neil Rushton chuckles. 'He came back three times with new versions, each with progressively heavier bass. Mark said, "This is ridiculous - you'll ruin club soundsytems!" We knew we had a record that was heavier than some of the Sheffield records, so in typical Network fashion we thought we'd take the piss and pretend that it was from Sheffield.'

To get people to buy into the lie, Network sent out initial copies of the single with labels that claimed it was the work of "0742 Records", a previously unheard of imprint whose name referenced the then Sheffield dialling code. For added authenticity, Mark Gamble asked his friend Robert Gordon to provide an "Edit with extra bass".

'For me, it all started in Sheffield, so the 0742 Records thing was a way of showing respect,' Gamble says. 'I had so much respect for Sheffield, and if people thought the record was from there, even better. It wasn't our intention to mislead people - it was just the sort of thing Network did. We even did a Soul-flavoured remix at one point that Neil [Rushton] jokingly named the R-Soul Mix.'

Behind the scenes, Network and Warp actually enjoyed a good relationship. Several former Warp artists, including the latter's first act, the Forgemasters, ended up releasing records on Network. The hype surrounding both imprints and the Bleep & Bass sound meant that the British clubbing public was eager for a taste of the action. Because of this, there was a collaborative Warp and Network tour featuring a mix of DJ sets and live performances from the likes of LFO, Rhythmatic, Nexus 21 and Nightmares on Wax[5].

'We did lots and lots of shows and to be honest from week to week I couldn't tell you where we were,' Mark Gamble admits. 'I remember that after one show a reviewer commented that our live set was the most convincing, but in truth, it was the most unconvincing live show you could imagine. Apart from the microphones, not one thing was live - it was just our tracks being played by a DAT machine. It was fantastic to be on that tour though and being around musicians who were doing something genuinely exciting.'

Aside from visiting the four corners of the UK, the tour also visited Germany for shows in cities with vibrant underground Techno scenes such as Berlin, Frankfurt and Cologne. Those gigs were a rip-roaring success, but that wasn't always the case thanks to a North-South divide that had been simmering away in society since the early '80s.

'We had two dates at the Mean Fiddler down in London, but after the first night they cancelled the second,' Mark Archer remembers. 'Everyone stood there with their arms folded looking up at the stage, like, "Go on, impress us!" Another time we did something for Channel 4, which was filmed at

---

5   Forgemasters didn't appear on the tour and instead went and did a mini-tour of their own, where Robert Gordon and Sean Maher performed live and Winston Hazel DJed.

Brixton Academy during the day. There were all these little kids down the front shouting, "Fuck off back up north, you wankers!" The North-South divide was very prevalent back then.'

Yet by the time the Warp/Network tour finished in early 1991, the once distinctive scenes in the Midlands/North and London/South East were coming closer together - musically at least. This was in part down to clubs such as Shelley's in Stoke and the Eclipse in Coventry, whose promoters embraced both Bleep & Bass and the growing Hardcore rave sounds now emerging from London and continental Europe.

Eclipse's opening night in October 1990 became legendary for a number of reasons, not least the fact that it was one of the first 'legal raves' to stay open all night[6]. The line-up represented the best of what was happening both 'up north' and 'down south', with Manchester rapper MC Tunes and Shelley's resident Sasha being joined on the bill by London Hardcore and Jungle Techno pioneer Fabio and leading Acid House/Techno DJ 'Evil' Eddie Richards[7].

Over the two years that followed, Eclipse became one of Britain's most talked-about and popular venues. Its central location made it an ideal meeting place for DJs, live acts and ravers from both the North and South. The club's up-for-it crowd was universally high on ecstasy and amphetamines, leading to a euphoric atmosphere that the DJs and live acts could exploit. To keep punters coming back for more, Eclipse's promoters ensured a steady stream of performances from the likes of LFO, the Prodigy, K-Klass, SL2, Moby, Shades of Rhythm and Nexus 21.

It was also at Eclipse where Mark Archer and Chris Peat debuted their second, and ultimately more successful, alias, Altern8. The pair recorded the tracks that made up their debut single, the "Overload EP", during studio downtime towards the tail-end of their time working at Blue Chip. These sample-heavy productions were much cheekier and altogether more full-throttle than the smooth and melodious Nexus 21 tracks the pair had been making, so Neil Rushton suggested they adopted a new moniker. He was also keen for the EP to sport all eight tunes they'd made in that style, making it more of a mini-album than a 12" single.

'It was Network's answer to [Frankie Bones and Lenny D's] "Looney Tunes" releases,' Mark Archer says. 'It was great value for money and very good for DJs who wanted releases where you could play multiple tracks off one record during a set. Network didn't promo it at all - when it came out, it sold well purely on its value for money merit.'

---

6   The promoters took advantage of a legal loophole by serving no alcohol and selling tickets only to "members" – people who had signed up a few weeks earlier.
7   Jobson, Daz: Eclipse: *The Club To Eclipse All Others*, Covert Mag, 2009 (http://www.covertmag.com/2009/07/eclipse-the-nightclub-to-errrrr-eclipse-all-others/)

When the Eclipse came looking for Altern8, Archer and Peat's second effort under the alias was doing the rounds on promo. It was called "Infiltrate 202" and was the product of a jokey studio session in which the two Stafford producers decided to throw as many of rave samples into the pot as possible, including riffs lifted from various recognizable club hits, a snatch of a pirate radio show by Sheffield DJs Asterix and Space ("Watch yer bassbins I'm telling ya!") and some suitably twisted electronics. This madness was underpinned by bustling, Hardcore style breakbeats and a bassline so heavy it could have been plucked from "LFO" or "The Theme".

'In the press, they called it 'rave by numbers', but it was never meant as a piss-take,' Mark Archer says defensively. 'If you were going to make a big tune without going overly commercial, you'd put everything on there that you liked at that moment.'

Altern8's Eclipse debut came just a few weeks after Archer and Peat's Nexus 21 performance at the club, so the duo were worried that the crowd would work out who they were. They decided to cover up and disguise themselves using masks and NBC suits - used as protection against chemical warfare attacks - borrowed off a relative in the RAF. Altern8 now had a distinctive look, albeit one that they didn't initially plan to use in future.

'There was no big plan to have a certain image, we just wanted to hide,' Archer admits. 'We honestly thought that the first PA we did as Altern8 would be our last. I guess it was a case of 'right place, right time' - it captured what was happening and just took off.'

The rapid rise of Altern8 in 1991 - a year in which they bagged two big chart hits in "Infiltrate 202" and "Activ8", which got to number two in the charts - was certainly indicative of the way British dance music was changing. In a little over 12 months, the influence of Bleep & Bass had diminished, while breakbeat-powered Hardcore records made with clubs like Eclipse in mind were becoming increasingly common.

Tracks were becoming faster, too, and while the sub-bass that had been such a prominent part of Bleep records remained, they were unrecognizable from the weighty, minimalist cuts that emerged from Yorkshire and the Midlands between 1988 and 1990.

When it came to promoting Altern8, Neil Rushton and John McCready were in their element. The duo's distinctive outfits and celebratory, rush-inducing records were an easy sell. While Techno purists dismissed Peat and Archer as "cartoon rave monkeys" - a particularly harsh charge given the undoubted quality of their Detroit-inspired Nexus 21 records - the British media loved them. A big money deal with Virgin America followed after Rushton and McCready likened the pair to dance music's premier pranksters the KLF, a duo that sold more records worldwide in 1991 than any other British act.

The runaway success of Altern8 didn't quite signal the end of Network's involvement with Bleep & Bass - there were occasional gems in 1991, including Cyclone's underrated "Sonic Cycology EP", the delayed release of XON's fantastic "Mood Set EP", the Forgemasters' "Black Steel EP" (featuring Unique 3's remix of "Track With No Name") and some weighty Robert Gordon reworks of Energize's "Report to the Dancefloor" - but the Birmingham label was now travelling in a different direction.

'Looking back, today has crystallized my thoughts about the Network years,' Neil Rushton says before downing the remnants of his pint at Café Artum. 'After I left my job I had to succeed with Kool Kat and Network. I was consumed by wanting to run the best possible label. I really enjoyed getting great deals for artists and being able to pay them quickly. Although we didn't take ourselves seriously, we took the music very seriously.'

CHAPTER FOURTEEN

NORTH OF WATFORD

THE STORY OF CHILL MUSIC

'It's important to set the record straight. Normally when people talk about the early UK scene, the same few things get mentioned. The real underground never gets talked about.'

TIM RAIDL Chill Music

When Britain's dance music revolution gathered pace in the final years of the 1980s, it was not just those in the biggest cities who felt the full force of Acid House and ecstasy culture. There were new converts to the cause the length and breadth of the country, with micro-scenes popping up in sleepy towns and mid-size cities with little or no previous dance music pedigree.

Perhaps the most significant growth came within the Home Counties, that band of mostly sleepy shires nestled within the London commuter belt. It was here, in farmers' fields and abandoned airfields close to the M25 and M1 motorways, that many of Britain's biggest raves took place between 1988 and '92.

The size and frequency of events was astonishing, with thousands - and sometimes tens of thousands - of people drawn to the colossal unlicensed parties run by a new breed of promoters such as Sunrise, Energy and Back To The Future. Another promoter, World Dance, held their first rave off junction six of the M25, not far from the picturesque village of Chalfont St Peter in Buckinghamshire, while another crew, Biology, hosted their first large scale shindig in fields near Aldernam, north of Watford and close to junction five of the M1[1].

The latter location, like so many selected by rave promoters, was just a short drive from South Mimms Services in Hertfordshire. This rest area, which opened alongside the completed "London Orbital" motorway in 1986,

---

1   *Revisiting The UK's Most Iconic Rave Spots with RMBLR*, Huck magazine, 2016
(https://www.huckmag.com/art-and-culture/style/rmblr/)

became a regular meeting point for ravers before and after events, much to the disgust of confused commuters and holidaymakers. 'We always gravitated to South Mimms in the morning along with hundreds of other ravers,' Bristolian Acid House enthusiast Alex White told *Red Bull Music* in 2018[2]. 'I will never forget the look of shock horror on one woman's face as our convoy of wacky racers pulled into the car park blasting beats, bleeps and basslines.'

Some of the promoters of these raves may have been based in the big city[3] [4], but the dancers came from far and wide, not least the sprawling suburbs of greater London and the post-war "new towns" of Hertfordshire, Buckinghamshire, Essex and Sussex. There were significant clubs, record shops and pirate radio stations[5] dotted around this network of new towns, allowing access to the emerging culture for those turned on by Hip-Hop, Electro, Chicago House and Detroit Techno.

Perhaps the most famous example was weekly Sunday party the Outer Limit, which took place at Rayzels in Bletchley, south of Milton Keynes, between April 1989 and July 1990. It was run by local lad 'Evil' Eddie Richards, whose DJ sets at the Camden Palace had helped turn Londoners on to the joys of House and Techno earlier in the decade[6]. Richards brought a host of hot American and British DJs to Bletchley, including Jeff Mills, Todd Terry, Derrick May and Richie Hawtin[7].

Then there was Bedfordshire, where the sizable town of Luton had long been a hub for black music in the region. Thanks to post-war immigration, Luton was home to one of the biggest Afro-Caribbean communities outside of Britain's major cities. During the 1960s and '70s, there was plentiful work in the town's hatmaking and motor manufacturing industries, making it a strong pull for those heading to the UK from elsewhere in the Commonwealth.

As a result, Luton's black music scene was strong. There were numerous Reggae soundsystem operators, a thriving annual carnival and a handful of key Blues, including the popular 5-0 Club. 'During the 1980s Luton had two

---

2   MacNeill, Kyle: *The Road To Rave: How the M25 Paved a Path for Acid House*, Red Bull Music, 2018.
3   Some had even worked in the City of London. The most infamous of all rave-era promoters, Tony Colston-Hayter, once argued that cracking down on rave culture went against the 'free enterprise culture' advocated by the Conservative government. His PR man, Paul Staines, later resurfaced as self-styled 'libertarian' right-wing blogger Guido Fawkes.
4   Many involved with the Sunrise crew were actually from Milton Keynes and started their events after being refused entry to Shoom at the Fitness Centre (despite having been a number of times before).
5   As well as local stations such as Stevenage's Hardcore FM, which launched in 1989, listeners could also pick up leading London pirates like Kiss FM, which remained influential even after it started broadcasting as a commercial station in autumn 1990.
6   Richards was undoubtedly one of the leading exponents of House in London, championing the style long before ecstasy culture took over and the "Shoomers" who claim to have imported the sound brought it back from Ibiza in their mixed bag of Balearic beats.
7   Brewster, Bill/Broughton, Frank: *Eddie Richards interview*, DJHistory.com, 2012

key soundsystems, Positive Force and Soul Incorporated,' says Tim Raidl, then a Jazz-Funk, Soul and House music DJ looking to make his way in the music industry. 'They were based out of a youth centre for the West Indian community. You used to get a lot of Electro and breakdancing there. There was also another important youth centre called the Starlight, and there were semi-regular warehouse parties in the same couple of old buildings in town.'

Hip-Hop was also popular, with enthusiastic locals being joined at events by American service personnel stationed at the nearby RAF Chicksands airbase. From 1987 onwards the town also had its own dedicated 'black music' pirate radio station, Jive FM, where Raidl and 'Evil' Eddie Richards were amongst the resident DJs. There were two significant record stores, too: the Soul, Reggae and House focused Bluebird Records, and Soul Sense. It was behind the counter of the latter that one of Britain's most admired Bleep-era labels, Chill Music, was born.

• • •

Whereas record shops launching labels was becoming increasingly common, Soul Sense was a rare example of a label setting up a shop. It was opened 1989 by the team behind Jack Trax, one of the first labels to license and reissue Chicago House records in the UK. The imprint's founder and owner was a serial dance music entrepreneur called Damon D'Cruz, who some years earlier had previously co-founded the "Upfront" compilation series as a direct rival to Morgan Khan's hugely successful "Streetsounds" albums.

'Those "Upfront" compilations were phenomenally successful,' Tim Raidl says. 'The first few sold 100,000 copies apiece or close to those numbers. Then Damon fell out with his business partner and decided to launch Jack Trax to push Chicago House in the UK.'

When Jack Trax first emerged in 1987, D'Cruz rented office and studio space in a building on Middle Street[8], close to the Barbican in central London. Just weeks after moving in, D'Cruz decided to take on a new staff member, aspiring graphic designer and DJ Tim Raidl. 'He didn't know me, but when he found out I was from Luton, he offered me a job,' Raidl laughs. 'I did some design and then started getting involved in A&R. In the early days, Jack Trax releases were selling a couple of thousand copies a week. Then there was a sudden change when ecstasy came into the scene. Overnight we were selling 30,000 records a week. We couldn't keep up with demand.'

Just as "Streetsounds" and its offshoot label StreetWave had made it possible for those on low or modest incomes to get their hands on hot Electrofunk tracks from the USA, Jack Trax helped new Chicago House converts

---

8   Curiously the building's owners were Rock supergroup Asia, whose 24-track record studio was on the same floor as the Jack Trax offices.

get their fix of the latest tracks from the Windy City via affordable compilations and 12" singles that didn't come with a hefty import price. It was not
alone in doing this - London Records signed up other Chicago pioneers such
as Steve 'Silk' Hurley and Marshall Jefferson - but when launched, Jack Trax
was one of the few labels dedicated to the sound.

Yet by the time Jack Trax moved to Luton and set up Soul Sense two
years later, the dance music landscape had changed considerably. While
American releases were still popular, they were now merely part of a wider
movement that also encompassed New Beat and Hardcore from the Low
Countries, British-made mutations of House and Hip-Hop, the piano-driven
rush of Italian House and the alien, sub-bass driven sound of Yorkshire
Bleep. From his spot behind the counter at Soul Sense, Tim Raidl could see
the way the wind was blowing.

'You had quite a mix of things going on at that time,' he says. 'Some of
the Belgian stuff was trickling through, and we were seeing the odd record
from the North of England like Forgemasters' "Track With No Name" and
Sweet Exorcist's "Testone". There were our Chicago releases, the Garage-
House stuff from New York and New Jersey that Dave Lee was pushing at
Republic Records, the breakbeat things by Shut Up & Dance and that quite
leftfield House and Electro sound coming out of Vinyl Solution in Ladbroke
Grove. All of these different things were being played at the raves.'

Jack Trax's previously healthy position was threatened further by Rumour
Records' decision to launch the "Warehouse Raves" compilation series in
early 1990. 'It was a direct competitor to Jack Trax and definitely dented
sales,' Tim Raidl says. 'As well as American dance tracks they included
Italian and British things, including some early Techno releases. You could
see that all the dots were starting to join together.'

While D'Cruz had once been an innovator, his label was now in danger of
falling behind the times. Fortunately, Tim Raidl was on hand to try and talk
some sense into him. 'I told him that things were changing and that people
now wanted British music,' Raidl says. 'I could see it happening, not just
through the releases that were coming into the shop but also in the demo
tapes that kids were dropping off. Jack Trax was struggling at that point
because Mr Fingers type records were not what kids in the rave scene were
looking for. So I said to Damon, "We should start a British label." He said,
"It'll never work!" I told him I thought it would and eventually he agreed.'

Raidl needed strong music to launch the label, so on the suggestion
of a mutual friend got in touch with a self-taught producer and studio engineer he'd previously encountered during trips to a tiny recording studio in
Bedford called Budeaux's. It was an odd place: a fully functioning professional studio based in the converted garage of a suburban house in one of
Bedford's least affluent neighbourhoods.

From the moment it opened in 1986 until it closed towards the end of 1993, its owner never bothered advertising its existence. Instead, Budeaux's clients came from the local Rock and Reggae scenes and the rapping US airmen stationed at RAF Chicksands. Budeaux's also attracted clients from within the blossoming local dance scene, with would-be producers keen to work in an inexpensive space stocked with a small but adequate selection of samplers, synthesizers and drum machines.

'The area where the studio was, Ford End, was a big West Indian area,' Raidl remembers. 'Local Reggae guys used to go there to record. Bedford had the same kind of size West Indian community to Luton[9].'

Budeaux's in-house engineer and part-time producer was the man Raidl was looking for. Not only was he open to releasing music on what would become Chill Music, but he'd also been working on tracks with a client turned friend who shared his love of underground House and Techno. He handed Raidl a demo tape featuring nine tracks they'd made together. After listening intently, Raidl offered the duo a deal. After much prompting, the two men decided on a name for their project: Original Clique.

In early summer 1990, Raidl released the duo's first two EPs, "Ten To Midnight" and "North of Watford", in the same week. There was no fanfare or fuss, with Raidl eschewing marketing or promotion. Instead, he simply handed boxes of both EPs to the van distribution services that were then one of the primary methods of getting underground dance records to independent shops. Crucially, both of the four-track singles were quietly impressive. Although varied stylistically, they were rough, raw and surprisingly bass-heavy, drawing clear influence from minimalist, bleep-heavy Techno tracks that had been emerging from the North of England with increasing pace over the previous 12 months.

The undisputed highlight of both EPs was "Come To Papa", a sleazy late-night beast full of "Testone" style bleeps, head-cracking bass and a simple vocal hook repeating the track's title (a trick repeated on the lead cut from "North of Watford", "Now Hear Me Now"). Like much of the rest of the two EPs, it sounded so authentically "northern" that most DJs misguidedly assumed that Original Clique were from Sheffield, Bradford or Leeds. The highest profile person to get it spectacularly wrong was John Peel, who announced on his Radio 1 show that this hot new act hailed from Yorkshire. He later corrected his mistake, telling listeners that the producers behind Original Clique were Luton natives (an easy error to make, given that Chill was based in the town).

Within a week both EPs were riding high in *Music Week*'s influential "Cool Cuts" chart. Record Mirror's James Hamilton, an influential dance music journalist since the days of Jazz-Funk a decade earlier, also reviewed

---

9   Bedford also boasts one of the biggest Italian populations in the UK, with almost a third of residents having some kind of heritage as of 2001. Between 1954 and 2008 the Italian government had a consulate in the town.

them in his weekly column. 'He didn't know what to make of them,' Tim Raidl says. 'He said they were verging on industrial. I don't think he liked them at all. Both of those records rubbed some people up the wrong way because some of the tracks were virtually unlistenable.'

That's a little unfair - both "Ten To Midnight" and "North of Watford" are still amongst the best Bleep-influenced releases to come from the South of England - but the eight tracks spread across the two EPs certainly tended towards the noisier end of the House and Techno spectrum.

The records continue to be popular with British Techno enthusiasts to this day, with continued speculation as to the identity of the mysterious producers behind the Original Clique project. 'At the time they were adamant that they wanted to be anonymous,' Tim Raidl says. 'There were two of them, but the main guy was called Tony. He used a lot of different pseudonyms, but the main ones were Tony Bone and Tony Boninsegna. He's never given away his surname, and I don't intend to now, either. He prefers not to be known.'

● ● ●

On a mundane afternoon in June 2019, the mystery man in question is limbering up to tell all about his rave-era production career. He says it's the first time he's ever talked about it to anyone outside his circle of friends. 'I don't mind talking about all this for a book, because you're really interested, but I'd much rather be making music,' he says bluntly. 'To be honest, it was all so long ago and time has sped up a lot since then!'

He bursts out laughing before composing himself. I suggest starting with the small matter of his identity and where the "Tony Bone" moniker came from. 'It all started with people calling me Bonehead, which then became Tony Bone,' he chuckles. 'They were just nicknames. I got the Boninsegna thing from the surname of the first scorer in the 1970 World Cup final, Roberto Boninsegna. Somebody on Discogs decided that was my real name. It isn't, but we may as well stick with that.'

It would be fair to say that Tony Boninsegna[10] is a bit of a character. He's nowhere near as involved in music than he once was, though he does still release music digitally now and then. Back in the rave era, he was a prolific producer and an even more prolific collector of pseudonyms. Between 1990 and '94, he and regular studio partner Mickey Thomas[11] released a dizzying number of solo and collaborative records under an impressive array of names: Lab Technicians, the Enigmatist, Ministry of Fear, Unlimited Source, Napoleon, Sykosis 451, Mephisto, A.E.K, Return of the Living Acid and, of course, Original Clique.

---

10   For the record, he did tell me his real name but mischievously he'd rather keep people guessing. You can actually find the answer online if you look hard enough.
11   There was an occasional third member, too: James Hudson.

'Because I had a lot of things coming out on different labels, I thought using different names would help,' Bonisegna chuckles. 'I thought it would stop the labels knowing I was doing things for other people as well, but that didn't work. I didn't want all the politics - you know, "Why didn't you give that track to us?" I liked House, Techno and Hardcore and wanted to make music in all of those styles. Who would have let me do that under one alias?'

When Tim Raidl called in early 1990, the artist occasionally known as Tony Bone was not a musical novice. By that point he'd been playing and making music for well over a decade, having initially been inspired by a mixture of Dub Reggae and the do-it-yourself ethos of Punk Rock. 'I started to learn guitar and bass, but I couldn't really be arsed with it,' he says. 'When Kraftwerk's "Man Machine" came out I got that, and once I discovered electronic music, I was hooked. I got myself a WASP synth, which relative to wages was a lot of money in them days, and an AKAI reel-to-reel. I spent the next few years messing around with synths and doing my own thing.'

In 1983 Boninsegna met a local synthesizer enthusiast he calls "Gazza", the man who later became his boss at Budeaux's. 'Gazza had a lot of old synths and taught me a lot,' he remembers. 'By then I was really interested in dance music, Electro particularly. When Acid House came along it was just a logical progression from that.'

When the studio first opened, Bonisegna was called on to engineer or co-produce tracks for a variety of low-key local acts from the Hertfordshire scene. As dance music gripped the nation, DJs who dreamed of making music became regular clients. One of those was Mickey Thomas, and after a few successful sessions, the pair decided that working together on tracks was the way forward.

From the start, both were really inspired by the sound of the Bleep & Bass records they'd heard at local raves and, in particular, the game-changing thrills of Unique 3's "The Theme". 'Hearing that was a big moment,' Boninsegna says. 'It just sounded so different. I don't know how to describe it. There was just something about how the bleeps hung in the air.'

The pair worked quickly in the studio ('I don't think any track took us more than four hours,' he says), building up basslines, beats and, later, chords and lead lines on a small collection of mostly cheap synthesizers, samplers and drum machines. 'I didn't have much equipment, but I knew what I had inside out,' Bonisegna recalls. 'I also knew how to abuse it to change sounds and get what I wanted out of it.'

When their first swathe of demos was complete, the duo tried selling their tracks to Bleep & Bass' most recognizable label, Warp Records, after Thomas met Robert Gordon at a party in Sheffield. 'I thought our demos sounded really amateur, but Mickey said they were really into it and were thinking about signing us,' Bonisegna reveals. 'It was Steve Beckett he was dealing with. They were dithering, and when "LFO" came along they told us they had too big a backlog of tracks. Labels say they're interested in tracks all the time and do nothing about it, so I doubt Steve Beckett would remember now.'

It wasn't much of a setback, though: a few weeks later Tim Raidl called and the pair began what would become a prolific partnership with Chill Music. Between 1990 and '92 they delivered a string of impressive (and popular) underground club cuts for the label. As Return of the Living Acid, there was the Afrika Bambaataa-sampling Hardcore madness of "Get Funky", a mangled Acid-Bleep workout called "Twin Tub", and a skittish slab of Hardcore Rave known as "Creator". Under the MI7 pseudonym, they impressed with the Reggae-sampling breakbeat skank of "Rockin' Down The House", while as Lab Technicians they served up the high-grade Bleep & Breaks shuffle of "We Gave You Life".

While stylistically different, all were blessed with significant bass weight, a by-product of a shared love of Dub. 'It's funny that people say that they can hear Dub in my tunes because that wasn't a direct influence as far as I was concerned,' Boninsegna muses. 'I can't see it myself, but it must be in there. I did listen to a lot of Dub and Reggae.'

Direct influence or not, Boninsegna was on friendly terms with plenty of people in Bedford's Reggae scene, most notably Dennis "Mixman" Bedeau, a Dub producer who owned the Blakamix studio and label. Bedeau later founded two labels dedicated to bass-heavy Hardcore, Techno and rave music, Bass Sphere and Infrasonic. Predictably, Bonisegna and Thomas were amongst his most reliable artists. 'I think Dennis just saw dance music as something that was on the up,' Boninsegna says. 'I reckon he thought, "There's a bob or two to be made here". I'm not having a go though - he's a lovely old boy.'

Boninsegna's decision to work with Bedeau stemmed from his growing frustration with Chill, and specifically its evasive owner Damon D'Cruz. 'There was a bit of a misunderstanding when I had three different singles that I'd done with three different labels in the top 20 of the dance charts in the same week,' he says. 'Damon claimed that even though the Chill one was high up in the charts, it didn't sell as much as it actually did. Damon did all right for us, though, same as Tim. Some people did call him dodgy Damon though!'

He laughs uproariously at the memory. 'The money thing wasn't a big concern for me then,' he says. 'I just loved making music and wanted to get tracks out there. It was just about capturing the energy and the vibe of the time.'

• • •

Chill went from strength to strength following the success of Original Clique's label-launching EPs. There was a tidy EP by another mystery artist, Aural Exciter (in truth, one side was produced by Tim Raidl[12] and the other Tony Boninsegna) followed by a run of releases by local artists who came on to Raidl's radar after dropping off demos at the Soul Sense shop.

'The first one I signed up was 'Horrors' by Bogeyman, which was a Bleep & Breaks track by a guy called Darren Pearce[13],' Raidl says. 'I'd also got things lined up by Rotor, which was a really young guy called Andrew Wright making lo-fi tunes on his Commodore Amiga, and NRG, which was Neil Rumney[14]. He had been a London Hip-Hop DJ who gave me a tape. That was a Break-beat Hardcore tune that sampled *The Terminator*. There was also that great Electro/Bleep crossover EP from Sinewave, which was a bedroom producer called Mark Fletcher[15]. He was only a student at the time - very young.'

With an accomplished, ever-growing catalogue that joined the dots between the best aspects of Northern and Southern club culture, Chill quickly became one of the UK's most on-point underground dance labels. Many of the imprint's releases were big hits on the rave scene, with some even crossing the Atlantic to America's West Coast.

MI7's "Rockin' Down The House" and Return of the Living Acid's "Get Funky" earned heavy rotations on the Los Angeles rave scene, where a new breed of self-styled "candy ravers" danced all night in former factories and abandoned industrial units. Unlike most underground dance scenes elsewhere in the United States, Los Angeles' rave evangelists were just as inspired by European Techno and British Hardcore records as tracks made in Detroit, Chicago or New York. Because of this, British acts were often invited over to DJ or do simplistic, DAT-based "live" performances. Alongside fellow Chill artist NRG, Tony Boninsegna and Mickey Thomas headed off on a jaunt around the West Coast to perform PAs at giant raves full of overexcited dancers.

---

12   Bizarrely, Raidl's track was engineered by former UK Decay Punk bandmember Spon, who owned a studio in Luton.

13   Like many who made Bleep-influenced Hardcore records in and around London, Pearce had previously run a Soul and Rare Groove soundsystem.

14   Rumney would become one of the most successful Hardcore and rave producers of the era, later notching up a colossal hit with his 1992 jam 'I Need Your Love (Real Hardcore Mix)'. Like many of the other artists who passed through Chill, he eventually left for pastures new after becoming frustrated with Damon D'Cruz.

15   Note for nerds: The online music database Discogs erroneously credits the Sinewave release to an entirely different Mark Fletcher, an obscure British Jazz drummer. Raidl confirmed that this is incorrect, and therefore that the real Sinewave has no dedicated page. Feel free to correct that and quote this book if any of the other contributors and editors dispute it.

'I had a great time,' Bonisegna says enthusiastically. 'One of the ones we played at was properly out in the sticks. It was at this big warehouse on an Indian Reservation. There must have been 5,000 people there. I think they liked what we were doing because it had that funk that came from Hip-Hop as well as the heavy bass.'

Back in Luton, things were not going so well for Chill Music. Amongst the roster of artists Raidl had assembled there was growing disquiet about Damon D'Cruz's business practices. Raidl battled on for a while on their behalf before quitting his A&R role in 1992. He left Soul Sense, too, choosing instead to launch a label of his own called Bad Ass Toons.

'Damon was very generous in some respects, but he would often just say, "Yeah, come and see me and I'll give you some money",' Raidl remembers. 'He might say to someone, "Give me a track, and I'll give you 500 quid". The artist would get that money, but then no money in future. Of course, these kids [the producers] saw their records selling thousands, and they weren't getting royalties. After I left, I had little to do with Chill, but I kept in touch with the artists, and they still moaned that they weren't getting paid.'

While Chill's demise was arguably avoidable, the way it ended was not all that surprising. The dance music industry in the UK expanded rapidly was still finding its feet in this period, with independent labels coming and going with increasing regularity. In that regard, Chill was no different than countless others, despite the presence of a fired-up entrepreneur at the helm.

Looking back, it seems to me that Chill was not significant because of the music it released, however good some of it most certainly was, but rather what it signifies. Based in Luton, a multi-cultural hot-spot on the northern fringes of the Home Counties, the label drew strength and influence not from the town's vibrant West Indian community, but rather white teenagers and young adults from the suburbs fired-up by the life-changing experiences they'd had at raves in the region.

While some of these may have loved Reggae, for the most part, their love of sub-bass frequencies came directly from the Bleep & Bass records they heard at events and on the area's multiple pirate radio stations. Combine this with the funky breakbeats that were so prevalent on records made in and around London, and you have a hybrid sound that's not only undeniably British but also had the potential to sell in big numbers.

'Bleep & Bass was a big influence on the people I signed, but when breakbeats started coming in many of them thought, "Maybe I should use breaks on my tracks",' Tim Raidl says. 'We knew those breakbeat records sold well, so we did steer some of the artists that way. Maybe I shouldn't have done, but the records they made like that did sell.'

What had started in a Bradford bedroom in 1988 had now spawned countless imitations and mutations, with "Bleep & Breaks" - an early expression of what would become Hardcore Rave - being the next significant step in the birth of British Bass music.

CHAPTER FIFTEEN

RAGE AGAINST THE MACHINE

THE RISE OF BLEEP & BREAKS

'If you go to America a lot of people know nothing. In London there's so many knowledgeable fanatics who know their shit. And different kinds of music mix, definitely more than in the States.'

CARL 'SMILEY' HYMAN Shut Up & Dance [1]

For all the subsonic vibrations coming from other parts of the United Kingdom at the tail end of the 1980s, the focal point of British dance music remained within the seemingly never-ending sprawl of London. The city's underground music scene was naturally larger and more varied than anywhere else in Britain, with the sheer size of the city allowing micro-scenes to survive, thrive and expand at their own pace.

'Black music' in all its myriad forms was the lifeblood of London's dance music underground, with a network of pirate radio stations springing up in all four corners of the capital to support the rapidly expanding scene. With plenty of media outlets based in the city, particularly taste-making titles focused on music, art and fashion, the city's journey through the ever-changing dance music landscape was widely chronicled, often to the detriment of undeniably important scenes elsewhere.

---

1   Brewster, Bill: *"Experimentation All The Way" – An Interview With Shut Up & Dance,* DJ History/Red Bull Music Academy, 2019.

When Bleep & Bass first landed in the capital, it was primarily embraced by those with a similar set of influences to the sound's Yorkshire pioneers: young black and white Londoners from inner city suburbs who had grown up with the sounds of Reggae soundsystems, Jazz-Funk, Hip-Hop and, later, Acid House and Detroit Techno ringing in the ears. The subsonic bass frequencies, tough beats and simplistic electronic melodies of Bleep resonated more with these individuals than the glassy-eyed, loved-up mix of Europop, Chicago House and surprising records that were the hallmark of the much-celebrated Balearic Beat scene[2].

Initially, there were very few straight-up House and Techno records made in London that fully embraced the Bleep & Bass sound. There were though a handful of producers and labels that shared the ethos and parts of the style's aesthetic. Perhaps the most obvious example was Warriors Dance, an imprint born out of the Addis Ababa studio on Harrow Road in West London. The man behind both was Tony Addis, a self-styled 'African dreadlocks[3] who could sort people's musical problems[4]'.

When Addis first opened the studio in 1980 his clients mainly came from London's vibrant Reggae scene (think Big Youth, Aswad, Dennis Brown and Matumbi), but as time moved on it became a go-to recording spot for everyone from Wham!, Manu Dibango and S'Express to Schoolly D and Soul II Soul. Addis nurtured and mentored many young black musicians from the area, eventually putting together a fluid collective called the Addis Posse. When House music began to land in the UK, he was hooked.

'I first started hearing House music on the radio, stuff like Farley 'Jackmaster' Funk, Steve 'Silk' Hurley and "Acid Trax" by Phuture,' Addis told *Test Pressing* in February 2019. 'All those early tunes were amazing. House music just exploded - there was nothing like it. It reminded me of the '70s Punk movement as its vibration was incredible and similar.'

When Addis decided to launch the Warriors Dance label in late 1987, it was initially to release distinctive House music, both from his friend Kid Batchelor's Bang The Party group as well as his own Addis Posse collective. While much of this material drew influence from American Deep House, Acid, Chicago jack and New York style 'Garage-House', the sonic influence of

---

2   The importance of this scene, originally focused on clubs like Shoom, Spectrum and Future, is arguably more cultural and social than musical. Many who attended the events were so fired up that they promoted parties of their own. It also helped sell Ibiza as a party destination for successive generations of young British holidaymakers. In my opinion, the wider impact of London's Balearic Beat scene has been overemphasized due to a mix of the success of some of its chief instigators (Danny Rampling, Paul Oakenfold etc.), the widespread media coverage it got at the time, and lazy journalists and documentary filmmakers who have just accepted this one-eyed narrative.

3   Addis was born in Lagos, Nigeria and moved to the UK as a child. During his music career, he established links with exiled Nigerian musicians such as Fela Kuti's long-time drummer Tony Allen

4   Apiento (Paul Byrne): *Warriors Dance – An Interview With Tony Addis*, Test Pressing, 2019.

Reggae soundsystem culture was obvious. By the time 1989 rolled around, Warriors Dance had developed a trademark style that effortlessly joined the dots between ragging acid, African rhythms, Deep House and Dub.

This bass-heavy brand of British Afrofuturism was particularly evident on the superb label compilation "The Tuffest of The Tuffest", whose highlights included an early version of one of the imprint's most influential cuts, the polyrhythmic dancefloor voodoo that was No Smoke's incredible "Koro-Koro". It goes without saying that "Koro-Koro" hit home hard in Yorkshire, where many DJs championed it with as much vigour as their own home-made Bleep & Bass cuts.

Warriors Dance was rather atypical, though, standing out from other London labels and artists. There were occasional expressions from elsewhere in the capital of the same ethos that had driven the original Bleep & Bass pioneers, but these were generally outliers. This would change over time as existing House and Techno imprints tweaked their sound to incorporate heavier bass and alien bleeps[5], but as 1989 drew to a close, solid examples of London Bleep were few and far between. One of the rare examples was "Low Frequency Overload" by 100 Hz, a duo from South East London comprised of up-and-coming DJ James Chapman and electronic music enthusiast Lee Renacre.

Like so many others, Chapman and Renacre became converts to the Acid House cause as wide-eyed teenagers during the first flush of the rave movement. 'I was very young when I first went to one of the Biology raves - probably 15 or 16,' Renacre remembers. 'We used to meet in Catford, get into the back of a van and just drive all night and find somewhere. You'd go to Camber Sands sometimes and there would be little illegal parties there. We'd also go to Sterns in Worthing and midweek London clubs like Sound Shaft and Legends.'

Keen to make their own music, the pair assembled a small selection of cheap, mostly second-hand drum machines, synthesizers and sequencers and spent many nights jamming together at home. In the summer of 1989, Chapman decided to book a day in Vons Studio on the Holloway Road in Islington and invited Renacre along. 'It was James's idea - I initially just went along for the ride,' Renacre remembers. 'I got into it though and had a fair bit of input into the first couple of tracks we made. We tinkered around on keyboards to get ideas that the engineer then translated. He helped us with the arrangement as well. After that, I was hooked.'

---

5   An excellent example of this is Catt Records, an East Ham-based outlet that had been offering up deep, mind-altering Acid House, dreamy dancefloor deepness and chunky early UK Techno since 1988. Some of its 1990 releases sound like their producers had been listening to a lot of Bleep, even if the resulting tracks are nowhere near as weighty as those made in Yorkshire.

The first completed track they were happy with was "Low Frequency Overload", a delicious fusion of warm, loved-up Deep House melodies, electronic bleeps, sporadic blasts of sampled breakbeats - a product of their love of Hip-Hop - TR-808 machine drums and one of the weightiest basslines so far seen outside of Bradford, Leeds and Sheffield. 'It was a bass war,' Renacre says. 'You had to have the biggest bass, and we always tried to make sure that we did.'

Having enjoyed Forgemasters' "Track With No Name", Chapman and Renacre sent a tape demo of "Low Frequency Overload" to Warp Records. It was rejected, so they pressed up 300 white labels in December 1989 and sold them directly to record shops in London. The record sold out in record time, leading to a reissue on Optimism Records in early 1990.

It was by no means pure Bleep & Bass - it's much more loved-up and melodic than many of the classics - but "Low Frequency Overload" got closer to the sound of Yorkshire than any other record made in London had done before. Renacre and Chapman later made some other suitably weighty 100 Hz tunes - "Catching Spiders" being the most notable - while Renacre also delivered some dark, sub-heavy Bleep-influenced EPs alongside Byron Lewis as Exodus (1991's white label only "The Dark Spirits" being the standout). By then, British dance music's obsession with speaker-rattling basslines was hitting fever pitch.

'Everybody was just bass crazy,' Renacre says. 'It was about the loudest bass you could get, but we soon learned that once you go to cutting studios, there are limits. In terms of inspiration, I guess it was just the records of the time. Every one was completely bass-heavy.'

● ● ●

The lack of records coming out of London that matched the specific swing and style of the Bleep & Bass tracks being made elsewhere is not that surprising when you consider the popularity of Hip-Hop, Soul and Rare Groove in the capital. When Bleep-influenced records began emerging with increasing frequency from 1990 onwards, many of those behind the tracks had spent their formative teenage years running soundsystems dedicated not to pure Dub Reggae[6], but rather a more mixed sound that became much more Hip-Hop focused as the decade progressed.

One of the leading exponents of this developing sound was Shut Up & Dance, a Hackney-based soundsystem, party crew and DJ outfit whose reputation was red-hot in 1989. They'd been a feature of the local scene since 1982, when the trio behind the project - school friends Philip 'PJ' Johnson, Carlton 'Smiley' Hyman and Kevin Ford aka DJ Hype - hand built their first Reggae style "sound".

'You had to have a sound if people were gonna hear you and take you seriously,' Hyman told Bill Brewster in 2005[7]. 'As you know, Hackney is a big soundsystem place. It was mainly Reggae and Dub we were playing to begin with because Jah Shaka was very big then. The sound was called Heatwave. We played the odd Soul thing, but the only big Hip-Hop tunes were [Afrika Bambaataa and the Soulsonic Force] "Planet Rock" and "The Birthday Party" by Sugarhill Gang.'

When Hip-Hop increased in prevalence, Johnson, Hyman and Ford became converts to the cause; not only did they re-focus their sound to play more Rap records with breakbeats, but Hyman and Johnson also took to the mic as fast-talking hosts with rhymes for days. They took the job of putting on parties seriously, frequently breaking into abandoned houses to run their own Blues style events with the aid of Hyman's electrician brother. They also out-did other sounds by including Ford's impressive scratch routines in their sets.

'We actually did it like a performance, with Hype cutting up two breaks and doing his thing on the decks,' Hyman explained to Brewster. 'We were the first sound to do that. And we had a Reggae MC, which was my brother Daddy Earl, and me and PJ rapping. We thought we was a Hip-Hop soundsystem. We wasn't, but we thought we were.'

Those impressive routines and relaxed rap flows over dancefloor-focused Hip-Hop beats were enough to win them a London-wide competition in 1987. Their prize was a week's worth of recording in a professional studio. Taking the name Private Party, they delivered a double A-side single that boasted Hyman and Johnson's tribute to Run DMC's "My Adidas", amusingly

---

6   One of the exceptions was Tony Thorpe, a South London musician and producer who graduated from the Reggae soundsystem scene to Post-Punk Electro/Dub fusion. He made a number of superb records in the mid-1980s as one-half of 400 Blows, before donning the Moody Boys alias. He became friends with the KLF's Jimmy Cauty and Bill Drummond and acted as their "groove consultant" and link with contemporary club culture. Thorpe made one superb, Bleep style Dub-House mini album with Cauty as The Moody Boys – the brilliant "Journeys Into Dubland" – while his remixes of the KLF's hit singles tended towards the freaky and bass-heavy. His 1990 remix of "What Time Is Love", a 128 BPM monster full of distorted bass and wonky bleeps, is particularly potent, while his Dub and Ragga-tinged 1991 reworks of "3AM Eternal" come from a similar sonic place to Yorkshire style Bleep & Bass.

7   Brewster, Bill: *"Experimentation All The Way" – An Interview With Shut Up & Dance*, Red Bull Music Academy Daily, 2019.

titled "My Tennents" (a reference to the super-strength beer so beloved of street drinkers), on one side and a silly cut-and-paste affair from Ford called "Puppet Capers" on the reverse. This featured all manner of snippets from puppet-based TV shows and, like the A-side, was an early warning of the tongue-in-cheek silliness and outrageous sample sources that would become a hallmark of their later production work.

'Obviously, we wanted to pursue it, get a proper deal and make more demos, but nobody wanted to know,' Hyman explained to Brewster. 'No major label, no indie, because they were all like, "This is too fast. This isn't going with the norm." So we thought, "Fuck you lot - we're going to do it all ourselves".'

When they re-entered the studio 18 months later, their style had significantly altered. While still dedicated to the Hip-Hop cause, they were operating at a significantly faster tempo than the toe-tapping, head-nodding 95-105 beats per minute tempo preferred by most Hip-Hop heads. The rise in popularity of House music in Hackney in 1988 made Hyman, Johnson and Ford push the tempo further; regardless of how fast a Hip-Hop record was, they'd push it up to 120 or 125 beats per minute, roughly the same as most jack-tracks from Chicago.

'We liked fast Hip-Hop, like what Big Daddy Kane was doing,' Hyman told Brewster. 'We liked the breaky stuff that was a bit faster, but we still wanted to take it further because we wanted to be able to dance to it. So we made our music much faster. The sort of Rap we made, at that House tempo, was unheard of then. There wasn't even such a thing as Hip-House back then.'

Hyman and Johnson's first single as Shut Up & Dance, "5 6 7 8", was a perfect expression of their very particular take on Hip-Hop. Heavy, rolling and undeniably dancefloor friendly, it was a chunky, breakbeat-driven treat that quickly became a club anthem in their native Hackney. 'My younger brother was well into House, and he was down at [key local club] Dungeons[8] every week,' Hyman explained. 'One week he came home and wouldn't stop talking: "They played your fucking tune! The place was going crazy! You have to come next week".'

The buzz around the record in London was such that major labels came calling. Having previously had their demos rejected by the very same label, the pair told them to 'fuck off'. Instead, they founded Shut Up & Dance Records, pressed up the record themselves and sold a shed-load of copies.

---

8   In the interview with Brewster, both Johnson and Hyman insisted that the importance of Dungeons, one of a number of key clubs in Hackney at the time, has been overlooked. They say it should be considered 'the birthplace of rave' due to the sweaty mix of Hip-Hop, House and Techno that was played there.

People were clamouring for a follow-up, so they headed back into the studio and recorded a pair of tracks that became big records in 1990: "£10 To Get In", a comment on the rising cost of entry to raves that fused Acid House with Funk breakbeats, Suzanne Vega and a brief snatch of The Beatles, and the bass-heavy, Bleep-influenced breakbeat jack of "Lamborgini".

While popular and influential, I'd argue that the two records Hyman and Johnson produced for the Ragga Twins the same year were far more significant. Although not known outside of the Capital, brothers Trevor and David Detouche were well known in North London as Flinty Badman and Deman Rocker, the fast-rapping, patois-speaking MCs involved with the popular Unity soundsystem. Thanks to their involvement with Shut Up & Dance, the brothers would soon become unlikely rave royalty.

'When we got the Ragga Twins down I said to 'em, "What we're going to try and do with you has never been done before",' Hyman told Bill Brewster. 'We wanted to give a Reggae feel into it to see if it worked. We didn't know what people will think and we didn't know what would happen.'

Those two early Ragga Twins records were undeniably groundbreaking. Joining together contemporary Ragga style Reggae sounds - complete with booming sub-bass frequencies - with Shut Up & Dance's beloved breakbeats and nods towards the hottest British Techno and House, they were almost as influential as the Bleep & Bass records that had been arriving in the Capital since the beginning of 1988. In terms of the scene in and around London, they were even more influential, offering a fusion of soundsystem culture and rave that was more in keeping with local tastes than anything that had previously been made up north.

Arguably the best track across the two EPs was "Hooligan '69", a track that owed a debt of gratitude to the Bleep & Bass records that had come before it. The track was the epitome of what would become "Bleep & Breaks", the end of the developing Breakbeat Hardcore spectrum that owed more to records from Yorkshire and the Midlands than some of its creators would now admit[9]. The track was naturally powered by a House-tempo breakbeat, but its booming bass and alien electronics were straight out of the Robert Gordon playbook.

Another to apply similar ideas to his early studio productions was Kevin Ford, their school friend and long-time crew DJ. By the time "Hooligan 69" came out, Ford was one of the biggest DJs on rave-focused pirate station Fantasy FM, which became a must-listen for fans of Acid House, Techno and breakbeat-driven club cuts after it launched in August 1989. 'Other cities

---

9   One Bleep & Breaks producer, who will remain nameless, refused an interview, and told me to "fuck off" when I suggested that he'd been influenced by records from Yorkshire. Given that this particular individual made a record that sampled "LFO", I was a bit surprised by his attitude.

didn't have pirate radio like we had,' Ford told Marko Kutlesa in 2017[10]. 'New ideas don't come out of Radio 1 and the like, they come from the little guy doing his pirate radio station with his crew, which in the beginning is probably awful, but he builds on it and then all of a sudden it builds.'

Ford's first forays into the studio were alongside another pirate radio presenter, Lightning FM regular Phivos Sebastiane aka The Scientist. The two met at a party at the Fridge club in Brixton through mutual acquaintances - Lightning founder members Jumpin' Jack Frost and Bryan Gee - and began working together on tracks for the freshly founded Kickin' Records imprint.

First was "The Exorcist", a Hype arranged beast that peppered a sped up James Brown breakbeat and nagging bassline with Bleep style lead lines, glassy-eyed synth chords and plenty of cheeky vocal samples. There were fewer bleeps on speedy follow-up "The Bee", but the fuzzy, industrial strength bass underpinning Hype's funky breakbeats recalled the raw energy of tracks such as "The Theme" and "Soul Thunder". It was accompanied by an alternative "Base Mix" that was stripped-back and heavy, sounding like a particularly funky Hip-Hop head's take on the Bleep & Breaks sound.

Both records were enormous, reportedly selling well over 35,000 copies apiece. The pair followed it up with an even more Reggae-influenced chunk of Techno/Breakbeat fusion as Kicksquad, the booming dancefloor Funk of "Champion Sound". It was another excitable Bleep & Breaks roller, with "Testone" style electronic melodies rising above more up-tempo Hip-Hop breaks and moody bass that sounded like it had been plucked from a Dutch Gabber record.

All three records were indicative of a growing trend. Record labels dedicated to this kind of heavy, House-tempo Breakbeat Techno were springing up at a rapid rate across the capital, while others gradually adapted their style to match. In this category was Production House, a label initially founded in 1987 by former Galaxy member Phil Fearon. While the label's early releases mixed Reggae, Soul and House, by 1990 in-house writer/producer Floyd Dyce was happily working with artists whose tastes lay in the developing Bleep & Bass and Bleep & Breaks sounds.

One of the first Dyce-produced singles from future rave heroes Baby D, "Daydreaming", was a rare vocal Bleep & Bass outing - complete with heavy Steppers drums, dialling tone bleeps and SH-101 clonks - while DMS's "Brand New World" came with a "Dubplate Mix" that explored similar sonic territory to Ability II's "Pressure Dub". Production House's 1990 releases also included The Brothers Grimm's "Soul Thunder" style workout "Déjà vu", whose three mixes added snatches of the Apache break to driller-friendly bass and intergalactic bleep melodies.

10   Kutlesa, Marko: *An Interview With DJ Hype – Still Smokin'*, Skiddle, 2017 (https://www.skiddle.com/news/all/DJ-Hype-interview-Still-Smokin/31904/)

Of the new breed of London labels that popped up to rival the likes of Production House, there's no denying that Reinforced Records was one of the most significant. It was founded by a quartet of North London DJs collectively known as 4 Hero (Mark Clair aka Mac Mac, Dennis McFarlane aka Dego, Gus Lawrence and Ian Bardouille). Like others in London, they had a background in both soundsystem culture (Clair and Bardouille ran the Soul, Hip-Hop and later US House focused Solar Zone sound from 1986 onwards) and pirate radio, joining forces to establish the Strong Island station in Camden[11].

'We played a lot of Rare Groove, Soul, Funk and Hip-Hop, but there was a guy on there called Funky Militant who was the first person I ever heard play Acid House,' Mark Clair remembers. 'Then one of the guys on the soundsystem started to play House, and you'd hear it in a whole new light. The bass on those early Chicago records was weak, but the soundsystem made the bass sound heavy, and people liked that. The input from the soundsystem almost morphed those records into something they weren't. We took that on and ran with it.'

When they started hearing the sub-heavy Bleep & Bass records from the North, Clair and his 4 Hero colleagues were smitten. 'Ital Rockers' "Ital's Anthem" was a big favourite with us at the time, because it had massive dub bass,' Clair admits. 'It was like a Jah Shaka sort of bass sound. What they were doing up north was almost "dub-ifying" House. Those Bleep & Bass tracks from Yorkshire featured drums that were almost like dancefloor dub records. That was unique and totally different to the swing of American House records and Detroit Techno.'

4 Hero's first few EPs - released in 1990 and early '91 - drew far more influence from the Bleep & Bass sound than those by The Scientist and Shut Up & Dance. "Combat Dance" was a Kraftwerk-sampling, sub-heavy Electro workout, while "The Scorcher" peppered one of Hip-Hop's most recognizable breakbeats (naturally sped up to the rave-friendly tempo of House) with Reggae MC samples and addictive Bleep melodies. That was backed with "Kirk's Back", which was arguably the most ludicrously subsonic of the lot.

None of these were quite as influential as their most famous early record, "Mr Kirk's Nightmare". Thanks to its dialling tone bleeps, surging breakbeats, quirky vocal samples, booming bass and razor-sharp synth stabs, it became one of the biggest Bleep & Breaks/Hardcore rave tracks of the period. 'We used to go to raves up north and think, "Where's the breaks man?",' Clair says. 'We took the influential sound of Bleep & Bass and brought it down to London. We made sure we had a heavy sub thing going off the synths, and

---

11   According to Mark Clair, the transmitter was based in a block of flats in Swiss Cottage whose residents including later Drum & Bass heavyweight Goldie.

the bleeps, and mixed them with the drum breaks of Hip-Hop. We loved the Yorkshire sound, but there was definitely a divide between what they were doing and what we were doing.'

The inspiration provided by Bleep's obsession with weighty dub bass was explored on another early Reinforced Records 12" single, Dennis McFarlane's 1991 "Kingdom of Dub" EP as Tek 9. This sported heavier Dub bass than almost any other early Reinforced release, offering a break-beat-powered take on the music of Robert Gordon, Mark Millington and the Bassic Records crew.

'Down here we were listening to those Yorkshire records and going, "How the hell do they get the sub-bass like that",' Mark Clair laughs. 'If you took all of the music that was playing on pirate radio at the time, you just couldn't join the dots together. It was the sound systems that joined everything together because of the sub-bass frequencies. It was making everything make sense. The heavy bass of the soundsystems made one thing lead to another.'

• • •

Out east in Essex, another micro-scene inspired by the triple delights of rave culture, Bleep & Bass and early Breakbeat Hardcore was begin-ning to take shape. Here, another dedicated band of mostly white working class rave converts - most of whom had come through the by now inter-twined House and Hip-Hop scenes - took the opportunity to forge successful careers from their all-encompassing passion for dance music culture.

They were not the first generation from Essex to throw themselves into club culture - after all, the southern Soul and Jazz-Funk all-dayer scene of the late '70s and early '80s had been partly driven by Essex-based DJs and dancers - but the success they ultimately achieved dwarfed anything enjoyed by their predecessors.

When it first developed, the small but growing Essex scene was loosely based around the Boogie Times record shop in Romford. Bossman Danny Donnelly and his friends Mark 'Ruff' Ryder and Andre Jacobs were particu-larly excited by the potential of fusing recycled Funk breakbeats, the cut-and-paste sampling techniques of Hip-Hop and the rave-friendly throb of Techno and Acid House. They were not dedicated soundsystem culture enthusiasts by any means, but wholeheartedly embraced the bass-heavy direction in which British dance music was headed.

Ryder was the first to make his way into a recording studio, working alongside his London record shop colleague (and fellow Essex native) Dave Lee. Along with Emmanuel Cheal they made a string of records as M-Dee-M in 1988 and '89, offering up a mixture of US-style Garage-House and Acid.

Their most potent concoction, "Get Acidic", was released by Transmat, in the process becoming the first UK-made track to feature on Derrick May's Detroit-based label[12].

'When I first met Mark in 1986 he was the in-house DJ at the Smithers & Leigh record shop where I worked,' Dave Lee remembers. 'His main skill as far as I was concerned, was the fact that he could scratch, which was a rare thing back then. I got him down to scratch on a track me and Mike were making and Mark being the kind of guy he is, he was heavily involved within about half an hour. Mike and Mark got on each other's nerves and had a difficult working relationship, so sometimes we'd sneakily do tracks behind Mark's back. That's not to say that Mark didn't contribute something in the studio - he definitely did.'

By now Lee was working for Republic Records, a House-focused offshoot of Rough Trade Records where he had control over signing tracks. Several M-Dee-M records subsequently appeared on the label, slipping effortlessly into a catalogue that contained both UK-made tracks inspired by Garage-House and records licensed from American imprints including Easy Street, BCM, Movin Records and Nu Groove.

As has been proved in the three decades that have passed since[13], Lee has both business sense and an ability to spot trends, so when Bleep & Bass began to dominate the British dance music landscape, he set up an ultimately short-lived subsidiary of Republic called Made On Earth.

'There were a lot of big warehouse parties at that point and some of the DJs who played at a lot of those, particularly Jack Frost and Bryan Gee, used to come into the Republic office to get promotional records,' Lee recalls. 'They would tell me how big records like "Dextrous" and "Testone" were for them at these events and on pirate radio. When "LFO" came out, it was the pinnacle of that Bleep sound. It was the ultimate record, and it was every-where. It was the boom tune of that month. Everybody liked it - even if you liked soulful House, Hip-Hop or R&B, you liked it because it had that low bass. I'd never heard a record before that had bass that low.'

In the end, Made On Earth only released a handful of records before getting caught up in the collapse of Rough Trade Distribution in 1991. All of these were heavily Bleep-influenced. There was "T.T.O" by Turntable Over-load, an unashamed tribute to "LFO" by the artist formerly known as Turnta-ble Orchestra that came accompanied with remixes by Ryder and Lee in a variety of guises. While Lee is now dismissive of it, "T.T.O" was a big club hit in Europe as well as the UK.

---

12   According to Dave Lee, Ryder did not attend the sessions in which he and Cleal made "Get Acidic".
13   Under aliases including Joey Negro, Akabu, Raven Maize, Doug Willis and the Sun-burst Band, Dave Lee has produced countless club classics and hit singles in the last 30 years.

Another Made On Earth highlight was F-X-U's "Steel City EP", a five-track exploration of Detroit Techno/Bleep & Bass fusion by a Sheffield duo William Goring and Mark McCormick that Lee describes as 'a poor man's Sweet Exorcist'. That's perhaps a little harsh; the EP has stood up far better than many second-wave Bleep records from that period, with the deep and sub-heavy grooves and sci-fi bleeps of "The Scheme" and smooth Bleep-Funk of "Dominator" remaining charming and well-made excursions. The EP wasn't particularly groundbreaking, but then little was in comparison to the jaw-dropping brilliance of the earliest Bleep & Bass tracks.

The sound of "LFO" and the Made On Earth releases seems to have influenced Mark Ryder. Around the same time in 1990, he headed into the studio to create his own take on the Bleep & Bass sound, Fantasy UFO's "Fantasy". This joyfully stuck limpet-like to the "LFO" blueprint, offering up the same style of changing basslines (a raw Derrick May inspired section, followed by a big sub-bass drop and deep frequencies for the remainder of the track), similarly starry chords and ear-catching bleeps that could have been lifted from a Warp or Bassic release. It's a terrific example of a record made in tribute to "LFO", of which there were many in the autumn of 1990.

Ryder initially intended to release it on the Strictly Underground imprint he'd established a year earlier for the Masters of the Universe records he'd made with Dave Lee, but the popularity of the first white label run of "Fantasy" was such that XL Recordings snapped it up for a wider commercial release. XL was fast becoming one of the most popular and on-point UK dance labels of the age, with DJs responding positively to its giddy mix of bass-heavy music from the South East and licensed cuts from New York heroes Frankie Bones, Tommy Musto and Lenny D.

"Fantasy" was big, but it was by no means the first Bleep-influenced cut from Essex to appear in stores. Ryder's close friends Andre Jacobs and Danny Donnelly got their first with an arguably superior record called "Dance Tones". Like Ryder, Jacobs had moved from Hip-Hop to House and was a successful DJ both in Essex and London. The previous year he'd spent the summer season DJing in Tenerife[14] alongside future Jungle and Drum & Bass hero Simon 'Bassline' Smith, so had built up a healthy bank balance. He decided to use some of this to book studio time.

---

14   It was here that he met a dancer that would become his girlfriend for a period, future Spice Girl Geri Halliwell. When his Tekno Too records became popular and rave promoters booked him to do PAs, Jacobs sent her out to dance on stage while two of his friends pretended to play keyboards and drum machines to a pre-recorded backing track.

'A guy called Des Mitchell introduced me to a guy called Mike Gray[15],' Jacobs remembers. 'The three of us went into the studio and made some tracks, which were quite poppy. One of them I released a couple of years later credited to F/B/K which sampled Todd Terry Project's "Weekend".'

Jacobs quickly became a studio regular, booking multiple eight-hour sessions in order to produce and mix as many tracks as possible. Unfortunately the sessions for what would become "Dance Tones" started badly when Jacobs' car was stolen and he had to call Danny Donnelly to get him out of a hole. The Boogie Times boss subsequently dropped what he was doing to give his friend a lift to the studio.

'If he'd not given me a lift I'd never have got the tracks done,' Jacobs admits. 'I already had the samples from the Speak & Spell machine and everything was ready to rock and roll. He did get slightly involved in the session, so to say thanks I have him a co-production credit and half the royalties.'

"Dance Tones" was a sub-heavy mixture of Kraftwerk style Electro-influenced drums, robotic vocal snippets, ear-catching futurist Bleep melodies and warehouse-ready synth stabs. It predictably became a huge club hit in the wake of "LFO", the record that had so obviously inspired it. Jacobs pressed it up on his freshly minted D-Zone imprint with a little financial help from Boogie Times. 'Danny managed to sell 1,000 copies of that in the shop within a few days,' Jacobs says proudly. 'That just got bigger when I gave it to the distribution vans and export.'

Like many of Essex's new wave of DJs, producers and record label owners, Jacobs was a driven individual blessed with an entrepreneurial spirit wholly in keeping with the times. In addition to quickly building D-Zone into an outlet for his own productions and those of his friends (see Mike Gray and Jon Pearn's release as Greed, "Give-Me", a funky Breakbeat-House affair that came with a weighty "Bleep Mix" on the flip), Jacobs also established a thriving dance music export business and was one of the first people to see the commercial potential of record label branded merchandise.

What made him successful as a producer though was his ability to tap into the then-hot Bleep & Breaks sound with productions that shamelessly sampled anyone and anything he could lay his hands on. Jacobs seemed to have an innate ability to capture the zeitgeist, with D-Zone releases selling in significant numbers throughout the label's existence. The imprint's biggest track - Bassix "Close Encounters" - sold over 15,000 copies before it was licensed for re-release by Champion Records, eventually reaching the lower reaches of the top 100.

---

15   Gray was a more experienced producer than the others. At the time he worked as a studio engineer at a studio called The Whitehouse. He engineered most of the early D-Zone material before later enjoying a successful and lengthy career alongside production partner Jon Pearn as Full Intention.

Produced by Jacobs with the assistance of engineer Mike Gray, "Close Encounters" utilized the familiar sparse synth melody from John Williams' soundtrack to Steven Spielberg movie *Close Encounters of the Third Kind*, a fine example of Jacobs' ability to spot hooks and join the dots between different sample sources.

One of the key aspects of Jacobs success with D-Zone Records was the sheer weight of bass he managed to get cut into the grooves on the label's vinyl releases. At a time when producers were routinely trying to out-do each other by finding ways to get more low-end weight on to wax, D-Zone's releases were produced to be played especially loud.

'The bass was down to where I cut it, Jah Tubby's JTS mastering studio in Hackney,' Jacobs says. 'He cut the grooves wider. I also used a pressing plant in London that only ever used virgin vinyl and didn't 're-grind' like the others. Their records were also of a heavier weight than the EMI plant in Hayes that most people used.'

Many within the scene were impressed, with JTS becoming the go-to lacquer cutting and mastering studio for a string of labels including Shut Up & Dance Records and Boogie Times Records, a fresh imprint from Danny Donnelly's shop of the same name. He launched it via Phuture Assassins' "I Like Techno", a mighty slab of Bleep & Breaks that naturally came with the obligatory lo-fi electronic motifs and Kraftwerk-esque vocoder vocals.

Boogie Tribe released a handful of other sub-heavy, Bleep-influenced Breakbeat Hardcore cuts in early 1991 (most notably Austin's "I Get High (Munchies Mix)"), as did Donnelly's second imprint, Suburban Base. While that would go on to play a bigger role in the evolution of British dance music when Hardcore sped up and Jungle emerged, its early releases were peppered with Bleep & Breaks numbers. The label's first release, Kromozone's "The Rush", remains one of the most mighty Bleep & Breaks cuts of all time - in terms of the sheer weight of sub-bass at least.

For a short time between 1990 and '91, the volume of Bleep & Breaks records coming out of Essex and London was staggeringly high. Rumour Records, the compilation-focused imprint that had previously provided inspiration to DJs via the "Warehouse Raves" series, decided to cash in on the craze with a set entitled "Breaks, Bass & Bleeps". Mixing more traditionalist Bleep fare ("Ital's Anthem", F-X-U's "The Scheme" and Hypersonics' "Dance Tones") with Bleep & Breaks cuts from The Scientist, The Brothers Grimm and Urban Hype, Rumour's new compilation captured the excitement of Britain's hottest club sound. Three more volumes followed in 1991 and '92, with each becoming more Breakbeat Hardcore focused than its predecessor. These tracked the evolution of a scene and sound that was moving further away from the records that had inspired it, while retaining some of the key ingredients, most obviously the consistent presence of deep and booming sub-bass.

In truth, the quality of many of the tracks showcased on these compilations - and throughout the Bleep & Breaks/Breakbeat Hardcore scene in general - was not up to the high standards set by Robert Gordon, Martin Williams and other key players in the Bleep & Bass story. The sound did produce some breathtaking brilliant cuts, but also a lot of weak, sample-heavy workouts whose breathless sense of excitement is their primary redeeming feature.

Some of those involved in the Bleep & Breaks movement are willing to admit this, though. Andre Jacobs readily admits that he didn't always hit the spot with his productions. 'Looking back, I did release some shit,' Jacobs says candidly. 'I listened back to the D-Zone catalogue recently to prepare digital re-masters and not all of it has stood up. I did try and get more original as I went on and that meant some of the records were quite off the wall. At the time, I didn't give a fuck because I was having fun and experimenting rather than ripping people off as I had done.'

• • •

Back in London, British dance music's sub-bass revolution was now being championed in one of the most unlikely of spots, 2,000 capacity West End gay club Heaven. The club was no stranger to thrilling new forms of dance music, and in 1987 and '88 played a key role in the development of the London House scene by playing House to a number of important nights that giddily joined the dots between Balearic Beat, Chicago Jack and the wild, TB-303 driven sound of Acid. 1989 saw the dawn of a new weekly night that dared to do things differently. It was called Rage and drew in a wide range of Hardcore Acid House and Techno enthusiasts from across the social and ethnic spectrum.

The story of Rage and the role it played as an incubator for British dance music's first homegrown styles has been told countless times before, but it's a story worth briefly re-telling. The party was the work of promoter Kevin Millins, a scene veteran that had been booking live shows and club nights since the dawn of the decade. Heaven's management recruited him to produce and promote a follow-up to Paul Oakenfold's celebrated weekly party Spectrum.

When it launched in the autumn of 1989, Rage's resident DJs were similar in ethos to those that had preceded them. Danny Rampling and Trevor Fung were renowned for playing a role in the Balearic Beat movement that had helped kick-start London's love affair with ecstasy culture, Mark Moore was a popular figure having tasted chart success with the S'Express project, and the late Colin Faver had previously been one of the first DJs to champion Techno in the capital. To complement his roster of resident DJs, Millins flew in guests from across the Atlantic including Derrick May, David Morales, Frankie Knuckles and Kevin Saunderson.

JOIN THE FUTURE

Rage differed from its predecessors because it was intended to be tougher and rougher - a Thursday night shindig for Hardcore ravers who wanted to party hard and dance harder. Yet, to begin with, it was not that much different to what was being offered elsewhere. As you may be aware, it took the arrival of two new resident DJs to give Rage a distinctive musical identity.

Fabio and Grooverider (real names Fitzroy Heslop and Raymond Bingham) already had a strong reputation on the rave scene, where they could regularly be seen playing at the hottest events. Like many of their DJ peers in South London, they'd grown up inspired by a mix of Reggae, Soul and Disco before taking to DJing and making a name for themselves on pirate radio.

'We'd play anything that was new,' Fabio explained to Laurent Fintoni in 2016[16]. 'German Techno, Belgian Techno, New York House - we just played anything we liked. We never sat down to plan it. Music came out, we'd buy it. We didn't put labels to anything.'

The two DJs initially came onto Millins and Fung's radar via regular DJ appearances in Brixton, where they'd become local heroes via riotous sets in pubs, clubs and at Blues style after-parties for big-name events including Heaven's own Spectrum. They were given an audition in the club's second room, the smaller but still sizable Star Bar, before being offered a residency.

Fabio and Grooverider's style was distinctively different from their fellow residents (their warm-up man John Digweed included), offering a more intense blend of sounds that tended towards the dark and serious. When they were subsequently moved downstairs to become the Rage's headline residents, the party's vibe changed completely.

'It was just a darker sound than other places,' DJ/producer Noodles told journalist Joe Muggs in a 2019 article celebrating three decades since the launch of Rage[17]. 'Tracks by Fast Eddie, Joey Beltram, Orbital's "Chime" and Little Louis's "French Kiss". The crowd was off their heads, proper dancing, but they were serious about the music.'

When Bleep & Bass emerged from Yorkshire, Fabio and Grooverider hammered the records at Rage, putting them in context with similarly raw and intense records of the period. Ability II's "Pressure", Juno's "Soul Thunder" and DJ Martin and DJ Homes' remix of Man Machine's "Animal" all became anthems at Rage, alongside a string of Bleep & Breaks cuts and sub-heavy expressions of British dance music's growing love affair with deep low-end frequencies.

16   Fintoni, Laurent: *Nightclubbing – Fabio & Grooverider's Rage*, Red Bull Music Academy Daily, 2016
17   Muggs, Joe: *London's Legendary "Rage" Party Is Celebrated In a New Compilation Series*, Bandcamp Daily, 2019.

Given a choice, the pair often prioritized instrumental dubs over vocal cuts and were not averse to layering breakbeats over four-to-the-floor House and Techno tracks to get an even denser sound. 'It was about chasing that intensity,' Grooverider told Joe Muggs. 'Because we had that intense feeling to begin with, people wanted more - darker, more bass, faster beats - just to keep that feeling.'

In the years that followed, Rage would play a key - and some would say decisive - role in shaping the future of British Bass music. As Bleep & Bass and its early breakbeat derivatives began to fade from prominence, other darker, faster and even more bass-heavy mutations emerged. Fabio and Grooverider would be front and centre, championing what some of their dancers dubbed "Jungle Techno". A new age of British dance music had begun.

ELEMENTS OF TONE

BLEEP OVERSEAS AND TECHNO'S TRANS-ATLANTIC CONVERSATION

'It's just evolution - it happens in the most unlikely places. We grew up in the middle of nowhere and then realized that maybe we did have our own ideas. Sometimes provincial people restrict themselves. I don't care where you live, you're still a global citizen. Those are the people who make things happen. You don't have to live in London.'

JOHN ACQUAVIVA

One of the most significant by-products of the rapid growth in creativity within British dance music was the way in which the most revolutionary records were sought-after overseas. While British-made music had long been popular abroad, it tended to be Rock and Pop music that struck a chord rather than dance music. Because of this, the growth in sales and influence of UK-made House and Techno around the world between 1989 and 1992 was a notable first.

British record shops had previously relied on imports from the United States to service the growing DJing community, but now the nascent UK dance music industry was exporting records on a scale never seen before. It was evidence of the global growth of dance music as an artistic and cultural force, with records from other rapidly expanding scenes in Europe - reunified Germany, Italy, the Netherlands and Belgium in particular - arriving in the UK in similar volumes.

Those within Britain's changing rave scene responded enthusiastically to many of these subtle European variations on dance music's major
themes, from the piano-driven loved-up bliss of Italian House to the post-
New Beat throb of the tough, intoxicating and mind-altering records emerging from Belgian cities such as Ghent and Antwerp.

The most dominant Belgian Techno label of the time was R&S Records,
an imprint founded by couple Renaat Vandepapeliere and Sabine Maes in
response to what they thought was the overly commercial nature of their
country's club scene at the time. They began by issuing a swathe of Acid
House influenced New Beat records, but soon starting championing tracks
full of buzzing synth stabs, druggy grooves, subtle Detroit Techno references
and bags of strobe-lit, wide-eyed energy. Vandepapeliere developed relationships with key labels in both the UK and US, delivering licensed European
releases of tracks that had previously appeared on Transmat, Metroplex,
Network, Ten and a clutch of other labels based in London, Detroit, New
York and Chicago.

The developing UK Techno scene provided plenty of inspiration for Vandepapeliere, Maes and the artists who passed through the doors of the
label's in-house recording studio in Ghent. With its minimalist structure,
brain-melting low-end frequencies and distinctive rhythmic swing, Bleep &
Bass provided just as much inspiration as the breakbeat-powered sounds
of London Hardcore and the groundbreaking sounds of Motor City Techno.

'Renaat just used to license anything he liked, whether it was from the US
or the UK,' says Per Martinsen, a Norwegian producer who not only recorded
for R&S as Mental Overdrive but also spent much of 1989 and 1990 acting
as their in-house studio engineer. 'There were a few Bleep style tracks that
he licensed, such as Fantasy UFO "Fantasy", Autonation "Sit On The Bass"
and Turntable Overload "T.T.O". Those European clubs pretty much played
anything that was good and interesting, so any tracks that were big in the
UK would be played a week or two later. Things moved really fast, and everybody was influencing each other. There was this dialogue all round: if one
place came up with a new sound, then ten records were made the next
month with that sound as an influence.'

Dig hard enough and you'll find plenty of examples of (mostly lesser-known) Bleep-influenced records that emerged from Europe between
1990 and '93, from the warm and weighty Dutch Deep House/Bleep &
Bass fusion of Quazar's "The Seven Stars", and the dubbed-out deep space
Breakbeat Techno of Norwegian[1] artist Biosphere's "Baby Interphase", to
the early Italian Techno grooves of The True Underground Sound of Rome

---

1   According to Per Martinsen, the deep bass and stripped-back construction of
Bleep struck a chord with the first wave of Norwegian House and Techno producers, most of
who emerged from the icy northern outpost of Tromso. The dubbiness of Bleep's best records is
certainly something that has remained a significant feature of underground dance records made
in Norway.

("Secret Doctrine" on Male Productions) and MBG (whose "Speed 127" EP came in Warp-aping purple sleeve). There was also the work of Moritz Von Oswald and Mark Ernestus, whose Dub Techno records - the first of which appeared in 1993 - mined similar sonic influences to the early UK Bleep & Bass sound whilst offering up something decidedly different.

'It was very exciting the way these different scenes around Europe existed alongside each other,' Per Martinsen says. 'When they discovered each other, they started talking to each other. Pre-internet, there was a great joy in communicating through the records - like including a secret message for such and such producer, or sampling their tracks to present back to them.'

Even more significant was the trans-Atlantic Techno exchange between Britain and North America. Historically, the United States had led the way when it came to dance music, with a multitude of British artists creating tracks made in tribute to everything from Soul, Disco and Jazz-Funk to Electro, Chicago House and Motor City Techno. It should be noticed that there were British and European influences that fed into the birth of these later genres - New Wave, Industrial Music, Italo-Disco and the German Tech-no-Pop of Kraftwerk being particularly important to Detroit's Techno pio-neers - but this was the exception to the rule.

By 1990 the roles had yet to fully reverse, but it was certainly no longer one-way traffic. Surprisingly, there were pockets of DJs and producers creat-ing their own mutations of Bleep & Bass and Breakbeat Hardcore scattered across Canada and the northern United States. Like the sound's Yorkshire pioneers, North America's Bleep evangelists were self-proclaimed outsiders who went against the grain and took on the established order, often with remarkable results.

• • •

It may be 3,400 miles from Bradford to Brooklyn, but the subsonic waves created by the first flush of Yorkshire's Bleep & Bass movement reverberated hard in New York City. Throughout the latter half of 1990 and beyond, American dance music's most storied metropolis played host to its own small scale Techno revolution, with a dedicated band of producers, DJs and party-starters doing their bit to bring UK style rave culture - and all that went with it, from strong ecstasy pills to illicit, all-night events - to the heart of the Big Apple.

At the fulcrum of the action stood Brooklyn's Groove Records, later renamed Sonic Groove, the first music store in the city dedicated to Techno music, and its small band of enthusiastic rave evangelists. Through their work and, more intriguingly, a clutch of records made by a a host of DJs and producers more associated with the city's globally celebrated House scene,

Bleep & Bass and the earliest Breakbeat Hardcore helped usher in a new era in US dance music, where imported rave culture marginalised some of the black American records that had initially inspired it.

The man who kick-started New York's UK-inspired Techno movement was Frankie Mitchell, a DJ and graffiti artist who earned his stripes on the mid-80s Electro and freestyle scene as Frankie Bones. 'You couldn't escape Electro if you lived in New York in the 1980s,' says Adam Mitchell, Frankie's younger brother. 'It was street music. That's what we listened to. But with the industry that existed and all the clubs that had been there since the Disco era, dance music was always there. We grew up around it.'

In 1988, Frankie Mitchell joined forces with fellow freestyle DJ and House enthusiast Lenny Dideserio to produce the first in a series of "Bones-breaks" albums: collections of dancefloor-focused tracks mostly forged from sampled beats, basslines, riffs and drum breaks. While the first collection embraced Electro, Freestyle and House, later volumes saw Mitchell and new collaborator Tommy Musto offering up the kind of cut-and-paste Hip-Hop-meets-Acid-House fare that would soon become hugely popular in the UK.

Even more influential was the first volume in Mitchell and Musto's "Looney Tunes" series. Released in early 1989, it featured the kind of cut-and-paste sample collages that had been the preserve of scalpel-wielding Hip-Hop pioneers such as Double Dee and Steinski. Crucially, though, Mitchell and Musto were not making cheeky Hip-Hop tape mixes, but rather applying the same techniques - stealing and re-using drums, basslines, synth stabs, melodies and vocal snippets - to make tracks that appealed to Acid House-inspired dancefloors.

The fact that the pair made extensive use of sped-up Funk and Hip-Hop drum breaks and fused them with New York and Chicago House sounds did not go unnoticed in the UK. When reissued on XL Recordings, "Looney Tunes Volume 1" sold in high numbers, with the Brooklyn-based duo's cheeky blends becoming staples in the sets of DJs on the orbital rave circuit.

Such was the popularity of both the "Bonesbreaks" and "Looney Tunes" releases that Energy, promoters of some of the biggest raves of the era, invited Mitchell over to DJ at their August Bank Holiday weekend bash. It was a transformative experience for Mitchell. After taking his first ecstasy pill, playing to 5,000 screaming punters at dawn and feeling the love and energy of Britain's Second Summer Of Love, Mitchell returned to New York a changed man. He was soon travelling back and forth across the Atlantic at regular intervals, returning from jaunts to UK raves with a fresh batch of British and European records and a bag full of mixtapes and recordings of DJ sets from raves and pirate radio shows.

Two aspects of UK rave culture particularly excited Mitchell: the loved-up, ecstasy-fuelled parties and club events where perfect strangers interacted in a spirit of 'peace, love and unity', and the rapidly changing European Techno sound. This included the post-New Beat style promoted by Belgium's

R&S Records (occasionally known outside the country as "Hardbeat"), and British Bleep & Bass. Mitchell became a rave evangelist, quickly converting his brother Adam to the cause as well as friends Joey Beltram, Tommy Musto, Heather Hart (who launched her own fanzine dedicated to rave culture), Jimmy Crash and Ray Love.

'When we first heard the early Bleep & Bass stuff we were blown away,' Adam Mitchell says. 'We'd never heard bass like that in regular dance music. That sound resonated really loudly in New York.'

It was inevitable that some in New York would "get" Bleep; after all, elements of the musical culture that inspired it had long been a feature of NYC nightlife. The city had spawned Electro and Freestyle, while the syncopated drum machine rhythms associated with House and Techno had long been a feature of locally made electronic Disco records and the mid-to-late '80s Garage House sound associated with DJ Larry Levan and the legendary Paradise Garage club where he played.

This sound, like many others, had organically developed following a series of groundbreaking, post-Disco "Proto-House" records that contained many of the stylistic traits associated with Dub Reggae (think extensive use of tape delays, reverb, and sparse, heavyweight grooves). Many of these records were made by self-proclaimed "Garage kids" - enthusiastic weekly dancers who produced tracks they thought would be popular with Levan, a DJ who regularly reached for records smothered in dub delays and produced remixes (usually with the assistance of legendary NYC studio engineer Bob Blank) full of echoing synthesizer lines and vocal snippets.

Many of these Garage kids had some kind of West Indian heritage, with one of the leading protagonists, Paul Simpson, spending his early years in Brixton surrounded by family members who ran Reggae soundsystems. The records he made with Winston Jones, alongside others by Timmy Regisford and the late Boyd Jarvis, became hugely popular in the clubs of Sheffield, Leeds and Bradford following their release between 1983 and '86[2]. Yet, while these were far more dubby than any other dance records that came before them, they still lacked the subsonic deepness of records that emerged from the Bleep & Bass scene.

"I think in New York, because of our history with Electro stuff - low-end bass, 808 kicks, deep frequencies - and the fact that we're a very multicultural city, Bleep was always likely to appeal,' Adam Mitchell says. 'I grew up

---

2   British-born Paul Simpson spent his early years in Brixton and had an uncle who ran a Reggae soundsystem. His synthesizer and drum machine-heavy productions of the mid-1980s were amongst the most Dub influenced to come out of the city at a time when soulful post-Disco records dominated. For more about his career and those of his NYC "Proto-House" contemporaries, check my 2016 article on the subject for Red Bull Music Academy Daily: https://daily.redbullmusicacademy.com/2016/05/the-music-got-me-a-brief-history-of-the-birth-of-house-in-new-york-city

in a very multicultural area where there were a lot of Jamaicans and Haitians. The Jamaicans used to play a lot of Reggae in the neighbourhood. Bass in the music was definitely appealing to people in New York City.'

When the first Techno records began to make it from Detroit to New York in the mid-1980s, few native New Yorkers took much notice. But Bleep was something different: a high-tech style that mixed Steppers style rhythms, ultra-deep bass, the body-popping beats of Electro and the far-sighted futurism of the Motor City.

'I remember going into record shops in New York and the House people were really into the Warp stuff,' Adam Mitchell says. 'You'd see Network releases, and Ozone too, so the records were getting into the hands of DJs who weren't necessarily paying attention to, say, Belgian Techno. Most of these DJs and shops weren't digging deeper. You didn't see Chill releases for example, but because Warp had good distribution, their records were making it into the stores that weren't really carrying Techno records or pushing Techno music.'

The lack of a record store pushing Techno irritated Frankie Mitchell, so he found a vacant shop space in Brooklyn and opened Groove Records in April 1990. Due to his growing overseas DJ commitments, he roped in Ray Love and brother Adam to work behind the counter. 'That's when I started collecting records seriously,' Adam Mitchell says. 'I instantly got into the music. Frankie had been giving me mixtapes, but through working in the shop I was able to identify all of the tracks.'

Amongst the tracks on the tapes was Unique 3's "The Theme", and various early Robert Gordon productions and remixes on Warp. Both Mitchell brothers became enormous fans of Gordon's work, eagerly reading the fine print of incoming British Techno records to see if he was involved.

'In my opinion, Robert Gordon made better music than the Detroit guys,' Adam Mitchell says. 'The Bleep records he produced, mixed or remixed have genuinely high-level production. The production is just amazing on those records. Even with all of the technology that's around now, you can't take those records and make them better. There's no improving on that.'

The wider influence of Bleep & Bass on dance producers on New York's music makers would start to become more obvious throughout the latter stages of 1990. Strictly Rhythm and Nu Groove - both imprints famed for helping to establish House music in NYC - both released a number of Bleep-influenced records, most notably by a young Roger Sanchez (under the Egotrip[3] and DV8[4] pseudonyms) and the Burrell Brothers (as Equation).

---

[3]   "Dreamworld" on Outer Limits, which blends deep and dreamy House with clear Bleep & Bass influences, is particularly special. In fact, it may well be Roger Sanchez's best record.
[4]   "Thoughts of the Future", from the 1990 "Freedom" 12", is one of the most authentic American takes on Warp style Bleep & Bass, while "The Future" from 1991's "The Ego Trip EP" does a great job in doffing a cap to the Bleep-influenced Dub/Deep House fusions of NYC contemporary Bobby Konders.

Bobby Konders, one of Nu Groove's most prolific producers of the period, also recorded a number of superb EPs that fused his twin loves of atmospheric Deep House and Dub Reggae. Two of these, "My Sound" and "Unauthorized Conceptions", ended up being released on the UK's XL Recordings. A little later in 1991, Todd Terry, then one of US House music's biggest names, went so far as to produce a Bleep-inspired "Techno Todd" remix of Sub Sub's dancefloor anthem "Space Face".

'Most of the guys [around at the time] seemed to be influenced by the sound,' Adam Mitchell says. 'I know [Joey] Beltram was really into the early productions - he was a huge fan of Robert Gordon in particular. Then you had guys like Damon Wild of Chapter 1[5] and How & Little, who did stuff on Nu Groove, City Limits and R&S. [Frankie] Bones was definitely sampling - outright sampling - a lot of Bleep stuff. I think almost everybody was bitten by that bug'.

To begin with, it was Brooklyn's obsessive Techno heads - Tommy Musto, Frankie Bones and Joey Beltram specifically - who would do the most to push forward America's take on Bleep & Bass, albeit in a style that owed an equal amount to Breakbeat Hardcore and Belgian Techno. The vast majority of the tracks released on Musto and Silvio Tancredi's Atmosphere Records imprint in 1990 featured some element of Bleep & Bass influence[6]. Mental Mayhem's "Joey's Riot", a pre-"Energy Flash" Joey Beltram production that boasts similar drums to his famous anthem with the addition of some typically Yorkshire bleeps is arguably the best example, though there are plenty of others among the catalogue.

Chief among these is P.L.U.M's "Make You Feel It (Feel The Wrath)", a joint venture between Adam Mitchell - who by now was DJing as Adam X - and fellow Groove Records regulars Jimmy Crash and Ray Love, under the watchful eye of big brother Frankie.

'My brother wanted to put us in the studio to do a remix for Mr C, something for The Shamen I think,' Adam Mitchell remembers. 'I was really new to the studio - I didn't really understand the structure of dance music or how to make an arrangement. I was so new to it that when we went to the studio, I was told we were going to take a bunch of samples, work with what they gave us, and make a track out of it. I had to be shown how to use the sampler.'

---

5   Chapter 1 was a trio made up of Wild, Gene Hughes aka Bluejean and Lea M. Beak aka DJ Moneypenny. Their 1990 debut on Strictly Rhythm, "Unleash The Groove", came with a "Love In Sheffield Mix" that cannily paid tribute to the early Warp Records sound, albeit in a manner closer to Roger Sanchez's Egotrip records rather than Forgemasters, Sweet Exorcist or LFO.
6   One of the duo's other labels, Fourth Floor, also licensed and reissued The Moody Boys' Bleep-influenced Dub House workout "Lion Dance" in 1991. The original was one of the highlights of the XL Recordings released "Journeys Into Dubland" EP. The Fourth Floor reissue included new mixes from Tommy Musto and Frankie Bones.

All three wanted to include heavy bass and distinctly British bleeps. Frankie had told them that Gordon and others within the UK scene had extracted the bleep noises from the test tones hidden deep within AKAI samplers[7], so they did just that. Along the way, there were numerous disagreements about the arrangement, so they agreed to do two different mixes: Crash and Love would handle what would later become the A-side "Crashing Mix", with Adam "directing" his own "Brooklyn Bassline" version.

'I didn't have that much of a clue what was going on, but the other guys were making a version, so I got to do a version too,' Mitchell says. 'I kept saying, "No, you should put the bass here." They understood how to arrange music much better than I did. We were taking all the samples we liked, each of us, and somehow we made it.'

All these years on, it's Adam X's version that still resonates. While it contains numerous distinctly New York style elements - cut-up Hip-Hop vocal samples, occasional blasts of fizzing breakbeats and so on - it's as authentic an early Bleep & Breaks record as you'll find. The bass is deep, rich and ridiculously weighty, while the bleeps sound like they could have been stolen wholesale from an early Unique 3 record.

Despite all involved being proud of their achievements, The Shamen weren't keen on these revolutionary remixes and refused to release them. 'I remember there was a version with vocals - once we took those out, it didn't really have any musical samples from the original Shamen track,' Adam Mitchell admits. 'Frankie decided to put out the two vocal-free versions as a standalone single. It was my first studio work, and I'm still super-proud of it.'

Despite the growing weight of Bleep-inspired material emerging from New York - including more Frankie Bones tracks that sampled "The Theme" and "Track With No Name", amongst other UK Bleep and Hardcore tracks - the DJs and producers behind the records remained virtual unknowns on the city's club scene. Frankie Bones and Joey Beltram were fast becoming big stars in Europe but struggled to break through in NYC.

'It was pretty bleak actually,' Adam Mitchell sighs. 'You had my brother, and you had our little posse. There was a small crew of us and we'd go out partying. We had friends who had really big sound systems in their cars. We would take some party supplies and just bug out to Techno music under a highway.'

All that changed in the summer of 1990 when local legend Mark Kammins - most famously resident DJ at the seminal Danceteria club - offered Frankie Bones the chance to cover for him at one of the city's smaller venues. 'My brother played all the bass and Bleep stuff,' Adam Mitchell recalls. 'We were all wired up in there on E or whatever, hearing that stuff over the sound system. It was incredible. No clubbers had really

---

7   Most at the time were convinced this is how Sweet Exorcist got the distinctive electronic sounds used on "Testone", though when asked about this theory Richard Barratt told me it was incorrect.

heard music like this before, but there wasn't really a rave scene yet. These were normal New York people - the only people that were onto the British sound was us. We wanted to break the UK style rave scene in the US - or in and around New York, at least.'

They would, of course, later do that, with the infamous Storm Rave parties that began in 1991. During 1990, though, they were ploughing a lone furrow, in New York at least. Yet, as the year drew to a close, they became aware of another pair of outsiders equally as inspired by the low frequencies of Bleep & Bass. They were not based in a colossal metropolis, but rather in a mid-sized Canadian city a short paddle across the Detroit River from Techno's spiritual home.

● ● ●

As he is keen to point out in interviews, John Acquaviva was one of Can-, ada's most successful DJs between 1982 and 1989. Playing a mixture of Electropop, New Wave, Industrial music and, later, Hip-House, Acquaviva DJed five times a week year after year, seamlessly beat-matching the best grooves he could find when most Canadian DJs were happy to act as glorified selectors.

'I probably did 2,000 gigs just in the 1980s,' he proudly says over the phone. 'I have one of the most voracious appetites for music and subsequently one of the biggest collections. I still have the original DJ ethos I had in the 1980s - if it's got a good groove, I'll play it.'

To get cheaper records 'on a discount' to play in his sets, Acquaviva took a job with a chain of record shops called Doctor Disc. They had outlets in London [Ontario], St Catherine's, Hamilton and Windsor, a border city that sits directly opposite the Motor City on the south bank of the Detroit River. 'One of my friends in Windsor, Karl Kowalski, told me that I had to meet this friend of his called Rich,' Acquaviva recalls. 'He got me to go down there to see this 19-year-old rock the basement of this club called Shelter.'

The DJ in question, Richie Hawtin, was British by birth. He moved to Windsor from Oxfordshire at the age of eight when his robotics engineer father got a job at General Motors in Detroit. Hawtin became obsessed with electronic music as a teenager, moving from Electro and breakdancing to the sci-fi sounds of early Detroit Techno via the clanking, intense and throbbing sounds of European Industrial and Electronic Body Music.

In 1985, aged 15, he started sneaking out of the house to dip across the border and talk his way into club nights in Detroit. Hawtin was fixated by the hardware-driven musical futurism emerging from the Motor City, so when he finally bagged his first DJ gigs in Windsor it was these records he pulled for first. When Acquaviva came to the Shelter to hear him play in 1989, he had already been DJing in clubs for two years. He was naturally regarded as a DJ on the rise in his home city and was a familiar face across the river thanks to nights spent dancing at Detroit's most Techno-focused clubs.

But it wasn't just Techno in its purest form that Hawtin enjoyed. Like Acquaviva, his head had been turned by some of the formative Bleep & Bass records. 'Unique 3's "The Theme" was one of the first three or four records that me and Richie bonded over,' Acquaviva says. 'We used to sit and day-dream about the clubs they were playing in because we'd read about how incredible the scene was there.'

Acquaviva and Hawtin were kindred spirits. Both were fascinated by the inherent futurism of Detroit Techno and its emphasis on technology. 'Techno is special because one of the key components is technology,' Acquaviva says enthusiastically. 'When I bought Kraftwerk albums like "Computer World", I saw myself in the future living in a world with my home computer. Techno was always about the future, and we're futurists. There was always that visionary component that went beyond clubbing. Our vision became reality.'

That vision was Plus 8 records, an imprint the pair founded in late 1989 to serve as an outlet for their productions. Acquaviva had previously estab-lished his own small recording studio, stuffing it with various drum machines and synthesizers including a Sequential Circuits Pro One and multiple Roland SH-101 units. 'I liked the gravelly sound you could get from the Pro One and I knew that a lot of New Wave bands had used another synth by the same company, the Prophet 5,' he says. 'I was really deep into the SH-101 though: I had a grey one, a red one and a blue one, with the modulation grip and the shoulder strap. When I met Rich, he told me that A Guy Called Gerald's "Voodoo Ray" came from the SH-101 and that I could get a similar sound. I loved that sound - "Voodoo Ray", with its midrange, almost melodic vibe, was a real touchstone.'

The first record the pair made together was "Elements of Tone", an expansive EP that contained audible nods to their major musical obses-sions: twisted, TB-303 powered Acid House, the sci-fi Techno of Detroit and the alien minimalism of Bleep & Bass. The title track was offered up in a quartet of bleep-heavy mixes, with the "Raw Tone Mix" - a stripped-back affair full of "Testone" style melodies, head-cracking drums and heavy low-end - sounding like a Canadian equivalent of Unique 3's earliest experi-ments. 'We collected all the pieces of equipment we thought the Bleep guys used,' Acquaviva says. 'We could literally play the Sweet Exorcist tones.'

"Elements of Tone" became the first release on Plus 8, slipping into stores in Windsor and Detroit in May 1990. The label's second release was another debut 12", this time from a young black producer from Detroit called Kenny Larkin. Engineered by Acquaviva, 'We Shall Overcome" adeptly added UK style bleeps to the skittish machine drums and futurist Funk that had long been a hallmark of Motor City Techno productions. Acquaviva and Hawtin then joined forces with friend Daniel Bell as Cybersonik, releasing an EP that expertly set out the Plus 8 agenda.

Lead cut "Technarchy" was riotous: a stomping chunk of raw, intense, rave-ready Techno smothered in fuzzy Belgian style synth stabs and mind-altering industrial electronics. Yet the tracks that accompanied it, "Algorhythm" and "Melody 928.V2", owed much to the trio's love of Bleep & Bass, with the latter sampling a snatch of a spoken word track tucked away on the flipside of Roger Sanchez's debut as Ego Trip, "Dreamworld". The EP quickly became hugely popular in the UK, leading to a reissue on Champion Records.

Plus 8's following release, a solo debut from Hawtin as F.U.S.E (short for Futuristic Underground Subsonic Experiments), contained the label's clearest expression of purist Bleep & Bass yet, "Approach and Identify". Powered by deep Dub bass, Robert Gordon-esque drum programming, intergalactic electronics and Unique 3 style lead lines, it remains one of the greatest Bleep records made outside of the North of England.

It was, of course, hugely popular in the sound's Yorkshire heartlands, with Warp Records selling countless copies in their Division Street store. When Hawtin and Acquaviva first headed to the UK for DJ gigs in early summer 1990, they made sure they visited Warp Records and checked in with Robert Gordon. The friendships they developed not only resulted in a handful of eventual collaborations with both Gordon and LFO but also the release of a F.U.S.E single on Warp, "Train Tracs", in 1993.

Interestingly, Plus 8, and Acquaviva and Hawtin in particular were not embraced quite so enthusiastically in Detroit, despite spending a lot of time there and running regular parties in the city. Some within the tight-knit Techno scene there resented the Canadians presenting themselves as members of their community. 'We definitely got some grief,' Acquaviva sighs. 'We didn't badmouth or talk trash about anyone, because we wanted to be around a long time. When Detroit felt that we were interlopers - even though Richie was living closer to the centre of the City than the guys in the suburbs that made some of the earliest records - we just changed our logo and became more global. We had no problem leaving Detroit to Detroit. I love the city and have a profound respect for the electronic community there, but some people don't understand beyond their arm's length.'

As Plus 8 was trying to make its mark in Detroit, the Godfathers of the original Techno scene were becoming international stars. Thanks to the work of Neil Rushton and John Mostyn, Juan Atkins, Kevin Saunderson and Derrick May were spending more time in Europe than they were at home. In their absence, a new generation of DJs and producers made their mark in the Motor City.

Leading the charge was an extended crew called Underground Resistance, whose founders Mike Banks, Jeff Mills and Robert Hood were far more politically engaged than their predecessors. They wanted to represent and champion Detroit's black working class - Techno's founding fathers were black middle class suburbanites - and frequently talked of using electronic music to inspire people out of the cycle of poverty that had long gripped the Motor City.

Underground Resistance's first releases on their self-titled imprint were impressive. The "Sonic EP", which arrived in the latter half of 1990, contained two Motor City translations of Bleep & Bass: the sub-heavy weight of "Orbit", and the off-kilter Techno-Funk of "Predator". This was a particularly timely and fitting trans-Atlantic exchange: what had begun in working class black communities in northern England, inspired by electronic futurism from Detroit, had now inspired a response from their equivalents in the style's spiritual home.

Back in Brooklyn, Frankie and Adam Mitchell looked on smugly, impressed by the records but adamant that they got their first. 'In North America, it was people in Brooklyn who were the first to be influenced, then came the Canadians[8] and the Detroit guys,' Adam Mitchell says. 'When my brother got a copy of the "Sonic EP" in the UK in December 1990, we had no idea it was by Underground Resistance out of Detroit. Richie [Hawtin] was a little earlier on it, but the Bleep sound was already in Brooklyn by then - we were definitely first!'

---

8   Aside from Hawtin and Acquaviva, there was also an outpost of Bleep-influenced Deep House and Techno in Toronto, where the Hi-Bias Records crew (including producers Nick Holder, Nick Anthony Fiorucci and Michael Ova) released a number of now sought-after records infused with audible references to key UK Bleep & Bass records.

PART FOUR

AFTERMATH

'In hindsight, it was a massive illusion.'

GEORGE EVELYN Nightmares On Wax

COMING DOWN

THE DEATH OF BLEEP AND THE CONTINUING ALLURE OF BASS

'When we were making music, we were making it to play it in clubs, because we had to go to clubs to hear that music. All of a sudden it was everywhere, it was selling, and it was making money. The whole reason for making music then begins to be diluted because of outside influences.'

WINSTON HAZEL

When it comes to documenting significant social and cultural movements, there's long been a tendency to focus on selected events: moments in time that marked highs, lows or clear turning points away from what had been considered the norm. With regards to popular music, many of these events - seismic or otherwise - are so woven into the fabric of our shared culture that even those with only a passing interest could name them.

Lonnie Donnegan releasing "Rock Island Line"; the Beatles on the Ed Sullivan Show (and/or their Royal Variety Performance appearance); Jimi Hendrix performing "Star Spangled Banner" at Woodstock; the Sex Pistols at the Lesser Free Trade Hall in Manchester; Live Aid; Malcolm McLaren and the World's Famous Supreme Team on Top of the Pops. Whether you were there or not, you instinctively know what happened and why it was important; in most cases, you could probably even explain how things changed as a result.

For the rave movement that sprung up in the wake of Britain's ecstasy-fuelled Acid House revolution, that moment took place at Castlemorton Common on the second May bank holiday weekend of 1992. It was the not so triumphant conclusion of a movement that had been growing

CHAPTER SEVENTEEN

^ WARP Records' co-founders
# ROB MITCHELL & STEVE BECKETT

for five years; a spontaneous weeklong shindig attended by an estimated 20,000-50,000 people, all drawn to a site in the sleepy Malvern Hills by a simple answerphone message and a desire to hang out, dance and have a good time.

What this 'free festival' represented was a meeting of the tribes, where those on the non-conformist traveller and free party scenes came together with ravers, music enthusiasts and festival freaks from all walks of life for a gargantuan, self-policed party that was little less than a massive two-fingered salute to accepted societal norms. Music was provided by a swathe of large and popular travelling soundsystems run by crews who sought not to profit from dance music culture as rave and club promoters did, but put on free parties for like-minded individuals from the margins of Britain's divided society.

Some of those at Castlemorton Common had fought bitterly - and would continue to do so - for their right to party in the face of the British government's crackdown on rave culture; for others, it would be their last hurrah. Regardless of what those who attended did next, Castlemorton was the last big expression of rave music's underground, anti-establishment roots. It occurred at a time when dance music culture was hitting its first commercial peak. What had started in a handful of clubs scattered around the UK had now become an established part of the music industry machine, with the previously united and loved-up scene below splintering off in dozens of different directions. With a new generation of DJs and producers snapping at the heels of those who had once been innovators, the pace of change would only increase in the years that followed.

When Castlemorton took place in 1992, "rave music" was much more sharply defined than it had been when the first wave of illegal parties took place in the mid-1980s. Although the soundsystems involved in the weeklong event each had their own style - contrast the deep, dubby and druggy House preferred by Nottingham's DIY crew and the insanely fast, intense and psychedelic Techno championed by London lunatics Spiral Tribe - "rave" as a term was usually applied to Breakbeat Hardcore, which by now was operating at a far faster tempo than the Bleep & Breaks records that had proved so popular a year or two before.

Whereas Bleep-influenced early Hardcore records had barely strayed above 130 beats per minute, with 120-125 BPM the preferred tempo for most, by 1992 Hardcore rave music started at 135 beats per minute and got faster. Many producers were happy to conform to a tried-and-tested formula that relied on the same few stylistic traits, from sped-up female vocal samples and over the top piano riffs, to grating electronic stabs and thunderous Techno kick-drum patterns overlaid with sweaty Funk breakbeats.

The music was energetic, wild and perfectly pitched for those coming up on ecstasy, with tracks structured to provide moments of rush-inducing release and surging sensory pleasure. Each Hardcore rave record came with sign-posted moments where hands could be raised towards the heavens in celebration. The biggest Hardcore records naturally transcended the club scene, becoming top-selling Pop hits that endure to this day.

Not all have lasted the test of time, with the flurry of so-called "toytown rave" records that emerged in 1991 and '92 being amongst the worst examples. No doubt plenty of chemicals were consumed during the making of these tracks crafted from samples of children's TV shows. If not, it's hard to fathom why anyone would think it was a good idea to make rave tracks inspired by Sesame Street (Smart E's Suburban Base-released "Sesame's Treet"), Trumpton (Urban Hype, "A Trip To Trumpton") and Roobarb (Shaft's "Roobarb & Custard")[1].

Given the direction of musical travel, it's unsurprising that Bleep & Bass had all but disappeared as a standalone sound, with those pioneers involved in the style's inception scratching their heads about where to go next. 'Dance music went so big with ecstasy and rave, pushed forwards by a large amount of young people who had no background in the kind of things we experienced before making our records,' Richard Barratt says. 'They weren't interested in why our records sounded the way they did. They came in at that entry point where there were these dark, bleepy, bass-heavy records and thought, "How do we make it more exciting?" They wanted more and more excitement. They made it faster and noisier with more midrange [sounds]. They did right - we were old men by that point as far as they were concerned. If you're 16, someone who's 27 is like your granddad.'

• • •

The rapid musical and cultural changes shaping the dance music scene in 1991 and 1992 were keenly felt in Sheffield, where a new generation of Hardcore loving DJs was threatening the old order. Jive Turkey, once the biggest show in town, was entering its final phase at the City Hall Ballroom. Richard Barratt and Winston Hazel's days as Sheffield's favourite DJs were coming to an end, with a new breed of younger DJs with rising reputations on local pirate station Fantasy FM rapidly rising up the pecking order.

The subtle variations between regional scenes that had been so important a few years earlier were no longer quite as evident either, thanks in no small part to the first flush of what would later become "superstar DJ" culture. Younger clubbers wanted to see well-known DJ heroes from the UK

---

1   Shaft's Mark Pritchard has long since redeemed himself by releasing some staggeringly good music in the 28 years that have passed since that was released, both on his own and as part of other influential electronic acts (Global Communication, Jedi Knights, Africa-HiTech etc.).

and abroad, rather than head to the same club week after week to share collective moments with hard-working local DJs who shaped scenes by playing extended sets in residencies that lasted months or years.

'When we decided to stop Jive Turkey we could see what was happening musically and within the scene,' Richard Barratt sighs. 'Everything got fucked up when travelling DJs began to become the norm. How are you going to build a night with a different person there each week playing different records? How does that contribute to a local scene? We got our thing built up over many, many years, just as DJs before us had built their sound in the clubs that they played. That just doesn't happen any more.'

These changing times seemed to affect Warp Records particularly hard. In 1990, anything they touched turned to gold; even Tricky Disco's "Tricky Disco", a playful, tongue-in-cheek track that GTO members Lee Newman and Michael Wells allegedly originally intended to be a piss-take of the Bleep & Bass sound[2], earned the label at top 20 chart position.

As the year drew to a close they'd already built up a backlog of quality material to release in 1991, including a suitably dub-wise single from The Step ("Yeah You", a collaboration between Winston Hazel, Richard Barratt and their friend Sarah Jay that came backed with some of Robert Gordon's heaviest remixes yet), the rock-hard explorations of Leeds' Tomas Stewart (the "Mindsong EP") and Nightmares On Wax's most Techno-focused EP yet, "A Case of Funk". To top it all off, they'd also signed a track by Robert Gordon's friends Glyn Andrews and Zye Hill, who went by the artistic alias Tuff Little Unit. The track Warp signed, "Join The Future", was artful, deep, loved-up and formidably bass-heavy.

Yet trouble was brewing. Rob Mitchell and Steve Beckett were getting increasingly frustrated with the pressing and distribution deal they'd signed with Rhythm King offshoot Outer Rhythm on the back of the success of the first white label pressing of Forgemasters' "Track With No Name" in 1989.

Naturally, some of the label's artists felt short-changed, too, as their royalty cheques - reportedly 'a couple of grand at most' for the 130,000-selling "LFO", according to Gez Varley - seemed a lot smaller than they ought to be. This was not due to any foul play on the part of the label's owners, though, but rather a deal that was skewed much more in favour of their backers in London.

'When we first met Rhythm King we signed everything away for £10,000 and walked out of their office going, "Yes, we've done it",' Steve Beckett explained in Richard King's 2012 history of the indie music scene, *How Soon Is Now? The Madmen and Mavericks Who Made Independent Music*

---

2   The separately released remix 12" was arguably far more "pure" in its approach to Bleep & Bass. The "Inner Space Mix", with its ghostly chords, deep space electronics and stabbing bassline, is particularly alluring. It was accompanied by the "Saxy Mix", which included some snaking, suitably bluesy saxophone parts played by one of Michael Newman's relatives.

1975-2005[3]. 'It's the classic story - you're into your little mind-set going, "Some idiot's given us 10,000 quid to release our records", and then not realizing that after a while you're selling 100,000 records and not seeing a penny. We were going, "Hold on... my God, what have we done?"'

They eventually extracted themselves from the deal thanks to the intervention of Mute Records founder Daniel Miller, who had financed both Rhythm King and the Outer Rhythm offshoot. But Warp's problems didn't end there, as a series of blazing rows and disagreements over potential signings led to Mitchell and Beckett parting company with fellow label co-founder Robert Gordon.

Getting to the bottom of exactly what happened between the three men is not an easy task. Robert Gordon is naturally still angry after all these years, accusing Beckett and Mitchell of a variety of sins that can't be published here for legal reasons. Rob Mitchell sadly passed away in 2001 and Steve Beckett refused all requests to be interviewed for this book, making cross-referencing their differing accounts impossible.

In Rob Young's 2005 illustrated history of Warp Records for Black Dog Publishing's short-lived *Labels Unlimited* series, Gordon is quoted as saying that the trio first clashed over which Tricky Disco tracks to sign; he wanted to sign a second track from the duo ("Pure", subsequently an enormous track for Wells and Newman as GTO) but Beckett and Mitchell outvoted him. Further rows followed, including one over Gordon's idea to license a Chicago House track by Plez, which was getting an amazing reaction in his friend Winston Hazel's DJ sets.

'They replied, "We don't license tracks!",' Gordon told Young. 'I said, "We do now - let's license it!" Plez had no idea it was so big in Sheffield, so they'd have accepted 500 quid. "We can't afford it!" Of course we can, phone them up, ask them... Massive row. Shortly after that Rob Mitchell says, "What we've decided is that we're 66 per cent of the company and you're only 33 per cent of the company - we're voting you out".'

Almost 30 years on, Robert Gordon can barely contain his rage at what happened and feels that his contribution to the formative years of one of the world's most successful electronic music labels has been airbrushed out of history. 'I got expelled from Warp Records, a label that I founded,' he fumes while sat in his recording studio. 'I was running it by myself, but it got so big. I was supposed to be producing Human League and The Fall and Yazz and all that stuff, so I just couldn't do it [run the label]. So I went to the local record shop and said, "Do you fancy running this label with me?" Obviously I was young, and they did a number on me.'

---

3   King, Richard: How Soon Is Now? The Madmen and Mavericks Who Made Independent Music 1975-2005, Faber & Faber, 2017

Had Gordon, Beckett and Mitchell sorted out their issues, it's fair to say that Warp - for better or worse - would have ended up being a completely different beast than it is today. Gordon's absence certainly signalled a new direction for the label, with responsibility for signing tracks and artists falling to Beckett and Mitchell, two former Indie kids turned electronic music enthusiasts whose musical interests were vastly different to Gordon's.

His vision was based around signing and releasing club-friendly records that appealed to both his black and white friends, which meant Acid House and Techno influences fused with the very particular aesthetics of Dub; for Beckett and Mitchell, it was more about building a label and a roster of artists through albums and singles that could appeal to people other than club DJs.

'When I went clubbing, I could only go to this club to see my black friends, or this club to see my white friends,' Gordon complains. 'So I thought, "What if there was a kind of music both of my friends liked, then I could see them in the same club. What I did worked - the clubs were 50-50 black and white. They destroyed that with their actions.'

It's fair to say that Beckett and Mitchell did eventually find their own voice for Warp, turning it into an outlet for a wide range of alternative, underground music styles. In the near three decades that have passed since, the label has gone through many stages of evolution, moving through 'intelligent dance music' and sofa-bound Electronica, to academic Ambient, glitchy Hip-Hop, alternative Rock, future R&B and much more besides.

In 1991 this was all still ahead of them, and it's fair to say that the label stuttered a bit in the 18 months following Gordon's departure. A good example of the label's changed priorities, and how it affected local artists, can be gleaned from the experiences of Tuff Little Unit's Glyn Andrews and Zye Hill. They signed a contract with Warp around the same time as their good friend Rob Gordon was being shown the door, something that still rankles with them to this day.

'When we signed, Steve and Rob wanted to get "Join The Future" edited for some reason, and even though Robert was our friend it was hard to get him to do the edit because of what had happened with Warp,' Glyn Andrews says. 'In the end, Robert did it, which is the version that came out and people know. We still think our version is more hard-hitting. When we finished "Join The Future", we were bouncing off the walls in the studio. When we first heard Robert's edited version we thought he'd taken all the momentum out of it.'

"Join The Future" remains one of the most magical of Warp's early releases, with a rich vein of musicality surging through it that marks it out from some of the label's more raw and industrial Bleep & Bass era tunes. In some ways, it also feels more personal and human thanks to the presence of a simple vocal from Warren Peart.

'We had a friend called John, who had also been to Hurlfield School like us, and he told us about this guy called Warren who'd come up from London and had a reputation for being a really good singer,' Zye Hill says. 'He had a good voice - he was compared to Seal at the time.'

Glyn Andrews nods in agreement. 'Warren was a lovely guy with a great voice,' he says. 'Steve Beckett and Rob Mitchell heard the track with his vocal and said to us, "If you put vocals on the tracks you're making you'll be massive".'

It wasn't exactly what Hill and Andrews wanted to do. Although they came from a background playing in Reggae bands and were far more musically adept than many of their label-mates, they were drawn more towards off-kilter instrumental music. In fact, they say that by the time "Join The Future" came out they'd been working on more 'experimental, hard-edged' tracks.

'Warp saw what we'd done with Warren and decided they wanted to make us into a band that they could market,' Andrews says. 'That's where second single "Inspiration" comes in. It was Steve's idea to send us down to London and get Jazzy M to produce it.'

Released later in 1991, "Inspiration" is something of a curiosity: a loved-up vocal record on Warp underpinned by London style breakbeats and smothered in the sort of organ stabs more associated with New Jersey Garage. While Peart's positive lyrics - an impassioned plea for peace, love and unity - are fully in keeping with the glassy-eyed ethos of rave, the track not only sits uneasily on Warp but also seems out of step with Tuff Little Unit's previous record. More in keeping with the duo's thinking at the time is B-side "Rush To The Beat", which mixed the duo's love for deep Dub bass and electronic Ragga rhythms with curious electronic noises and lo-fi synth-sax lines.

'That was the starting point of what we wanted to do with the album that was meant to follow "Inspiration",' Andrews explains. 'As part of the promotion for the single we ended up playing at a rave in Ayr[4] and Tim Garbutt from Utah Saints was there, filling in for Sasha who didn't turn up. After he heard our set, he turned to us and said, "You're not a rave act, are you?" I said, "No, we're fucking not! I don't know why we're here. We should be in a dark warehouse with a few purple lights playing deep, deep music". That's what we should have been doing.'

---

4   Streetrave in Ayr was one of the biggest events nationally during the rave era. Many of those interviewed for this book DJed or performed PAs there in 1990 or '91. The promoter behind the event continues to put on large-scale dance music events in Scotland to this day.

Warp pressed on with sending them down to London to record[5], racking up significant studio bills in the process. 'That stuff Jazzy M produced just wasn't our sound,' Hill sighs. 'It wasn't like what we'd been working on and it wasn't what we wanted to do. When someone else does something with your work, it doesn't feel it's you.'

Beckett and Mitchell's attempts to turn Tuff Little Unit into something they weren't seems wholly in keeping with their muddled thinking in the period after Robert Gordon left the label. They signed some good dance-floor material in 1991 and '92 - see Coco, Steel & Lovebomb's "Feel It", which they licensed from Instant Records, plus a clutch of EPs from producers associated with the Fourth Wave record store in Huddersfield - but also surprisingly deviated towards Breakbeat Hardcore via Manchester producer Kid Unknown's "Nightmare" and "Devastating Beat Creator".

Much to Robert Gordon's irritation, Beckett and Mitchell also licensed their first records from abroad: DSR's "Miami" EP, a collection of deep and occasionally wonky club cuts named after the city in which it was made and, more puzzlingly, the Progressive House meanderings of German producer THK ("France").

More on-point though was "Artificial Intelligence", Beckett and Mitchell's game-changing compilation of "home listening music" that tapped into the new wave of so-called Intelligent Techno[6] records being made by artists who were thinking beyond the boundaries of clubs and raves. Some of these, such as B12 (as Musicology) and Black Dog had emerged from the anti-Hardcore end of the London Techno scene[7], while others were based elsewhere around the UK (Autechre across the Pennines in Lancashire, Richard D James down in Cornwall) or even overseas (Jochem Paap aka Speedy J, and Richie Hawtin as Up!). There was even a nod towards the vibrant Ambient House and Chill-Out movement that had appeared in response to the increasing tempo and intensity of the rave scene[8], fittingly via a track by one of the DJs who started it, Orb man Alex Paterson.

This was, of course, the direction that Warp would embrace in the years that followed. While Beckett and Mitchell kept offering up club-focused Techno (and occasionally House) records in parallel to album releases from

---

5   Beckett also booked in more live appearances for them, including a stint supporting The Shamen on a five-date national tour.
6   Chill-Out DJ Mixmaster Morris, then clubbing correspondent for the NME, claims to have invented the term 'Intelligent Techno'. He says he was the first person to use it in print. It caused a stink, though, with those whose records weren't associated with the style naturally feeling grumpy with the negative connotations (i.e. that their records weren't intelligent).
7   For further detail on the Detroit-influenced London Techno scene, I urge you to read Oli Warwick's brilliant history of its formative years on the *Red Bull Music Academy Daily* website: https://daily.redbullmusicacademy.com/2015/07/london-techno-untold-story
8   A few years back I wrote a detailed piece charting the rise of this scene for RBMA, which I'd like to point you in the direction of: https://daily.redbullmusicacademy.com/specials/2016-ambient-house-feature/

the artists involved in their "Artificial Intelligence" movement until the mid-1990s, few made a significant impact. It was Electronica that the label's listeners now wanted, and they were more than happy to oblige.

Sadly, for Tuff Little Unit's Glyn Andrews and Zye Hill, they'd already parted company with Warp Records by the time Steve Beckett and Rob Mitchell decisively changed direction. 'Reflecting on it in the past couple of weeks, I've come to the conclusion that Rob and Steve tried to make us something we weren't for the good of the label at the time,' Andrews says. 'It just wasn't what we wanted at the time because we wanted to be more experimental. After we left, that's when they went more experimental. Maybe if we'd stuck around we'd have been involved with that stage of the Warp Records story.'

• • •

The festivities at Castlemorton in May 1992 came at a time when the previously united Hardcore rave scene was beginning to fracture. At the heart of the issue was a widening divide between those who wanted unbridled release - think endless sped-up piano riffs, squeaky female vocal samples and cartoonish electronic motifs -and those who preferred a moodier, darker sound built on thundering sub-bass pressure, raw synth hooks (more akin to the "Hoover" sounds of Belgian Hardcore techno) and sweaty, chopped-up drum breaks.

For the DJs, producers and dancers keen on the latter blend of musical elements, rave music was becoming too silly and cheesy. In their eyes it was becoming detached from the roots of both Bleep & Bass and Breakbeat Hardcore, eschewing the bass weight and Dub aesthetic borrowed from soundsystem culture in favour of a multi-coloured, laser-lit approximation of Hardcore Techno favoured by lads in hot hatchbacks and lasses in fluffy bras and day-glo face paint.

The inevitable split was decisive. The more carefree and exuberant end of the scene moved towards Happy Hardcore, a rushing sound popular at commercial raves and in provincial clubs, and in some areas bouncy Techno, a kind of precursor to what would later become the Yorkshire-founded sound of "Donk". Those wedded to heavy sub-bass and grittier sounds gravitated towards "Darkcore", a key stepping stone in British Bass music's move from Bleep & Bass to Jungle and Drum & Bass.

In all honesty, Darkcore had a relatively brief existence as a standalone genre, but it forms part of the organic development of Drum & Bass culture that would become the dominant form of British Bass music in the decades that followed.

Just as Bleep & Bass could be seen as a product of its environment and a musical reaction to life in impoverished, inner-city suburbs of forgotten post-industrial cities, Darkcore and the growing Jungle movement can be considered a later musical by-product of similar societal pressures.

Of course, not all of those who made Darkcore records were from crime-ridden housing estates in London, or for that matter young black men surrounded by gang warfare over the lucrative illegal drugs trade - it was a mixed scene, not just racially but also in terms of the gender of its acolytes - but it's certainly true to say that it was a far more edgy and intense than any Rave music that had come before it.

This darker, heavier and more bass-heavy variation of Breakbeat Hardcore was just the latest marker on the evolutionary journey being played out in Fabio and Grooverider's DJ sets at Rage. It was here where punters would scream the word "Jungle" when heavy breakbeat science was dropped, and where the combination of surging sub-bass and high-speed breakbeat rhythms inspired a whole generation of dancers and DJs and take to the studio and create their own fast, intense and sub-heavy records. If they succeeded, they might even hear their tunes over Heaven's sizable soundsystem.

'Rage had an amazing soundsystem, big bass bins on the floor and mids and tops flying around the balcony,' club regular and later Jungle and Drum & Bass pioneer Storm told *Red Bull Music Academy Daily* in 2015[9]. 'I've not heard many soundsystems like it in my whole career - everything about it was perfect. And the lighting in there... That was the first time we experienced the whole assault on the senses. Each week they'd bring something new.'

Fabio and Grooverider did not champion anything remotely like Happy Hardcore in their sets, instead preferring to dig for B-sides, instrumental dubs and weighty reworks that captured the seriousness and intensity they were after. Between 1990 and '92 there were plenty of tracks around that hit the spot, many of which drew power from rumbling, Dub style bass and a soon to be ubiquitous drum break original lifted from The Winstons Funk workout "Amen, Brother".

The two DJs could draw on some of the first releases from Rob Playford's Moving Shadow label, which the Hip-Hop kid turned Rave convert initially ran from the living room of his Stevenage home. The label's earliest singles in 1990, created by Playford as The Orbital Project/The O Project, featured Breakbeat Hardcore tracks peppered with samples from big records, including numerous Bleep & Bass ones (see "Dubstle" and "Hustle", which lifted the "Testone" bleeps), as well as insanely heavy low-end frequencies.

No doubt Fabio and Grooverider would also have reached for some of the label's superb 1991 releases, from the heavily Bleep-influenced, Dubwise breakbeat minimalism of Earth Leakage Trip's "Psychotronic EP", to the Proto-Jungle funkiness of Kaotic Chemistry's "Drumtrip" and 2 Bad Mice's colossal "Bombscare", which is now one of the most revered rave tracks of the era.

Then there was the output of Forest Gate's Ibiza Records, whose 1991 and early '92 releases from Noise Factory distilled the essence of rave culture's bass-heavy variants and packaged them in a form that would now be considered Jungle. Noise Factory was the work of a producer called James Stephens, who cut his teeth making electronic Reggae dubplates for Tottenham's Unity soundsystem before moving towards Breakbeat Hardcore. Through tracks like "Imperative" and "Warehouse Music", Stephens delivered his take on Jungle Techno, fusing the Dub bass and alien electronics of Bleep with the bustle of Breakbeat Hardcore. "Be Free", a 1992 B-side, could also be considered one of the first Dub-powered Jungle records[10].

'Producers in England were trying to recreate what Groove and Fabio were putting in the mix with Techno, Acid, Breakbeat and House all together,' Storm explained to RBMA. 'It became our religion. Goldie was infected by it like we were. We would come home from Rage and he was like, "Right, I'm gonna make this music, you two are going to play it, we're going to make a label, we're going to find a club".'

Goldie, real name Clifford Price, grew up in the West Midlands obsessed by Electro, breakdancing and Hip-Hop culture. He'd been a familiar face on the all-dayer scene in the region in the mid-1980s, before moving to New York. When Price returned, he ended up in London, where he soon became a Rage regular and an active member of the extended Reinforced Records crew in Dollis Hill.

By this point Reinforced had yet to fully move away from the Bleep & Breaks sound they'd helped popularize - see the "LFO" chords and melody samples on Nebula II's "Anathema" - but like many within London's Rage-infected Hardcore community, their releases were getting progressively darker. The label's Rufige Cru collective, whose members included Goldie, led the way in this regard, beginning with the "Darkrider EP" in 1991. Their tracks were formidable cut-and-paste affairs, where drums, bass, hooks, stabs and melodies were often lifted wholesale from past and present records. Listen hard enough to the first few Rufige Cru records, and you'll spot elements from Sweet Exorcist's "Clonk's Coming" and Brothers Grimm's Bleep & Breaks workout "Deja-Vu".

Goldie would go on to help to define Darkcore further in 1992 and early '93 with a string of Rufige Cru and Metalheadz tracks. The latter's debut EP contained two key cuts, "Terminator" and "Sinister", which became foundation records of the sound alongside tracks by DJ Hype, Nasty Habits,

---

10   Robert Gordon cites Paul Ibiza, who ran the label, and James Stephens as two of the London producers who got what he and his colleagues were trying to achieve with Bleep & Bass. He also says he put 'musical messages' into some of his productions as a response to Stephens' Bleep references.

Boogie Times Tribe (one of a number of Suburban Base-signed acts exploring the moodier and more bass-heavy end of the Hardcore/Proto-Jungle
spectrum), EQ and Origin Unknown (the peerless "Valley of the Shadows").
Combined with the parallel Ragga-Jungle movement that began to gather
pace in 1993, Darkcore defined the blueprint for what would become Jungle
and Drum & Bass.

It's interesting to note at this point that some of the earliest Proto-Jungle
records - those tracks produced and released before Jungle was considered
a specific genre, but which bear many of the same aural hallmarks - were
made by Gerald Simpson, the man whose timeless "Voodoo Ray" release
helped inspire the birth of Bleep & Bass. From 1991 onwards, Simpson
started making booming, bass-heavy records with breakbeats that were
more in keeping with the London-focused Darkcore scene than the still
baggy and loved-up sound that was popular in his home city of Manchester.

Simpson's 1991 and '92 releases on Juice Box, in particular, are peppered with Proto-Jungle jams of the highest quality. The most potent examples include "28 Gun Badboy", a record that sounds like a bridge between
Bleep, Breakbeat Hardcore and what would become Jungle, and the heavily
Reggae and Ragga influenced "King of the Jungle" and "Free Africa". The
fact that Simpson was drawn towards this sound and helped shape its
development offers further proof of the thread running through from his
earliest singles and Yorkshire Bleep & Bass to the explosion of Jungle
and Drum & Bass culture that was such a feature of British dance music
in the mid-1990s.

Some sonic aspects of the growing Jungle movement also inspired
Robert Gordon, though it would take a while for any of his experiments in
the style to see the light of day (you can hear some on his 1996 solo album
"Robert Gordon Projects", which contained tracks produced at different
points in the years following his expulsion from Warp).

'I loved Jungle and bought a lot of it for my own pleasure[11],' Gordon
enthuses. 'During the Jungle era, I didn't make any records because I was
enjoying everyone else's. I went partying and enjoyed all of it. The systems
got fitted for heavy bass so they could handle it, and I got some bass massag-
ing and did some stepping. My attitude was: you don't need me, this is good.'

Gordon kept in close contact with the many friends and kindred spirits
he made within the Jungle scene when it began blossoming in 1993[12] and
'94. He's keen to point out that the scene's predominantly black creators -
those from London and Bristol - suffered in the sound's early years thanks

---

11   He also says he bought a number of bass-heavy London Hardcore records in 1990
and '91, much to the disgust of his friends Winston Hazel and Richard Barratt, who outright
hated the style at the time – or at least the earliest expressions of it and what they saw as weak
breakbeat copies of Bleep.
12   Rage shut its doors at the end of 1993, by which point the movement Fabio and
Grooverider helped inspire had outposts of its own in clubs and bedroom studios throughout the
UK.

to a combination of negative media coverage (it was portrayed as being associated with inner-city violence and gang warfare) and what he saw as racist attitudes within the music industry.

'The attitude [from the music industry establishment] was, "Go back home and do your own jungle bunny music",' he rages. 'That's why we adopted the phrase and used it ourselves. What I'm trying to say is that the BBC and Radio 1 especially ignored it for four years. There was Jungle-mania and the mainstream media ignored it. All the Jungle labels were frustrated and the DJs and producers seemed to feel the same way. We felt that we'd been pushed out by the big labels. So we put it to a vote at a meeting in London and agreed not to sign major label deals. We wanted to freeze out big business. Then Goldie walked into a major label contract and became a media darling.'

More intriguingly, Gordon also says that had he still been involved with Warp during the time when Darkcore and Jungle were mutating from Bleep & Bass and Breakbeat Hardcore, the label would have proudly represented the style. 'Jungle is basically that first Warp compilation, "Pioneers of the Hypnotic Groove", with drum breaks on it,' he asserts. 'That's Jungle. Warp should have been a pioneer in the Jungle scene. It would have been if I was still there, but ours wouldn't have been dirty street music, it would have been accurately produced and very well mixed.'

JOIN THE FUTURE

THE ENDURING LEGACY OF BLEEP & BASS

'Bleep provided the essential elements: the building blocks of the UK sound that followed. You can take these elements and do something new, but the fundamentals are still there.'

NEIL LANDSTRUMM

On a muggy, windswept night in August 2019, three veterans of Sheffield's original Bleep & Bass scene are sat in the living room of a cramped house in the Heeley area of the city, just down the hill from the secondary school where they first met. Zye Hill, Glyn Andrews and Sean Maher have got together to listen back to a box full of DAT tapes dated 1990 and '91.

Hill and Andrews produced the music contained on the tapes when they were working towards the possible release of a Tuff Little Unit album that never materialized. I've been invited along to share the experience, in part to get a sense of the direction they took following the release of the record whose title has been borrowed for this book, "Join The Future".

With a glass of Guinness in hand and a notebook full of scribbled lines at his feet, Andrews methodically works through tape after tape of eye-opening tracks. In front of him on the coffee table is a vintage TASCAM DAT machine, which in turn is connected to an especially beefy-sounding home soundsystem. As the tracks play, both he and Hill sit quietly with their eyes closed and soft smiles on their faces.

While the rush of nostalgic memories is powerful, their pleasure seems to be derived primarily from the sounds surging from Andrews' over-sized speakers: subsonic vibrations, densely layered off-kilter electronics and tough - sorry, 'tuff' - rhythms that have not been aired privately or publicly for the best part of three decades.

Aside from the heaviness and skewed funkiness of the surprisingly experimental music, what strikes me is how ahead-of-the-times many of these unreleased, mostly un-named tracks sound. One features Zye Hill's younger self uttering the words 'blow up the system' in a heavily accented Jamaican accent above a booming fusion of punchy, Dancehall-influenced drums, surging synthesizer motifs and bass so heavy it can rattle your teeth. In fact, such is the subsonic intensity of one of the bass parts that I wouldn't be surprised if dogs within a four-mile radius were sent scurrying behind sofas and below kitchen tables in search of cover. 'You might want to re-edit that to take out that frequency,' Sean Maher says to Hill while holding a sizable spliff. She nods in agreement.

Another track sounds like a blueprint for what would later become Drum & Bass, though Hill and Andrews' particular brand of leftfield industrial futurism is miles apart from the typical D&B club sound. As the evening moves on and more tracks are aired - including a handful made with their regular vocalist Warren Peart - I'm struck by how it is possible to hear elements of later British Bass music developments, including Dubstep and the kind of broken Techno so beloved of the producers associated with Bristol labels such as Livity Sound and Idle Hands. It brings me neatly back to the idea that first inspired this book, namely that British dance music - and its sub-bass-heavy variations in particular - owes a huge, largely unacknowledged debt to the pioneers of the short-lived Bleep & Bass sound.

Before heading to Andrews' house for this surprise listening session, I'd spent a couple of hours hanging out with Robert Gordon in the backyard of the terraced house he's lived in since the late 1980s. When I arrived, he was discussing building a new PA system with two elder friends from the Sheffield Reggae scene. One, a smiling pensioner called Wesley, founded the Steel City's first Reggae band in 1971, introducing South Yorkshire to the delights of Bob Marley and the Wailers via covers of the band's early Jamaican hits. To prove his point, he sings a snatch of "Small Axe" with a soulful inflection that fills the early evening air.

It's a timely reminder of the groundwork that was laid for later British dance music developments - and Bleep & Bass in particular - by the generations that came before Robert Gordon and his contemporaries: first or second-wave Caribbean immigrants whose parents headed to Britain's industrial towns and cities in order to secure work. Wesley's father worked for British Steel and later Laycocks, while his mother was a nurse at Nether Edge Hospital[1]. All of his family suffered racist abuse in those early years, but he says it has never really gone away: just days before our meeting, he was drenched with liquid thrown by the driver of a passing car.

---

1   It turns out she was still working in the maternity unit when I was born, so there's a possibility she may even have been in the delivery room when I entered the world bawling and screaming with severely jaundiced skin. How's that for synchronicity?

Sat on his back step, Robert Gordon listens intently. We discuss his youth in the late 1970s and early '80s, a time when racial barriers were breaking down within the city. He grew up within the Brutalist 'streets in the sky' of the Park Hill housing estate, the remnants of which are currently undergoing redevelopment courtesy of gentrification specialists Urban Splash.

From where he's sat, Gordon can see the concrete-clad complex a few hundred metres away, its angular frame covered in scaffolding. He says that race was not an issue amongst the young people who lived in Park Hill and its partner complex at Hyde Park; what united them was their ordinariness and membership of Sheffield's sizable working class. 'Bleep & Bass was not black music or white music,' he says. 'It was made by black people and white people, but they were working people. It was working people's music.'

● ● ●

Framing Britain's late-1980s/early-90s Acid House revolution as a primarily working class movement is not a new idea, but it does have much merit. The artist Jeremy Deller has extensively explored the idea in his work, first joining the dots between early UK dance music culture and brass band music - an earlier expression of working class musical culture popular in the North of England - on his 1997 collaboration with Stockport's Williams Fairey Band, "Acid Brass".

More recently he expanded his theory via the 2019 BBC4 documentary *Everybody In The Place: An Incomplete History of Britain 1984-92.* In it, Deller frames Acid House and UK rave culture, including the thrilling new musical genres it birthed, as a social and cultural uprising from within the 'left-behind' working class communities of post-industrial British towns and cities.

While this does not tell the whole story - the impact of ecstasy and dance music culture was felt throughout society, inspiring young people from different backgrounds - it is a hypothesis that rings true when it comes to Bleep & Bass and the similarly-minded electronic music movements that quickly erupted in the months and years following the release of A Guy Called Gerald's "Voodoo Ray" and Unique 3's "The Theme".

The emergence of Bleep & Bass was the logical conclusion of a story that had been building within the North of England, and Yorkshire in particular, since the dawn of the 1980s. The groundwork was laid during the Northern Soul era, when predominantly - but not exclusively - white working class men took drugs and danced all-day or all-night to mostly obscure black American Soul records made in and around Detroit, America's most notorious example of a once mighty industrial city decimated by factory closures.

By the early-80s, this all-dayer-driven scene had mutated into something entirely different, where young black dancers raised on Jamaican soundsystem culture began dominating dancefloors while demanding DJs played the hottest Jazz-Funk and, later, Electro records. They travelled all over the country to dance, walking from their homes in racially mixed inner city neighbourhoods to catch coaches to Manchester, Sheffield, Huddersfield, Leeds, Birmingham, Nottingham and Leicester.

Electro, in turn, drew in more dance music converts from different ethnic and social groups, from kids in tower blocks and low rise council estates to middle class suburbanites and young people from towns and cities with little or no black music pedigree.

When Chicago House - and later Detroit Techno - records first hit the UK, they were championed by DJs who came from, and played music to, this audience. The same could be said of the way House slowly took root in London, where soundsystem culture and a love of Hip-Hop and Electro were common within the mixed-race working class communities dotted around the metropolis.

Once the groundwork had been laid, all it needed was a spark to ignite an entire musical movement. That came from a handful of pioneering records, many of which are covered in detail in this book, whose raw, sparse and intense sounds not only reflected the shared backgrounds of their creators but also the declining industry and bleak economic conditions of the cities in which they lived.

Thanks to an inherent sense of local and regional rivalry, something evident in wider society but particularly prevalent within both Hip-Hop and soundsystem culture, it wasn't long before "answer records" from crews in other towns and cities began appearing in stores. These breathtaking, mind-altering missives were then amplified and distributed to all four corners of the nation via a network of clubs, warehouse parties and illegal raves during the UK's ecstasy-fuelled Acid House revolution.

'There's an absolute direct line from the post-Northern Soul Electro scene to Bleep & Bass and beyond,' says Vaughan Allen, a former dance music and club culture journalist who first filed copy in the Acid House era. 'People forget the importance of that within communities in northern cities that otherwise had nothing else. That is totally ignored in the standard history of Acid House. It's usually written as if it came from these actually quite posh kids going to Ibiza and then recreating that when they came back.'

Setting aside the wider Acid House and rave movement, whose growth was driven by a number of other factors that aren't the concern of this book, the result of this 'direct line from the post-Northern Soul Electro scene to Bleep & Bass and beyond' was a distinctly British electronic music identity whose conception can be traced back to A Guy Called Gerald's "Voodoo Ray" and the records made in Yorkshire in response.

In other words, Gerald Simpson proved that it was possible to break the mould and instill British-made music with sounds and stylistic traits inspired by the specific experiences of young, mostly working class young people in post-industrial UK towns and cities. Bleep & Bass was the first major response to this revelation and therefore provided a neat set of sonic instructions which could then be built upon and twisted into new shapes to fit specific local, regional and eventually international audiences.

'Bleep gave a blueprint to society,' Winston Hazel asserts. 'People started making the equivalent of what they'd heard more and more and more. Stuff became popular on a regional scale and then nationally. Then you can't help but be influenced by that because it's everywhere.'

So what, then, was this blueprint? Listen to formative Bleep & Bass records from the likes of Unique 3, Forgemasters, Nightmares on Wax, LFO, Sweet Exorcist, Ability II, Ital Rockers and others and you'll find the following aspects in differing amounts: the body-popping punch of Electro; the sample thievery and aggressive rivalry of Hip-Hop; the sci-fi futurism and machine soul of early Detroit Techno; the clanking intensity of Industrial music; the driving and jacking rhythms of Chicago House; the mind-altering rush of the ecstasy experience and the attitude-laden strut of ground-level creative rebellion. The single most important ingredient of all, though, was Jamaican soundsystem culture. The expression of this influence in Bleep & Bass was the sound's most revolutionary aspect of all, and the aspect that still resonates to this day.

Listen to a range of Bleep & Bass - and later Bleep & Breaks - tracks and you'll hear a number of specific things drawn from Jamaican music and the soundsystem culture that grew up alongside it. Naturally, the importance of deep bass and subsonic sound frequencies is key, but also the rhythmic similarities between House and Techno and the 'Steppers' style of Reggae music.

The best Bleep records mimic the minimalist construction of Dub, where the space around the sparsely arranged musical elements is just as important as the bass and drums beneath. Those sparse, high register melodic elements - the famous "bleeps" - could also be compared to the echoing blips and electronic noises often used in both Dub records and via the simple effects units utilized by many soundsystem operators during performances.

From Bleep onwards, these elements borrowed from soundsystem culture have become, in differing degrees, the defining characteristics of a hatful of electronic music styles pioneered in the United Kingdom. They were there in the post-Bleep styles of Breakbeat Hardcore, Darkcore and Jungle, but also in later strands such as Speed Garage, Bassline - a style still sometimes referred to as "the Niche sound" in reference to the Sheffield club that made it famous - and UK Funky.

Pointing out these links is something that many analytical British music writers have done over the years, most notably Simon Reynolds. He calls this "the Hardcore Continuum", and it has much merit. Where I disagree with his analysis is the weight and emphasis he gives to different aspects of the story. For example, he acknowledges that Bleep & Bass was one of the earliest expressions of this but generally sees it as a kind of Northern sideshow to the main events of Breakbeat Hardcore and Jungle in London. I'd argue that many early Breakbeat Hardcore records were in fact responses to Bleep - and in particular "The Theme", "Ital's Anthem", "Track With No Name", "Testone", "Pressure Dub" and "LFO" - tailored to more accurately reflect the strength of the Hip-Hop scene in and around London.

There's no doubt that London is British dance music's spiritual home, and that many post-Bleep developments were primarily driven by those in the city with similar musical and social backgrounds to their predecessors up north. I'd still argue though that these developments can trace their roots back to a Bradford bedroom in the summer of 1988 and that Reynolds' natural focus on London is based more on what has happened in the three decades since Bleep than what actually created the 'Hardcore Continuum' in the first place.

Some will see this as pedantry, but I firmly believe that it is important to give due credit to 'the pioneers of the hypnotic groove' (to borrow the title of Warp Records' first label compilation). During the years spent researching this book, many DJs and producers from within British dance music have expressed similar sentiments. Scottish DJ, producer and label owner JD Twitch probably puts it most succinctly: 'You can trace a lot of things happening now right back to Bleep & Bass. A couple of years back I did a podcast looking at British Bass culture, and you couldn't tell which records were made in 1990 and which were made in 2012. It all seemed to merge into one.'

• • •

The day before I called in on Bleep pioneers Robert Gordon and Tuff Little Unit in early August 2019, I spent some time wandering around the Park Hill estate in which they grew up. These days, the vast site is partway through being completely transformed as part of a bid to update the listed site for the 21st century. That in itself has proved controversial within Sheffield, with plenty complaining that the utopian, meritocratic spirit in which it was first built - think futuristic 'streets in the sky' housing working people at affordable prices - has been ignored in favour of gentrified homes for the privileged and wealthy.

Although one of the vast blocks has been brought up to date, work on the rest of the site has yet to be completed. So while the front portion that looms over Sheffield city centre is impressively modern - 21st century Corbusier style Brutalism, perhaps - those that sit behind it are in various stages of disrepair. Aside from providing temporary homes to drug addicts, squatters and homeless people desperate for somewhere to shelter for the night, these blocks have not changed since the last permanent tenants moved out in the mid-1990s.

Nestled in the shadow of one of these blocks within a former car park lies the S1 Artspace, a gallery run by mostly local 20 and 30-somethings still wrestling with how to engage more of the local community. I stumbled inside out of pure curiosity and found a cluster of enthusiastic, knowledgeable staff whose leisure activities revolve around Sheffield's still vibrant underground Techno and Electro scene.

What struck me, aside from their passion for the estate in which they're based, was these young women's extensive knowledge of Yorkshire's electronic music history. They seemed to feel like they were part of a new wave of artists, event promoters, DJs, dancers and producers who are merely the latest custodians of the Steel City's electronic music heritage.

They knew the role that Park Hill, in particular, had played in Sheffield's musical history, though not that a number of Bleep & Bass pioneers had lived here during the late-70s and 1980s. Even more impressive was their instinctive understanding of how the music discussed in this book was still a big part of British Bass music's DNA.

They're not the only people of their generation to have spotted this. During the five years spent researching and writing *Join The Future*, I've encountered many others who have made the very same connections, each time thinking aloud what had long gone unspoken or unwritten. The links were always there but, for one reason or another, successive generations of writers and critics have not made them - or at least not in a particularly comprehensive manner.

'Bleep is mysterious, and it will always be slightly hidden away or covered up,' Luca Lozano told me in 2014. 'It's not like Detroit Techno, where there are so many documentaries and we know the whole story about the founding fathers. Bleep & Bass will always remain a mystery, which makes it all the more alluring.'

In the days leading up to my stroll around Park Hill, I'd enjoyed several conversations with a young Sheffield DJ, producer and radio host who goes by the artistic alias Utah[2]. He initially got in touch regarding an hour-long documentary he was making for online station NTS, which aimed to join the dots between Bleep & Bass and many of the records he's enjoyed since first becoming a passionate follower of British Bass music. These myriad influences - think Dubstep, Grime, UK Funky, Bassline and polyrhythmic Techno as well as original Bleep & Bass tracks - can be heard across the EPs he's delivered for Coyote Records and Symbols.

I'd long been hearing elements I'd associate with early Bleep & Bass tracks in contemporary Bass music releases, from the murky, late-night hedonism of Bruce's "Sonder Somatic" (check the clonks, surging sub-bass and off-kilter rhythms of "Cacao" and the rhythmic steel of "Meek"), and the sparse post-Dubstep, Dancehall-influenced creepiness of Peverlist and

---

2   It's actually "Utah?" on his releases for the avoidance of doubt.

Kowton's "Raw Code", to the buzzing rave-era revivalism of Paul Woolford's phenomenally successful Special Request project and the bleeping tunefulness of South African producer DJ Mujava's "Township Funk". Aside from Woolford, I doubt that many of these producers were specifically riffing on Bleep & Bass, but rather putting their own twist on the 'fundamental elements' that have been there since the style emerged in the late 1980s.

Utah was kind enough to provide examples of records that he thought expressed a conscious or subconscious influence from Bleep & Bass, or at the very least come from a similar sonic place. He started with Grime, a particularly raw, sparse and stripped-back style that has become one of the dominant forms of British popular music in the last decade.

'I definitely think you can hear it in some of Youngstar's records,' he explained. 'He stripped things down to the bare bones for "Pulse X" in a similar spirit to a lot of the minimalism found in early Bleep tunes, while "The Formula" to me has a proper Forgemasters sound - a bit industrial with plenty of bass and cowbell. Other tunes like "Raw To Da Floor" have that big focus on the sub, and when pitched down parts of it wouldn't go amiss in between two Bleep tracks.'

He went on to name further cuts by Alias, Ruff Sqwad and DJ Mondie, before talking in more general terms about Grime: 'The sound has several tunes with similar synth vocal motifs to Bleep & Bass, though it's hard to tell whether this was a direct influence or accidental. Some tracks have a moody atmosphere, industrial sounds, a sub-bass focus and a haunting sparseness.'

Utah also pointed me in the direction of UK Funky and bass-heavy Techno producers such as Champion, Lil' Silva, Walton and Beneath, whose darker tunes can be considered a more intense and mind-altering contemporary take on the Bleep & Bass template. 'With a lot of these records, what I hear is a clear influence from soundsystem culture, minimalism and really heavy sub-bass,' Utah said. 'A lot of functional early UK Funky tunes have the distinctive "electronic" quality I would associate with Bleep.'

If I asked the same question to a range of contemporary British DJs and producers, they'd no doubt point me the direction of hundreds of other records made in the last decade that can, in one way or another, be linked back to the sonic trademarks of Bleep & Bass. Whether deliberate or not, most bass-heavy British dance music can trace its roots back to the early creative rebellion that was Bleep & Bass. Perhaps now, 30 years on from the release of the first Yorkshire Bleep records, it's time that this was more widely acknowledged.

'I feel that those Bleep & Bass producers just hit upon the purest distilled essence of club music,' Scottish Techno producer Neil Landstrumm says. 'It's perennially valid, timeless and current sounding no matter what stage or phase of the musical cycle you're in. Every few years it seems to pop up: Grime, Sub-Low, Dubstep, Garage. The ghosts of Bleep are still there.'

BLEEPOGRAPHY

RECOMMENDED RECORDS
AND FURTHER LISTENING

What follows is a chapter-by-chapter breakdown of recommended tracks, records and releases that are in some way relevant to the story being told. Some influenced what became Bleep & Bass, while others were in turn influenced by Bleep. Others are referenced in the text, form part of the wider story or are simply interesting singles, albums or compilations worthy of mention. There are also a small number of recommendations for documentaries, television shows and video clips that provide further context or explore a particular avenue being discussed in a specific chapter.

Please note that this is not meant to be a comprehensive list of every single Bleep & Bass record ever made, though in some cases I have included lesser-known or overlooked releases that there wasn't space to fit in the main body text. In some cases, I've also included explanatory text to justify my selections. Note that many of the recommended releases included in this list, and referenced in the book, are not yet available digitally from services such as Apple Music, Spotify and Deezer. However, most of those that aren't can be listened to via the main YouTube website and app.

A more in-depth 'Bleepography' focused specifically on the style will be added to jointhefuture.net in due course.

GENERAL LISTENING

There are relatively few dedicated Bleep & Bass compilations currently available, aside from Join The Future: Bleep Techno & Early British Bass Music 1988-92, a companion release to this book available on Cease & Desist Records. Warp's Pioneers of the Hypnotic Groove and Warp 10+2: Classics '89-'92 collections provide a good overview of that particular label's Bleep-era output, while Network's Bio Rhythm: Dance Music With Bleeps collections (which have been reissued on vinyl in recent years) should also be essential listening.

Another good option is Richard Sen's This Ain't Chicago: The Underground Sound of UK House & Acid 1987-91 (Strut Records, 2012); although it's not Bleep-specific, it does give a good overview of the changing nature of UK House (and, to a lesser extent, techno) during a key period. The same could be said of Fabio and Grooverider's 30 Years of Rage compilations on Above Board Distribution, which effectively showcase tracks made and released during the earliest days of the British Bass music movement (Acid

House, Techno, Bleep, Breakbeat Hardcore, Darkcore, Jungle etc.). They selected both tracks from the UK and those from Europe/North America, so it's possible to hear the exchange of ideas that fed into the movement documented in this book.

CHAPTER BY CHAPTER RECOMMENDATIONS

INTRODUCTION: WEIGHT FROM THE BASS

Recordings of Winston Hazel and George Evelyn's DJ sets from Boiler Room's Sheffield Shaped The Future event at the Southbank Warehouse are available via the Boiler Room's Soundcloud account (https://soundcloud.com/platform/sets/boiler-room-sheffield-shaped).

PART ONE: RHYTHM TAKES CONTROL

CHAPTER ONE: CULTURE CLASH

There's not much in the way of recommended listening, but I would suggest watching the Taskforce Chapeltown (1986) and Chapeltown: One Year On (1987) documentaries, both of which can be accessed for free via the BFI Player (https://player.bfi.org.uk/). The same website also includes another excellent Yorkshire Television documentary from 1987 about residents of the Manor council housing estate. Titled Made in Sheffield, the 30-minute film focuses on the extreme lengths some jobless Sheffielders went to in order to get by as the city suffered through the effects of rapid de-industrialization.

CHAPTER TWO: THE DANCE

There are plenty of compilations available that will give you a good overview of the sounds that fired the all-dayer scene during the Northern Soul, Jazz-Funk and Electro era. Good places to start with Northern Soul include: The Northern Soul Story series on BMG/Sony/Music On Vinyl (each of the four volumes focuses on records made popular at a different iconic venue - the Twisted Wheel, the Golden Torch, the Blackpool Mecca and the Wigan Casino), Northern Soul Floorfillers (Demon Records, 2017), Northern Soul All Nighter (One Day Music/Not Now Music, 2014), Andy Smith's Northern Soul (BGP Records, 2005), Northern Soul Floorshakers (Music Club, 1996) and the six volumes in Kent Dance's Northern Soul's Classiest Rarities series (2001-2017).

As for Jazz-Funk, you can do no better than head for Mastercruts' Jazz-Funk Classics series (1991-94). The first five volumes give an excellent introduction to the kind of Jazz-Funk jams that were popular on UK dance-floors in the late '70s and early '80s. Also worth a listen are Z Records' Back Street Brit Funk compilations, which focus on UK-made variations of Jazz-Funk, Disco, Boogie and Electrofunk from the same period. In terms of Electro, I'd suggest exploring the Street Sounds Electro and Street Sounds Crucial Electro compilation series, which ran between 1983 and '88. Some are better than others, but all were hugely important at the time. 1984's Street Sounds UK Electro compilation is an absolute must.

The following albums and singles are also pertinent for different reasons and are well worth a listen:

• Afrika Bambaataa & The Soulsonic Force - *Planet Rock - The Album* (Tommy Boy, 1986)
• Chick Corea - *The Leprechaun* (Polydor, 1976) / *Tap Step* (Warner Bros. Records, 1980) / *Touchstone* (Warner Bros. Records, 1982)
• Cybotron - *Enter* (Fantasy, 1983) / *Techno City* (Fantasy, 1984)
• Hashim - *Al-Naafiysh (The Soul)* (Cutting Records, 1983)
• Herbie Hancock - *Head Hunters* (Columbia, 1973) / *Lite Me Up* (CBS, 1982) / *Future Shock* (CBS, 1983)
• Kraftwerk - *Trans-Europe Express* (EMI, 1977) / *The Man Machine* (Capitol Records, 1978) / *Computer World* (EMI, 1981) / *Tour De France (Remix)* (EMI, 1983)
• Malcolm McLaren - *Buffalo Gals* (with the World Famous Supreme Team) (Charisma, 1982) / *Duck Rock* (Charisma, 1983)
• Mantronix - *The Album* (Sleeping Bag/10 Records, 1985)
• Run DMC - *Run-DMC* (Profile Records, 1984)
• Various Artists - *Tommy Boy - Greatest Beats* (Tommy Boy, 1985)
• World Class Wreckin' Cru - *World Class* (Kru-Cut Records, 1985)
• Yellow Magic Orchestra - *Yellow Magic Orchestra* (Alfa/A&M, 1978) / *Technodelic* (Alfa/A&M, 1981) / *After Service* (Alfa, 1984)

CHAPTER 3: RIDDIM IS FULL OF CULTURE

The 1980s was a crucial time for soundsystem culture, with Dub and Reggae music undergoing significant changes thanks to the popularity of electronic instrumentation. This was naturally reflected in the music played at sound clashes and Blues parties, with each "sound" or illicit venue having their own particular blend (for example, some stuck to more traditional Roots Reggae records while others embraced the brave new world that accompanied the 'digital riddims' that increased in popularity as the decade increased).

My suggestion would be to listen to a wide range of Jamaican and British Dub, Reggae and Dancehall. If you can find a copy, Honest Jon's 2002 compilation of British Dancehall, Watch How The People Dancing - Unity Sounds From The London Dancehall, 1986-89 is a must (especially as some of the producers involved would later play a role in the rise of Bleep & Breaks, Darkcore and Jungle), while a number of key labels also released vinyl compilations during the period that offer neat introductions to their particular take.

Jammy's sets 1985 Master Mega Hits - Sleng Teng Extravaganza and Sleng Teng Extravaganza: 1985 Master Mega Hits Volume 2 showcase the significance and influence of the now-infamous "Sleng Teng Riddim". The Wackie's collections African Roots Act 2 (1982), African Roots Act 3 (1983) and Best of Champions (1990) offer an indication not only of how times were changing but also the influence of that imprint's Dub and Dancehall output. I'd also recommend hunting down some of the output of King Tubby's digital-era imprint Firehouse, particularly the Firehouse - Waterhouse II (1986) and King Tubby's Presents Soundclash Dubplate Style (1988) compilations.

Another important aspect of the story told in this chapter is the growing appreciation of early House and Techno by some within the British soundsystem scene, particularly in Yorkshire. Because of this, the list below also includes some key records from Chicago and Detroit.

* Adonis - *No Way Back* (Trax Records, 1986)
* Creation Rebel - *Starship Africa* (4D Rhythms, 1980) / *Creation Rebel vs New Age Steppers - Threat To Creation* (Cherry Red, 1981) / *Return From Space* (RCR, 1984)
* Hercules - *7 Ways* (Dance Mania, 1986)
* Jah Shaka - *Kings Music* (Jah Shaka Music, 1984) / *Commandments of Dub 4 - Dub Almighty* (Jah Shaka Music, 1985) / *Jah Dub Creator (Commandments of Dub Part 5)* (Jah Shaka Music, 1985) / *Commandments of Dub Chapter 9 - Coronation Dub* (Jah Shaka Music, 1989)
* Jah Shaka meets Mad Professor - *At Ariwa Sounds* (Ariwa, 1984)
* Mad Professor - *A Caribbean Taste of Technology* (Ariwa, 1983) / *Mad Professor Captures Pato Banton* (with Pato Banton, Ariwa, 1985) / *Dub Me Crazy 7: The Adventures of a Dub Sampler* (Ariwa, 1987) / *Dub Me Crazy 8: Experiments of the Aural Kind* (Ariwa, 1988)
* Model 500 - *No UFO's* (Metroplex, 1985) / *Sound Of Stereo / Off To Battle* (Metroplex, 1987) / *Interference/Electronic* (Metroplex, 1988)
* Mr Fingers - *Mystery of Love* (Alleviated, 1985) / *Amnesia* (Jack Trax, 1988)
* New Age Steppers - *The New Age Steppers* (On-U-Sound, 1980) / *Action Battlefield* (Statik Records, 1981) / *Foundation Steppers* (On-U-Sound, 1983)
* Playgroup - *Epic Sound Battles - Chapter One* (Cherry Red, 1982) / *Epic Sound Battles - Chapter Two* (Cherry Red/On-U-Sound, 1983)

- Steve Poindexter - *Computer Madness* (from *Work That Mutha Fucker EP*, Muzique Records, 1989)
- Prince Jammy - *Prince Jammy Destroys The Invaders* (Greensleeves, 1982) / *Computerized Dub* (Greensleeves, 1986)
- Reese - *Just Want Another Chance* (Incognito Records, 1988)
- Scientist - *Scientist Meets The Space Invaders* (Greensleeves, 1981) / *In Dub* (Jah Guidance, 1983)
- Scientist vs The Professor - *Dub Duel at King Tubby's* (Kingdom Records, 1983)
- Wayne Smith - *Sleng Teng* (Greensleeves, 1986)

CHAPTER 4: HOUSE PARTY

The changing nature of Yorkshire's club scene was in some ways reflective of wider trends in dance music in both America and Europe. The best way to quickly get a grasp of the most significant changes is to listen to a few albums and compilations representing each of the most significant musical movements and important sub-genres. We've already covered Electro and Jazz-Funk, so begin with checking out the Post-Disco/Proto-House era NYC vibes of Dimitri From Paris Presents Night Dubbin' on BBE (2009), before working your way through Dave Lee's excellent Washington Go-Go retrospective, Go Go Get Down: Pure Ghetto Funk From Washington D.C. (Z Records, 2012) and the first two volumes in the Classic Rare Groove series on Mastercuts (released in 1993 and '94 respectively). In terms of 1980s Hip-Hop, few compilations cover all bases, so I've included some of the most popular dancefloor tracks and influential albums in the list below, alongside other records popular in Yorkshire's clubs.

It feels like we all know the history of Chicago House instinctively, but there are still options for those who require an introduction to the sound. If you can find a copy of BCM's epic, 15-CD retrospective The History of the House Sound of Chicago (1988) then that's worthy of attention, primarily because it includes both tracks that influenced the style plus a whole heap of early Windy City House cuts; if not, then The House Sound of Chicago on London Records (1986) and any Trax Records retrospective (the Bill Brewster compiled Sources: The Trax Records Anthology on Harmless from 2015 is my current favourite) should provide a good overview of the formative years of that sound. For the harder end of the Chicago spectrum, Acid: Can U Jack? Chicago Acid & Experimental House 1985-95 on Soul Jazz Records (2005) is a great place to start.

10 Records' two Techno! The New Dance Sound of Detroit compilations (released 1988 and 1990 respectively) are historically significant primers for the Motor City sound, while the four-disc TSOB: The Sound of Belgium

(La Musique Fait La Force, 2013) does a terrific job in chronicling the country's dance music story from New Beat to Trance via EBM, Industrial, Hardcore and Techno.

Finally, should you want an introduction to the Balearic sound, then FFRR's infamous 1988 Balearic Beats compilation is a must - if only to read Terry Farley's slack-jawed, loved-up sleeve notes ("I'm on one, matey" etc.)

- The 45 King - *The Master of the Game* (Tuff City, 1988)
- Adonis - *We're Rocking Down The House* (TRAX Records, 1987) / *Acid Poke* (Desire Records, 1988)
- Rob Base & DJ E-Z Rock - *Get On The Dance Floor* (Profile Records, 1988) / *It Takes Two* (Profile Records, 1988) /
- Big Daddy Kane - *Long Live Kane* (Cold Chillin', 1988)
- Black Riot - *A Day In The Life/Warlock* (Fourth Floor Records/Champion, 1989)
- Circuit - *Release The Tension* (4th & Broadway, 1984)
- Colonel Abrams - *Music Is The Answer* (Streetwise, 1984) / *Trapped* (MCA Records, 1985)
- De La Soul - *Three Feet High & Rising* (Tommy Boy, 1989)
- "Fast" Eddie Smith - *Jack The House* (D.J International, 1987) / *Acid Thunder* (D.J International, 1988) / *Hip House* (D.J International, 1989)
- Cuba Gooding - *Happiness Is Just Around The Bend* (Streetwise/London Records, 1983)
- Hotline - *Rock This House* (Rhythm King, 1986)
- Kenny "Jammin" Jason & "Fast" Eddie Smith - *Can U Dance?* (D.J. International, 1987)
- J.M Silk - *Music Is The Key* (D.J International, 1985)
- King Bee - *Back By Dope Demand* (Torso Dance, 1990)
- Doug Lazy - *Let The Rhythm Pump* (Atlantic, 1989) / *Let It Roll* (Atlantic, 1989) / *Doug Lazy Gettin' Crazy* (Atlantic, 1990)
- LL Cool J - *Radio* (Def Jam, 1985) / *Bigger & Deffer* (BAD) (Def Jam, 1987)
- Mr Fingers - *Washing Machine* (TRAX Records, 1986) / Slam Dance (Alleviated Records, 1987) / *Amnesia* (Jack Trax, 1989)
- Main Source - *Looking At The Front Door* (Wild Pitch Records, 1990) / *Peace Is Not The Word To Play (Remix)* (Wild Pitch Records, 1991) / *Breaking Atoms* (Wild Pitch Records, 1991)
- Phuture - *Acid Tracks* (Trax Records, 1987) / *We Are Phuture* (Trax Records, 1988)
- Public Enemy - Yo! Bumrush The Show (Def Jam, 1987) / *It Takes A Nation of Millions To Hold Us Back* (Def Jam, 1988) / *Fear of a Black Planet* (Def Jam, 1990)
- Pushe - *Don't Take Your Love Away* (Partytime Records, 1984)
- Royal House - *Get Funky* (Idlers, 1989)

- Rhythim Is Rhythim - *Nude Photo* (Transmat, 1987) / *Strings of Life* (Transmat, 1987) / *It Is What It Is* (Transmat, 1988) / *Beyond The Dance* (Transmat, 1989)
- Serious Intention - *You Don't Know* (Easy Street Records, 1984) / *You Don't Know (Limited Edition Special Remix)* (Easy Street Records, 1984) / *Serious* (Pow Wow Records/London Records, 1986)
- The Paul Simpson Connection - *Treat Her Sweeter* (Easy Street Records/10 Records, 1985)
- Strafe - *Set It Off* (Jus Born Records, 1984)
- Subject - *The Magic, The Moment* (Pow Wow Records, 1985)
- Tyree - *Turn Up The Bass* (featuring Kool Roc Steady) (D.J International/ FFRR, 1988/89)
- Virgo/Virgo 4 - *Virgo* (Radical Records, 1989) / *Resurrection* (Rush Hour Recordings, 2011)
- Visual - The *Music Got Me* (Prelude Records, 1983; Note: the 2016 Ransom Note Records reissue of the 'original dub', credited to Boyd Jarvis, is worth picking up, if only for the Dan Tyler and Nick The Record re-dub on the flipside).

PART 2:
PIONEERS OF THE HYPNOTIC GROOVE

CHAPTER 5: BLOW YOUR HOUSE DOWN

To get an appreciation of Manchester House music during the period - or at least the specific strain covered in this chapter - take a trawl through the catalogues of T-Coy, 808 State and A Guy Called Gerald. Pretty much anything made between 1987 and 1990 will give you a good overview. Naturally, I've made some more specific selections below. Another key release is DeConstruction's 1988 compilation *North: The Sound of the Dance Underground*. If you want to get a feel of the more baggy and loved-up end of the "Madchester" spectrum, Happy Mondays' *Bummed* (1988), *Hallelujah* (1989) and *Pills 'N' Thrills And Bellyaches* (1990) naturally remain the touchstones.

- 808 State - *Let Yourself Go* (Creed Records, 1988) / *Newbuild LP* (Creed Records, 1988) / *Quadrastate EP* (Creed Records, 1989) / *90* (ZTT, 1989) / *The Extended Pleasure of Dance EP* (ZTT, 1990) / *Prebuild* (Rephlex Records, 2004; contains music recorded during the jam sessions with Gerald Simpson prior to the recording of *Newbuild*)
- A Guy Called Gerald - *Voodoo Ray EP* (Rham!, 1988) / *Hot Lemonade* (Rham!, 1988) / *Voodoo Ray [Remix]* (Rham!, 1989) / *The Peel Sessions* (Strange Fruit, 1989) / *Trip City* (Avenus, 1989) / *Automatikk* (CBS, 1990)
- Arnette - *Dream 17* (Deconstruction, 1988)

- Biting Tongues - Love Out (Cut Deep, 1989) / *Recharge* (Cut Deep, 1989)
- Candy Flip - *Evolution* (on *Space*, Debut Records, 1989; purist Bleep business from an unlikely source)
- Chapter & The Verse - *All This And Heaven Too* (Rham!, 1988) / *If I Knew Then (What I Know Now)* (Rham!, 1989)
- Grand Groove - *Let's Dance* (Rham!, 1988; a Chad Jackson style cut-and-paste jam co-produced by Colin Thorpe and Aniff Akinola)
- Hit Squad MCR/S-B-M & MC Tunes/Shure 4 - *Wax On The Melt EP* (Eastern Bloc, 1988)
- Inertia - *Nowhere To Run* (Retroactive, 1988; a lesser-known Gerald Simpson side project)
- Jupiter 6 - *The Tracking System* (Greyboy Records, 1990: a rare example of a Manchester Bleep record that sounds like the missing link between "Voodoo Ray" and "LFO")
- Kiss AMC/Ruthless Rap Assassins - *Kiss AMC/We Don't Care* (Murdertone, 1987)
- Lounge Jays - *Massage A Rama* (W.A.U! Mr Modo, 1989; a lesser-known 808 State side project)
- Mantronix - *In Full Effect* (10 Records, 1988)
- Ruthless Rap Assassins - *Killer Album* (EMI, 1990)
- *T-Coy* - *Carino* (DeConstruction, 1987) / *Night Train* (DeConstruction, 1988) / *Carino + Singles* (LCM, 2012; tidy compilation that draws together the trio's 12" singles)

CHAPTER 6: ONLY THE BEGINNING

The best introduction to the sound of Unique 3 is undoubtedly their 1990 debut album, *Jus' Unique*. It includes versions of "The Theme" plus their other singles from the period. Some of their EPs and 12" singles include some heavier alternative mixes, plus bonus cuts worthy of re-appraisal - the list below contains a few pointers.

- Mad Musician/X-Plosion - *Break Out* (Tribe Recordings, 1989-90; exact release date unknown) / *Together* (Tribe Recordings, 1989-90; "BFD Bass" is a bass-heavy beast in the style of "The Theme")
- Unique 3 & The Mad Musician - *Only The Beginning/The Theme* (Chill Records, 1988)
- Unique 3 - *The Theme* (10 Records, 1989) / *Rhythm Takes Control* (10 Records, 1990) / *Weight From The Bass/Musical Melody* (10 Records, 1990) / *No More* (10 Records, 1991) / *Activity* (10 Records, 1991; the overlooked title track is an aggressive fusion of dancehall, techno, dub and breakbeat hardcore)

CHAPTER 7: STATING A FACT

For a quick introduction to the early sound of Nightmares On Wax, the best place to start is debut album *A Word of Science (The 1st and Final Chapter)* (Warp Records, 1991). That said, I'd recommend checking out their early EPs and 12" singles to get a better grasp of their Bleep-era club cuts and the way their sound developed between 1989 and 1991. Naturally, if you can find their first self-released EP, it's worth a listen, if only for the ludicrously raw, "Voodoo Ray"-sampling version of "Dextrous".

• Age of Chance - *Kiss* (FON Records/Virgin, 1986) / *One Thousand Years of Trouble* (Virgin, 1987) / *Mecca* (Virgin, 1989)
• Breaking The Illusion - *Can U Understand/Drop The Mic* (Play Hard Records, 1989)
• CUD: *Robinson Crusoe (Friday Mix)* (Imaginary Records, 1990; lesser-known early N.O.W. rework, nestled on the B-side of the 12" single)
• Logarhythm - *Jungle* (Nightmares On Wax Remix) (on Various Artists - *Rewind*, Republic Records, 1990)
• Nightmares On Wax: *Nightmares On Wax EP* (Poverty Records, 1989; contains *Let It Roll* and *Dextrous* as well as Hip-Hop cut *Stating a Fact*) / *Dextrous* (Warp Records, 1989) / *Aftermath #1* (Warp Records, 1990; contains *Aftermath* and *I'm For Real*) / *Aftermath #2* (Warp Records, 1990; notable for sporting a very heavy LFO remix of *Aftermath*, though flipside *Sal Batardes* is deliciously wonky and bass-heavy too) / *Aftermath #3* (Warp Records, 1990; the remix of *I'm For Real* is the one to check) / *A Case of Funk EP* (Warp Records, 1991) / *Set Me Free* (Warp Records, 1992) / *Happiness* (Warp Records, 1993)

CHAPTER 8: WARPED VISION

If you have the time, it's worth browsing through the discographies of both FON Records and Mark Brydon and Robert Gordon as FON Force. This will give you a good grasp of how their productions - and the label they produced for - developed during the mid-to-late 1980s. Naturally, it's essential to gorge on the Forgemasters' few releases and remixes; while only their earliest work is covered in this chapter, I've listed later EPs and remixes below. Robert Gordon's later debut solo album, *Rob Gordon Projects* (Source Records, 1996) contains several Forgemasters tracks recorded in the period. I've also listed other essential Gordon releases under other aliases, primarily because they're worth a listen but also because it gives a fuller picture of his distinctive contribution to UK electronic music culture.

- Black Knight - *Black Knight* (Source Records, 1994; exceptionally good later solo material from Robert Gordon)
- Chakk - *Clocks & Babies* (self-released tape, 1982; CD and download reissue on Klanggalerie, 2016) / *Out of the Flesh* (Doublevision, 1984) / *You/They Say* (FON Records, 1985) / *Big Hot Blues* (MCA Records, 1986) / *Imagination (Who Needs a Better Life)* (MCA Records, 1986) / *10 Days In An Elevator* (MCA Records, 1986)
- Manu Dibango - *Abele Dance ('85 Remix)* (on *Pata Piya* 12", Celluloid/ Streetwave, 1985)
- Eric B & Rakim - *Put Ya Hands Together (Fon Force Mix)* (on *The Microphone Fiend + Put Ya Hands Together*, MCA Records, 1988)
- The Fall - *Shift Work* (Fontana, 1991)
- Fear by Force - *Space Is The Place* (Jam Today, 1990; FON Force remixing Atmosfear - the A-side remix of *Dancing In Outer Space* is particularly good)
- Forgemasters - *Track With No Name* (Warp Records/Outer Rhythm, 1989) / *The Black Steel EP* (Network Records, 1991) / *Quabala EP* (Hubba Hubba, 1994)
- Jaki Graham - *No More Tears (Fon Force Remix)* (EMI, 1988)
- Gwen Guthrie - *Padlock (Special Mixes)* (Garage Records, 1983)
- Inspiral Carpets - *Commercial Rain/She Comes In The Fall (Remixes)* (Cow/Mute, 1990; look out for the Forgemasters' "Rub-A-Dub Mix", which reportedly includes a short sample from Orbital's then massive club anthem *Chime*)
- Grace Jones - *Nightclubbing* (Island Records, 1981)
- Krush - *House Arrest (The Beat Is The Law)* (FON Records, 1987)
- Man Machine featuring Forgemasters - *Man Machine* (Outer Rhythm, 1989)
- Pop Will Eat Itself - *Box Frenzy* (Chapter 22, 1987; album produced by Robert Gordon) / *Def.Con.One* (Chapter 22, 1988; the 12" Robert Gordon-produced 12" version also includes scratches by Winston Hazel)
- Psychic TV - *Love War Riot (The FON Force Vocoder Mixes)* (Temple Records, 1989)
- Eric Random & The Bedlamites - *Ishmael* (FON Records, 1986; ace fusion of leftfield Dub and Electro co-produced by Robert Gordon)
- The Swanhunters with Chakk - *Bloodsport* (FON Records, 1986)
- Ten City - *Devotion (Paradise Revisited UK Mix)* (on *Suspicious*, Atlantic, 1989)
- Treebound Story - *My Life's Example* (FON Records, 1986; flipside cut *Forever Green* was Rob Gordon's first solo production at the FON studio)
- View To View - *Torus* (Source Records, 1994; rare collaborative EP from Robert Gordon and David Moufang aka Move D)
- Yazz - *Where Has All The Love Gone?* (Big Life, 1988; the "Ghetto Mix" in the UK 12" is the FON Force re-rub) / *Wanted* (Big Life, 1988) / *The 'Wanted Remixes!* (Big Life, 1989)

CHAPTER 9: THE TRUE CREATORS

LFO, DJ Martin and the Chapeltown crew are covered in two separate chapters (see below for the second), so I've split the lists into records covered in that chapter. In this first one, the key records are of course "LFO" and "LFO (Remix)", including all of the weighty and otherworldly B-sides. The list that follows also includes records that influenced LFO and some of the numerous tracks made in tribute or inspired by Mark Bell, Gez Varley and Martin Williams peerless classic.

- D-M-S - *Brand New World (Dubplate Mix)* (Production House, 1990)
- Fantasy UFO - *Fantasy* (XL Recordings, 1990)
- LFO - *LFO* (Warp Records/Outer Rhythm, 1990) / *LFO (Remix)* (Warp Records/Outer Rhythm, 1990)
- Lhasa - *The Attic* (Music Man Records, 1990)
- Mayday - *Wiggin'* (on Nude Photo '88, Kool Kat, 1988)
- Mind of Kane - *Out of Control/Frequency* (Déjà vu Recordings, 1990)
- Rhythim Is Rhythim - *The Dance* (on Rhythim Is Rhythim: Nude Photo 12", Transmat, 1987)
- Turntable Overload: *T.T.O* (Made On Earth, 1990)

CHAPTER 10:
ITAL ANTHEMS AND BASSIC BEATS

The key records this time round are those Bassic Records releases engineered/co-produced by Martin Williams/Homer Harriott (details below) and LFO's brilliant debut album, "Frequencies". There are some other fine releases worth checking - including a number of remixes by the Leeds producers documented in this chapter - so I'd suggest paying particular attention to the following list if you're after overlooked gold.

- Ability II - *Pressure/Pressure Dub* (Bassic, 1990)
- Botany 5 - *Love Bomb (LFO Mixes)* (Virgin, 1990)
- The Bridewell Taxis - *Spirit (LFO Mix)* (on *Spirit* 12", Stolen Records, 1990)
- Ital Rockers - *Ital's Anthem* (Bassic, 1990; don't forget to check flipside *Science (First Mix)* too) / *One Day EP* (Outer Rhythm, 1991)
- Juno - *Soul Thunder* (Bassic, 1990)
- LFO - *We Are Back/Nature* (Warp Records, 1991) / *We Are Back (Remix)* (Warp Records, 1991) / *Love Is The Message/Tan Ra Ra* (Tommy Boy, 1991) / *Frequencies* (Warp Records, 1991) / *What Is House EP* (Warp Records, 1991)
- LFO [Paul Hardcastle] - *Brainstorm* (Fast Forward Records, 1990) / *Sonic Attack* (Fast Forward Records, 1990)

- Man Machine - *Animal Remixes* (Outer Rhythm, 1991; look for the "Primordial Jungle" and "Neanderthal Dub" mixes by Williams and Harriott as DJ Martin and DJ Homes)
- Unit 93 - *Trust No One* (Bassic, 1990)

CHAPTER 11: PLAY THE FIVE TONES

For this chapter, I'd recommend first getting to grips with Cabaret Voltaire's catalogue, especially albums and 12" singles released between 1981 and '91. This will give you an idea how their sound developed, with Code (1987), Laidback, Groovy and Nasty (1990) and Body & Soul (1991) being essential listening with regards to the period covered in this book. For an introduction to the Sweet Exorcist sound, Warp's *RetroActivity* compilation (2011) contains the vast majority of the duo's Bleep and Clonk-era work.

- 23 Skidoo - *Last Words* (Fetish Records, 1981) / *The Gospel Comes To New Guinea* (Fetish Records, 1981)
- Cabaret Voltaire - *Mix-Up* (Rough Trade, 1979) / *The Voice of America* (Rough Trade, 1980) / *Red Mecca* (Rough Trade, 1981) / *The Crackdown* (Virgin/Some Bizarre, 1983) / *Yashar* (Factory, 1983) / *James Brown* (Virgin/ Some Bizarre, 1984) / *Sensoria* (Virgin/Some Bizarre, 1984) / *Micro-Phonies* (Virgin/Some Bizarre, 1984) / *Code* (Parlophone, 1987) / *Here To Go* (Parlophone, 1987) / *Hypnotised* (Parlophone, 1989; includes FON Force and Robert Gordon remixes) / *Easy Life* (Parlophone, 1990; there were two 12" singles of this, with one containing the "Jive Turkey Mix" and the other a trio of takes by Robert Gordon) / *Laidback, Groovy & Nasty* (Parlophone, 1990) / *Percussion Force* (Les Disques De Crepuscule, 1991; includes contributions from Parrot and Robert Gordon) / *What Is Real?* (Les Disques De Crepuscule, 1991) / *Body & Soul* (Les Disques De Crepuscule, 1991) / *Colours* (Plastex, 1991)
- The Funky Worm - *Hustle! (To The Music)* (FON Records, 1988) / *The Spell! (Get Down With The Genie)* (FON Records/WEA, 1988) / *U+Me=Love* (FON Records/WEA, 1989)
- Sweet Exorcist - *Testone* (Warp Records, 1990) / *Testone Remixes* (Warp Records, 1990; Robert Gordon's "high-tech" reworks) / *Clonk* (Warp Records, 1990) / *Per Clonk (Remix)* (Warp Records, 1990) / *CC EP* (AKA *Clonk's Coming*, Warp Records, 1991) / *Popcone* (Plastex, 1991) / *Spirit Guide To Low Tech* (Touch, 1994)
- Ultramarine - *Geezer (Sweet Exorcist Remix)* (on *Nightfall in Sweetleaf*, Rough Trade, 1992)
- XON - *The Mood Set* (Network Records, 1991)

PART 3: LOW FREQUENCY OVERLOAD

CHAPTER 12: HARDBEAT AND BASSLINE

Most of the Ozone Recordings' tracks mentioned in this chapter can be found –in some form or another - on the label's 1991 compilation, *Hardbeat + Bassline*. The imprint released a second compilation that year, *Technozone*; that too is worth a spin.

- 1703 - *Hypnotize* (Ozone, 1991) / *Let Yourself Go* (Ozone, 1993)
- Count Zero - *Silent Prayer* (Ozone, 1990) / *Positive Nuisance* (Ozone, 1990) / *Success* (Ozone, 1991)
- Ionic - *Global Mode* (Ozone, 1991)
- Simon Mark - *Say Aaagh!* (Ozone, 1990)
- DJ Mink - *Hey Hey! Can U Relate?* (Ozone, 1990/Warp Records, 1990; the latter contains Parrot and Mark Brydon's ace "Sunshine Dub Instrumental" mix)
- New Age Technology - *New Age Technology* (Ozone, 1990) / *You Say* (Ozone, 1991) / *Damn I'm Good* (Ozone, 1992)
- On A High - *Hot* (Ozone, 1991; debut single from another of Tim Garbutt and Pat Scott's aliases - Breakbeat Hardcore flipside "Hotter" is arguably the pick of the two tracks)
- Panic - *Voices of Energy* (Ozone, 1990) / *Voices of Energy II* (Ozone, 1991)
- Success - *Tripwire* (Ozone, 1990)
- Trak 1 - *Motion/Diffusion* (Ozone, 1990) / *For This* (Ozone, 1991)
- Utah Saints - *What Can You Do For Me* (FFRR, 1991) / *Something Good* (FFRR, 1992) / *Utah Saints* (FFRR, 1992)
- Zone - *Eternal* (Ozone, 1991)

CHAPTER 13: BIORHYTHMS

To get an overview of the music at the heart of the story told in this chapter, I'd recommend tracking down both of Neil Rushton's Detroit Techno compilations - *Techno: The New Dance Sound of Detroit* (10 Records, 1988) and *Techno 2: The Next Generation* (10 Records, 1990) - as well as both *Bio Rhythm* compilations on Network Records. If you can find them, Kool Kat's two *House Masters: US v UK Showdown* collections also make interesting listening. While the standard is hardly high, they give a good indication of the kinds of House music being made and released in the UK before "Voodo Ray" and the Bleep & Bass movement.

- Addis Posse - *Nice Up* (Kool Kat, 1988)
- Altern 8 - *Overload EP* (Network Records, 1990) / *Activ 8* (Come With Me) (Network Records, 1991) / *The Vertigo EP* (Network Records, 1991; contains Infiltrate 202) / *Full On Mask Hysteria* (Network Records, 1992) / *Brutal-8-E (Orange Edition)* (Network Records, 1992)
- Bang The Party - *I Feel Good All Over* (Kool Kat/Warriors Dance, 1987) / *Release Your Body* (Warriors Dance/Transmat, 1988; includes an early Derrick May remix as MayDay)
- Bizarre, Inc - *Technological* (12") (Blue Chip, 1989) / *Technological* (album) (Blue Chip, 1989) / *Bizarre Theme/X-Static* (Vinyl Solution, 1990) / *Such A Feeling* (Vinyl Solution, 1991) / *Playing With Knives* (Vinyl Solution, 1991)
- C&M Connection - *Another Night* (Blue Chip, 1990)
- Critical Rhythm - *I'm In Dub With You* (Network Records, 1990)
- Cyclone - *A Place Called Bliss* (Network Records, 1990) / *The Sonic Cycology EP* (Network Records, 1991)
- Demonik - *Labyrinthe* (Rham! Records, 1989; a rare treat - a high quality Bleep & Bass record from Birmingham, courtesy of then 17-year-old Peter Duggal)
- Doggy - *Psyche* (Rham! Records, 1990; a fine slab of Bleep/Electro fusion from Birmingham's Peter Duggal)
- Energize - *Report To The Dancefloor* (Network Records, 1990; the "Electro Mix" is particularly heavy) / *Report To The Dancefloor (Robert Gordon Remix)* (Network Records, 1990)
- Neal Howard - *Indulge* (Network Records, 1990)
- Inner City - *Big Fun* (KMS/10 Records, 1988) / *Good Life* (KMS/10 Records, 1988) / *Paradise* (10 Records, 1989)
- Gloria Jones - *Tainted Love* (Inferno, 1979)
- Mayday - *Nude Photo '88* (Kool Kat, 1988)
- MK - *Somebody New* (Network Records, 1990)
- Denise Motto - *I M N X T C (Jack Your Body To The Beat)* (Kool Kat, 1987) / *Doing It Properly (Is X T C)* (Kool Kat, 1987)
- Nexus 21 - *The Rhythm of Life* (Blue Chip, 1989) / *(Still) Life Keeps Moving (Club Mix)* (Blue Chip, 1989) / *Progressive Logic EP* (Network Records, 1990) / Logical Progression (R&S Records, 1990)
- Reese - *Rock To The Beat* (KMS, 1989) / *Funky Funk Funk/Bassline* (Network Records, 1991)
- Reese & Santonio - The Sound (KMS, 1987) / Back To The Beat (With 'The Sound') (FFRR, 1988) / Bounce Your Body To The Box (Kool Kat, 1988)
- Rhythim Is Rhythim - *Strings of Life '89* (Kool Kat/Big Life, 1989)
- Rhythm Mode:D - *So Damn Tough* (12") (Blue Chip, 1988) / *So Damn Tough* (album) (Blue Chip, 1988)
- Rhythmatic - *Take Me Back* (Network Records, 1990) / *Frequency/Demons* (Network Records, 1990) / *Take Me Back (Remix)* (Network Records, 1990) / *Beyond The Bleep* (Network Records, 1991)
- Risky Business - *Jammin' To New Orleans* (Kool Kat, 1987; the first release on Neil Rushton and company's House-focused label)
- Symbols & Instruments - *Mood* (Network Records, 1990)

- T-CUT-F - *House Reaction* (Kool Kat, 1987) / *House Reaction (Union Jack Mix)* (10 Records, 1988; includes two versions made by Mark Gamble and Derrick May)
- Two Men, A Drum Machine & A Trumpet - *I'm Tired Of Getting Pushed Around (Remix)* (Metronome, 1988; includes two lesser-known Derrick May remixes)
- Various Artists - *Acid Trance* (Blue Chip, 1988) / *Bio Rhythm: Dance Music With Bleeps* (Network Records, 1990) / *Bio Rhythm 2: 808 909 1991* (Network Records, 1990) / *Techno! The New Dance Sound of Detroit* (10 Records, 1988) / *Techno 2: The New Generation* (10 Records, 1990)

CHAPTER 14: NORTH OF WATFORD

Your best bet here is to take a trawl through the Jack Trax and Chill catalogues. One or two Jack Trax compilations will give you an idea of the Chicago House records they were sampling, while the label's various 12" releases include some stone-cold classics that no discerning listener should be without (e.g. Ralphi Rosario, Mr Fingers, Fingers Inc, etc.). Getting hold of Chill releases - especially the rare and sought-after ones - can be a little trickier, but helpfully there are clips of quite a few of them on YouTube. Tony Bonisegna released loads of music under a large number of aliases, so the list below includes the best (and most interesting) of these.

- A.E.K - Sudden Death EP (Bass Sphere, 1991) / The Bad Bwoy Breakout EP (Bass Sphere, 1992)
- Aural Exciter - *Step Back* (Chill, 1990)
- Blame & Justice - *Murderin' MC/Death Row* (Chill, 1991, promo only; obscure early outing from the future Drum & Bass heroes)
- Bogeyman - *Horrors* (Chill, 1991) / *Horrors (Part 2)* (Chill, 1991)
- Dr Caligari - *Freaks* (Chill, 1991; lesser-known Hardcore solo outing from Tony Boninsegna)
- Lab Technicians - *St Vitus* (Chill, 1991)
- MI 7 - *Rockin' Down The House* (Chill, 1991) / *No Contest* (Chill, 1991) / *The Great Leap Sideways EP* (Chill, 1992; includes a Return of the Living Acid remix of *Rockin' Down The House*)
- Ministry of Fear - *EP With No Name* (Contagious, 1991; lesser-known Tony Boninsegna/Mickey Thomas production that contains numerous wonky, Bleep-influenced cuts)
- Napoleon - *The Softcore EP* (Infrasonic, 1992) / *The Russian Front EP* (Infrasonic, 1992)
- N.R.G - *The Terminator* (Chill, 1991) / *Trip Switch* (Chill, 1991) / *The Hardcore EP* (Chill, 1992)
- Original Clique - *North of Watford EP* (Chill, 1990) / *Ten To Midnight EP* (Chill, 1990) / *3 Phase 415v/P.S.1* (Chill, 1991)

- Pierre Point - *The Executioner's Song* (Bass Sphere, 1991) / *The Fuzion EP* (Bass Sphere, 1992)
- Return of the Living Acid - *Twin Tub* (Chill, 1991) / *Get Funky* (Chill, 1991) / *Creator/Move Dammit* (Chill, 1991)
- Rotor - *Purely Rhythm* (Chill, 1991) / *Kaleidoscope* (Chill, 1991)
- Sinewave - *Sinewave* (Chill, 1991; a killer chunk of Electro/Bleep fusion)
- Sykosis 451 - *This Town/Hurricane* (Bad Ass Toons, 1991) / *Elemental Mayhem EP* (Infrasonic, 1992; both *Tornado* and *Monsoon* are bass-heavy Electro-influenced beasts) / *The Return To Space EP* (Infrasonic, 1992)
- Various Artists - *Upfront 1/2/3/4/5* (Serious, 1986-87; a taste of Damon D'Cruz's "Streetsounds"-rivalling dance comps) / *Warehouse Raves, Warehouse Raves 2/3/4* (Rumour Records, all 1990)

CHAPTER 15:
RAGE AGAINST THE MACHINE

Helpfully there many compilations chronicling the Bleep & Breaks and early Breakbeat Hardcore scenes, as well as sets that reflect the changing nature of British dance music at the time. In the latter category, a great place to start is Above Board's 2019 compilations celebrating the legacy of Fabio and Grooverider's weekly Rage night. Entitled *30 Years of Rage* and available in numerous formats (double CD, four double vinyl albums and download/streaming), they feature a mixture of tracks - some very hard to find - that detail the club's unique music policy and how bass-heavy British dance music was changing during the period.

Rumour Records' contemporaneous *Bass, Breaks & Bleeps* compilations are worth tracking down as they contain many of the biggest records in the style, as well cuts that have long been forgotten or may have stood the test of time. Four volumes were released between 1990 and '92. A number of the key labels mentioned in this chapter either released compilations at the time or later celebratory sets charting their contribution to the changing sound of British dance music. These include XL Recordings' *The First Chapter* (1990) and *The Second Chapter: Hardcore European Dance Music* (1991); Warriors Dance's *Acid Trax & Warriors Dance* (1988) and *The Tuffest of the Tuff* (1989, but reissued in expanded form in 2019); and the triple-CD *Suburban Base: The History of Hardcore, Jungle and Drum & Bass* (2014).

- 100 Hz - *Low Frequency Overload* (Optimism Records, 1990) / *Catching Spiders* (Optimism Records, 1991)
- II Exodus - *The Dark Spirits* (white label, 1991)

- 4 Hero - *Combat Dancin'* (Reinforced, 1990; includes *Combat Dance* and *Mr Kirk's Nightmare*) / *The Scorcher/Kirk's Back* (Reinforced, 1990) / *All B 3/Rising Son* (Reinforced, 1990) / *No Sleep Raver/Marimba* (Reinforced, 1991) / *In Rough Territory* (Reinforced, 1991)
- 4 For Money - *It's A Moment In Time (Rising High Dub)* (Tam Tam Records, 1990; Rising High stalwarts' Caspar Pound and Marc Williams weighty Bleep & Bass re-make cam be found on the UK 12" of this Italian House release)
- Addis Posse - *Nice Up* (Kool Kat/Warriors Dance, 1988) / *Let The Warriors Dance* (Warriors Dance, 1989)
- Austin - *Unity In Dub/I Get High* (Boogie Times Records, 1991) / *I Get High (Munchies Mix)* (Suburban Base, 1991)
- Autonation - *Sit On The Bass* (R&S Records, 1991; booming Bleep business on Belgian label R&S, as produced by David 'Ubik' Campbell)
- Baby D - *Day Dreaming* (Production House, 1990; vocal Bleep & Breaks, with the "Can U Handle It Mix" offering the heaviest bass)
- Bang The Party - *Bang-Bang You're Mine (Remixes)* (Warriors Dance, 1989)
- Bassix - *Close Encounters* (D-Zone/Champion, 1990)
- Bleeps International - *Bleeps International* (Fast Forward Records, 1990; more Bleep-inspired business from Paul Hardcastle)
- Brothers Grimm - *Déjà vu* (Production House, 1990) / *No Use Crying Now* (Production House, 1991; the "Soundbwoy Mix" is the one - Bleep & Breaks with soulful vocals)
- Danse City - *Lunar Tune* (on Together We Can Kick It, Danse City Records, UK; London Bleep with lashings of funky acid flavour)
- D.M.S - *Brand New World* (Production House, 1990; all about the "Dubplate Mix", a heavy, UK Steppers-influenced Bleep workout) / *Love Overdose* (Production House, 1991; Bleep & Breaks featuring samples from The Incredible Bongo Band and, more bizarrely, Fleetwood Mac's "Big Love")
- Djum Djum - *Difference (Remix)* (Outer Rhythm, 1990; sub-heavy CJ Mackintosh reworks of an early Leftfield co-production)
- Exocet - *Safety Zone* (on Lethal Weapon, Catt Records, 1989)
- Fantasy UFO - Fantasy (XL Recordings, 1990) / *Mind, Body, Soul* (Strictly Underground, 1991) / *Hypersonic* (Strictly Underground, 1992)
- Frenzied Bass - *Frenzied Bass EP* (S.O.R Recordings, 1990; cut-and-paste adventures in bleeps, breaks and acid)
- F.X.U - *Steel City EP* (Made On Earth, 1990)
- Greed - *Give Me* (D-Zone, 1990; check the B-side "Bleep Mix")
- Hypersonic - *Dance Tones* (D-Zone Records, 1990)
- Indo Tribe & The Future Sound of London - *The Pulse EP* (Jumpin' & Pumpin', 1991)
- Infamix - *Hypnotic FX* (Industrial Music, 1990: cheery early Bleep production from the duo that would later become B12) / *Ee45* (Industrial Music, 1990)

- The Inmates - *The Electric Chair/Electro Techno* (Buzz Records, 1991; heavily influenced by LFO's *LFO*)
- Jolly Roger - *Ulysses (The Groove)* (on *We Can't We Live Together*, Desire Records, 1989; bass-heavy, stripped-back House/Techno from 'Evil' Eddie Richards)
- Ju-Ju - *The Happy Dance/Daybreak* (OhZone, 1991)
- Kicksquad - *Sound Clash* (Champion Sound) (Kickin' Records, 1990) / *What You Searching For* (Kickin' Records, 1991)
- Kromozone: *The Rush* (Suburban Base, 1991)
- The KLF - *What Time Is Love? (Remodeled & Remixed)* (KLF Communications, 1990; the Moody Boys remix is a Bleep-heavy, sub-sporting classic) / *3AM Eternal (The Moody Boys Selection)* (KLF Communications, 1991; Bleep-influenced, bass-heavy reworks from Tony Thorpe)
- Language - *Renegade* (Boss Records, 1990; rush-inducing Bleep & Breaks cut with a loved-up Deep House feel)
- Mad Bas'tard - *I Am The Future* (Omen Recordings, 1991)
- Melancholy Man - *Joy* (Warriors Dance, 1989; all about the "Bassapella" on the flip)
- Moody Boys - *Journeys Into Dubland* (XL Recordings, 1990) / *Jammin (Ital Mix)* (on *Funky Zulu (You're So Fresh)*, XL Recordings, 1990) / *King of the Funky Zulus* (United We Conquer, 1990; sub-heavy breaks with dub bass, acid lines and a few occasional Bleep type sounds... seriously heavy)
- Nebula II - *Séance/Atheama* (Reinforced Records, 1991)
- The Neutral Zone - *Outer Space* (Optimism Records, 1990; "moodily intro'd and jazzily Bleeped" London Bleep & Breaks cut)
- Nicolette - *School Of The World/Single Minded People* (Shut Up & Dance Records, 1990) / *Waking Up/The Dove Song* (Shut Up & Dance Records, 1991)
- No Smoke - *Koro-Koro* (Warriors Dance, 1989) / *Koro-Koro (Remixes)* (Warriors Dance, 1989) / *International Smoke Signal* (Warriors Dance, 1990, reissued in 2018) / *Righteous Rule* (Warriors Dance, 1990; no bleeps, but tons of sub-heavy Reggae bass and Steppers influences. Includes two fine Dub mixes)
- N-R-G Posse - *Themes* (D-Zone, 1990; sample-heavy mash-up business that includes snippets of "The Theme", Kraftwerk's "Numbers" and "Strings of Life")
- Oribtal - *Omen Remixes* (FFRR, UK; the Hartnoll brothers' brief dalliance with Bleep & Bass influences)
- Phuture Assassins - *I Like Techno* (Boogie Times Records, 1990)
- The Predator - *The Outer Limits* (Industrial Music, 1990)
- Private Party - My Tennents/Puppet Capers (I.M.W, 1987)
- Project 1 - *Project 1 EP* (Tam Tam Records, 1990; "Ferrari" is a rock solid chunk of Bleep & Breaks)
- Q-Bass - *Dancin' People* (Suburban Base, 1991)

- The Ragga Twins - *Ragga Trip/Hooligan '69* (Shut Up & Dance Records, 1990) / *Illegal Gunshot/Spliffhead* (Shut Up & Dance Records, 1990) / *Hooligan '69 Remixes* (Shut Up & Dance Records, 1991) / *Reggae Owes Me Money* (Shut Up & Dance Records, 1991) / *Shine Eye* (Shut Up & Dance Records, 1992)
- The Scientist - *The Bee* (Kickin' Records, 1990) / *The Exorcist* (Kickin' Records, 1990)
- Secret Desire - *White Lies* (Vinyl Solution, 1990)
- Shut Up & Dance - *5 6 7 8* (Shut Up & Dance Records, 1989) / *Raps My Occupation/£10 To Get In* (Shut Up & Dance Records, 1990) / *Lamborghini* (Shut Up & Dance Records, 1990) / *Dance Before The Police Come!* (Shut Up & Dance Records, 1990)
- Smooth & Simmonds - *Our Theme/The Experiment* (white label, 1990)
- Tech-Aluco - *The Master/Overdrive Max* (Wax Factory productions, 1991)
- Tek 9 - *Kingdom of Dub* (Reinforced Records, 1991)
- Tekno Too - *Feel The Power* (D-Zone, 1990) / *Psycho* (D-Zone, 1991) / *The Remix EP* (D-Zone, 1993)
- Toxic - *The Toxic EP* (D.Zone, 1991: typical cut-and-paste fusion cuts with a heavy breakbeat hardcore/Bleep & Bass influence)
- Ubik - *Non-Stop Techno EP* (Zoom Records, 1990; more Electro than Bleep, but insanely heavy. *Bass Generation* is particularly good) / *System Overload EP* (Zoom Records, 1991; a patchwork of Techno, Electro and Hardcore influences that come together on a rock solid EP from David Campbell)

CHAPTER 16: ELEMENTS OF TONE

The North American take on Bleep & Bass and Bleep & Breaks was relatively short-lived and focused on a few key groups of producers. Because of this, a good overview of the movement can be gained by listening to the work of Frankie Bones (notably the *Bonesbreaks* series and *Looney Tunes* EPs produced in cahoots with Lenny Dee) made between 1988 and 1990, his brother Adam X (1990-91) and, of course, John Acquaviva and Richie Hawtin.

If you have the time, take a trawl through the early catalogues of Atmosphere Records and Plus 8. Belgian label Buzz's 1991 compilation *The Atmosphere Compilation* offers a good primer for the former imprint, while Easy Street's *Brooklyn Beats: Brooklyn's In The House* contains cuts from many of the key players in the early NYC Techno scene (Joey Beltram, Mundo Muzique, How and Little, Frankie Bones etc.).

- Biosphere - *Baby Interphase* (Apollo, 1993)
- Adam X & Frankie Bones - *Crossbones EP* (Fabulous Music, 1991)

- Frankie Bones - Bonesbreaks Volume 1 (Underworld Records, 1988) / Bonesbreaks Volume 2 (Underworld Records, 1988) / *Bonesbreaks Volume 2* (Underworld Records, 1989) / *Call It Techno* (Breaking Bones Records, 1989) / *Call It Techno Remixes* (X Records, 1990)
- Frankie Bones & Lenny Dee - *Looney Tunes Volume 1* (Nu Groove/XL Recordings, 1989) / *Just As Long As I Got You* (XL Recordings, 1989) / *Looney Tunes II* (Nu Groove/XL Recordings, 1990)
- Chapter 1 - *Unleash The Groove* (Strictly Rhythm, 1990)
- Cybersonik - *Technarchy* (Plus 8 Records, 1990) / *Revelation 928* (on *Backlash*, Plus 8, 1991)
- Delusions of Grandeur - *Touch Me In The Night* (City Limits, 1990)
- Digital Distortion - *Certain State of Mind* (Atmosphere Records, 1990; loved-up Brooklyn Bleep & Bass produced by Mike Lafferty with remixes by Frankie Bones) / *Shoombadooba* (Atmosphere Records, 1990; worth checking for the downtempo Deep House/Bleep fusion of *Mellow Bug* and Bleep & Breaks heaviness of *Take Your Soul*)
- DJ's Rule - *Serious EP Vol-1* (Hi-Bias, 1990; lush Deep House with occasional Bleeps)
- DV8 - *Thoughts Of Tomorrow* (on *Freedom*, Strictly Rhythm, 1990) / *The Egotrip EP* (Strictly Rhythm, 1991)
- Egotrip - *Dream World* (Outer Limits, 1990)
- Freedom Authority - *Unauthorized Conceptions* (XL Recordings, 1990)
- F.U.S.E - *Approach & Identity* (Plus 8, 1990) / *F.U* (on NMS Promo, 1991)
- Nick Holder - *Digital Age* (DNH Records, 1991) / *Soundwaves* (DNH Records, 1991) / *The Digital Age* (Double EP) (Strobe Records, 1992)
- How & Little - *Jammin' Breaks* (City Limits, 1990) / *The Formula* (R&S Records, 1991)
- MBG - *Speed 127* (MBG International, 1990)
- Mental Mayhem - *Where Are They Hiding/Joey's Riot* (Atmosphere Records, 1990)
- The Prince of Dance Music - *In My Kingdom We Dance In Peace* (City Limits, 1990; Nu Groove regular Lamont Booker delivers Deep House and Techno with surprisingly weighty bass and electro influences)
- P.L.U.M - *Make You Feel It (Feel The Wrath)* (Atmosphere Records, 1990)
- Psyance - *Motion* (Plus 8, 1991)
- Project '86 - *Industrial Bass* (Nu Groove, 1990)
- Quazar - *Day-Glo* (on *The Seven Stars EP*, Go Bang, 1991; Dutch Deep House/Bleep & Bass fusion)
- Revelation - *Chapter II* (Atmosphere Records, 1990)
- States of Mind - *Elements of Tone* (Plus 8, 1990)
- Sub Sub - *Space Face (Todd Terry Remix)* (10 Records, 1991; all about the clonking and bass-heavy "Techno Todd Dub")
- The True Underground Sound of Rome - *Secret Doctrine* (Male Productions, 1991)

- Underground Resistance - *Sonic EP* (Underground Resistance, 1990)
- Z-Formation - *Intense EP* (Hi-Bias, 1991) / *Frenzy* (on *Brutal EP*, Hi-Bias, 1991; LFO-influenced cut produced by Nick Holder)

PART 4: AFTERMATH

CHAPTER 17: COMING DOWN

Some of the compilations mentioned in the Bleep & Breaks chapter remain relevant to this one, particularly the *30 Years of Rage* and *Suburban Base: The History of Hardcore, Jungle and Drum & Bass* ones. The gradual transformation of Warp Records in 1991 and '92 is perfectly chronicled via the contrasting *Artificial Intelligence* and *Evolution of the Groove* compilations.

- 2 Bad Mice: *Bombscare* (on *Hold It Down EP*, Moving Shadow, 1991)
- A Guy Called Gerald - *28 Gun Badboy* (single) (Columbia, 1991) / *King Of The Jungle* (Juice Box, 1992) / *Free Africa* (on *The Musical Magical Midi Machine/Like A Drug*, Juice Box, 1992) / *28 Gun Badboy* (album) (Juice Box, 1993)
- Acen - *Trip To The Moon Part 2* (Production House, 1992; check the Bleep-influenced Darkcore heaviness of the A-side "Darkside" version)
- Boogie Times Tribe - *Real Hardcore/The Dark Stranger* (Suburban Base, 1993)
- Coco, Steel & Lovebomb - *Feel It* (Warp, 1991)
- DSR - *Miami* (Warp, 1992)
- Earth Leakage Trip - *Psychotronic EP* (Moving Shadow, 1991)
- E.Q - *In The Jungle* (on *The Graphic EP*, Formation Records, 1992) / *End of an Era EP* (Formation Records, 1993)
- DJ Hype - *The Trooper* (Suburban Base, 1993) / *Shot In The Dark* (Suburban Base, 1993)
- Kaotic Chemistry - *Five In One Night EP* (Moving Shadow, 1991; *Drumtrip* is the most Bleep-influenced of the bunch)
- Kid Unknown - *Nightmare* (Warp, 1992) / *Devastating Beat Creator* (Warp, 1992)
- Metalheadz - *Terminator EP* (Synthetic Records, 1992)
- Nasty Habits - *As Nasty As I Wanna Be EP* (Reinforced Records, 1992) / *No Dominator* (NHS Records, 1992)
- Noise Factory - *Loving You/Jungle Techno* (Ibiza Records, 1991) / *The Buzz/Imperative* (Ibiza Records, 1991) / *Noise Factory/Warehouse Music* (Ibiza Records, 1991) / *Be Free* (on My Mind, 3rd Party, 1992)
- The Orbital Project - *Orbital Madness* (Moving Shadow, 1990) / *Chinese Lollipops EP* (Moving Shadow, 1990)
- Origin Unknown - *Valley of the Shadows* (RAM Records, 1993)

- Plez - *Can't Stop* (Plezure Records/Loaded, 1990)
- Rhythm Invention - *Can't Take It* (Warp, 1992)
- Rufige Cru - *Terminator EP* (Reinforced Records, 1992) / *Darkrider EP* (Reinforced Records, 1992) / *Krisp Biscuit/Killa Muffin* (Reinforced Records, 1992) / *Ghosts EP* (Reinforced Records, 1993)
- The Step - *Yeah You!* (Warp, 1991) / *Yeah You! (Remix)* (Warp, 1991)
- THK - *France* (Warp, 1992)
- Tomas - Mind Songs (Warp, 1991)
- Tricky Disco - *Tricky Disco* (Warp, 1990) / *Tricky Disco* (Remix) (Warp, 1990) / *House Fly* (Warp, 1991) / *House Fly (Radical Rockers Remix)* (Warp, 1991)
- Tuff Little Unit - *Join The Future* (Warp, 1991) / *Inspiration* (Warp, 1991)
- The Warrior - *Babylon A Burn* (Strictly Underground, 1991; heavyweight DJ Hype production)

CHAPTER 18: JOIN THE FUTURE

You can listen to Utah's Bleep & Bass special, as mentioned in this chapter, on the NTS Radio website. Below I've listed various Bleep-influenced cuts mentioned in the main text; there are tons more out there, but there's not space here to mention everything.

- Beneath - *No Symbols 001* (No Symbols, 2012) / *No Symbols 002* (No Symbols, 2012)
- Champion - *Motherboard* (UK Urban, 2009) / *Lighter EP* (Formula Records, 2011) / *War Dance* (from *Rainforest EP*, Roska Kicks & Snares, 2011)
- ES-Q - *Enter The System [Forge Mix]* (on *Enter The System EP*, Dolly, 2019)
- Four Tet - *Love Cry [Roska Remix]* (Domino, 2010)
- DJ Fett Burger & Luca Lozano - *Electric Blue* (Sax Tags UFO, 2014)
- Kowton - *Basic Music Knowledge* (Idle Hands, 2010) / *Utility* (Livity Sound, 2016)
- Neil Landstrumm - *Bedrooms & Cities* (Tresor, 1997) / *Restaurant of Assassins* (Planet Mu, 2007)
- Lil' Silva - *Different* (white label, 2009)/ *Gobble That* (LS Whites, 2012)
- Luca Lozano - *And It Was Good EP* (Optimo Trax, 2014)
- Mosca - *Square One [Roska Remix]* (on *Square One EP*, Night Slugs, 2010)
- DJ Mujava - *Township Funk* (This Is Music/Warp Records, 2008)
- Peverlist - *Dance Til The Police Come* (Hessle Audio, 2011)
- Pev & Kowton - *Raw Code* (Hessle Audio, 2013)
- Utah? - *Bronze EP* (Coyote Records, 2019)
- Visionist - *First Love* (on *I'm Fine, Part II*, Lit City Trax, 2014)
- Youngstar - *The Formula* (DDJs Productions, 2002) / *Raw 2 Da Floor* (Musical Mob Royale, 2002)

ACKNOWLEDGEMENTS

During the five years spent researching and writing this book, there have been many people who have offered advice, support, help and encouragement. Without their contribution, I doubt you would be reading this book right now. Apologies to anyone I have forgotten; your encouragement and assistance was definitely appreciated.

First of all, I'd like to thank all of those who agreed to be interviewed for Join The Future and tell their story, sometimes for the first time. The following were all interviewed especially for this book, or for the various articles I wrote on the subject prior to starting work on Join The Future: Aniff Akinola, Vaughan Allen, Glyn Andrews, Mark Archer, David Bahar, Richard Barratt, Dave Beer, Tony Boninsegna, Chris Brown, Mark Brydon, Christian Cawood, Mark Cotgrove, Luke Cowdrey, Colin Curtis, Adrian Collins, David Duncan, Robert Gordon, George Evelyn, Mark Gamble, Kevin Harper, Tony Hannan, Homer Harriott, Drew Hemment, Winston Hazel, Zye Hill, Lucas Hunter, Andre Jacobs, Richard H Kirk, Neil Landstrumm, Ralph Lawson, Dave Lee, Sean Maher, Stephen Mallinder, Keith McIvor, Mark Millington, Adam Mitchell, Roisin Murphy, Pipes, Tim Raidl, Neil Rushton, Pat Scott, Ed Stretton, Tomas Stewart, Colin Thorpe, Gez Varley, Martin Williams, Greg Wilson, Jonathan Woodliffe.

The following people all offered advice, showed support, connected me with artists or commissioned articles about aspects of the style, for which I am grateful: Tony McParland at Juno Plus/Boiler Room, Aaron Coultate at Resident Advisor, Carl Loben at DJ magazine, Russell Deeks at IDJ, Todd Burns and Aaron Gonsher at Red Bull Music Academy Daily, Dave Jenkins, Oli Warwick at CRACK, Liam O'Shea at Hope Works/No Bounds, Chris Duckenfield, Brian Morrison at Above Board Distribution, Simon Purnell, Paul Cataneo, Andy Pye, Richard Hardcastle, Dan Wootton and the Southbank Warehouse crew, Matthew Collin, Bill Brewster, Paul Woolford, Neville Watson, Utah?, Sam Wild, Alex Wilson.

Extra special thanks to Kieran Walsh, Harry O'Brien and Jake Simmonds, whose enthusiasm set me on this road back in early 2016; to Colin Steven at Velocity Press for offering to publish and promote the book with such vigour and passion; and to Keith McIvor (aka JD Twitch) who has been on this journey with me from the very start and has offered further opportunities to tell this story in musical form.

ACKNOWLEDGEMENTS

Shouts to those friends in Bristol and beyond who put up with me banging on about Bleep & Bass for five years, particularly current and former housemates (Darren Grundy, Owain Hepple, Owain Kimber, Sean Kelly, Ali Carnegie), and fellow musical obsessives/DJ buddies (Anthony George, Tom Govan, Gareth Morgan, Oli Ackroyd, Darren Odell, Chris Farrell, Dan Kelly, Richard Carnes, Andrew Clarkson).

Finally, I'd like to dedicate Join The Future to my family, who showed belief in the project and my ability to deliver it from the very start. Mum, Dad, Mollie, Simon, Catherine and Oscar, this is for you.

MATT ANNISS September 2019

JOIN THE FUTURE

SPECIAL THANKS TO EVERYONE WHO PRE-ORDERED THE BOOK:

Nathan Adams, Mark Archer, Claire Ashton, Richard Austin, Nicolai Bähr, Dave Bain, Neil Baker, Martin Barraclough, Bognar Balazs, Rogier Barendregt, Daniel Berman, Matthew Berridge, Alexey Bessonov, Danilo Betti, Bob Bhamra, Raag Bhatia, David Birch, James Bowyer, Richard Brass, Jon Brent, Joe Brooke-Smith, BUNKERHEADZ, Neil Burdon, Markus Bürki, Adrian Burns, Todd Burns, Joshua Castles, Christian Cawood, Gabriele Cencig, Richard Chater, Pramesh Chauhan, Timothy Child, Richard Clarke-Hill, Dave Cotgrave, Trevor Cox, Paul Crognale, Oliver Crossan, John Crowley, Colvin Cruickshank, Antony Daly, Nick Davidson, Adrian Davies, Martijn Deijkers, Victor Dermenghem, Tommy De Roos, Cyril Desmoulins, Ben Devereux, James Dewey, Ashish Dhru, Mathieu Dionne, Garrett Doherty, Giovanni Dominice, Mick Donnelly, Ben Dornan, Graham Drennan, Simon Driscoll, Simon Duck, Matthew Duffield, Adrian Edwards, Neil Elkins, Sharon Embleton, Damon Fairclough, Tim Forrester, M L Fisher, Graham Fletcher, Francesco Fusaro, Rob Gear, Timo Gemmeke, Anthony George, Alan Gilby, Andrew Gillham, Kate Goodbun, Whitsitt Goodson, Richard Gorman, Jude Greenaway, Rob Hale, Ian Halliday, Nick Hamilton, Stuart Hammersley, Aidan Hanratty, Richard Hardcastle, Suridh Hassan, Alex Haydon, Winston Hazel, Paul Heath, Jason Hemmenway, Mark Henson, Owain Hepple, Conor Hickey, Lorien Houlton, Tom Houlton, Stephen Howe, Darren Hutton, Edouard Isar, Jamie Jerome, Stacey Keating, Santeri Laitinen, Jyrki Lappalainen, Rob Learner, Guillaume Legare, Luca Lozano, Dennis Lummer, Thomas Lye, Aly Lyon, John MacKinnon, Simon Mander, Melissa Maristuen, Eleanor Matthews, Jürgen Mayer, Jim McCormack, Dominic McKay, Nuutti-Iivari Meriläinen, Matthew Milner, Matt Milnes, Johnny Mooney, Adam Morris, Michael Moser, James Morgan, Johannes Moser, Tino Müller, Chris Murdoch, James Musselwhite, Dylan Nelson, Natalie Newman, Will Oakley, Peter O'Brien, Andrew O'Byrne, Kath O'Donnell, Hannah O'Neill, Davide Passaro, Anand Patel, Marie Patin, Joel Pearson, Phatmedia, Michel Plamondon, Tim Proctor, T Proefrock, Mark Pycraft, David Mark Rayner, Michael Reed, Paul Riggs, Tom Robbins, Joe Roberts, Leopoldo Rosa, Timo Rotonen, Ian Roullier, Jamie Russell, Lourenco Sampaio, Nimmo Sandilands, Sander Scheerman, Kaspar Schlueer, Ben Scott, Eileen Sheller, Adrian Shelley, Tim Sheridan, Shidashi-Ya, Connor Small, Mike Smalle, Pablo Smet, Chris Smith, Nicholas J Smith, Toby Smith, Karl Smout, Matthew Southwell, Elle Stocks, Philipp Steigerwald, Adrian Stewart, John Subsekt, Brion Paul Sutherland, Neil Sutherland, Nick Sutton, Liam Swaffield, Martin Thomas, Ryan Thompson, Fabian Tremmel, Jane Unwin, James Upton, Katherine Venn, Alex Waddington, Aidy Watts, Charles Weisfeld, Mathew Weston, David Wheeley, Alex Wilson, Danny Wootton, Matthew Wright, Sheen Yap, Chris Yeates

STATE OF BASS:
THE ORIGINS OF JUNGLE/DRUM & BASS
MARTIN JAMES

As UK government legislation, standardised music and bad drugs forced the euphoria of the rave into the darkness, a new underground movement emerged – jungle/drum & bass.

It was the true sound of the beating heart of 1990s UK. A melting pot of Britain's multi-cultural urban hardcore rave distilled via the journey from Jamaica's Tivoli Gardens soundsystem clashes, through the UK's inner city blues parties and onto jazz-funk all-dayers and soul weekenders. The jungle/drum & bass nexus was like nothing else the world had experienced before.

Drawing on interviews with some of the key figures in the early years, State of Bass explores the scene's social, cultural and musical roots via the sonic shifts that charted the journey from deep underground to global phenomenon.

Originally published in 1997, State of Bass: The Origins of Jungle/Drum & Bass extends the original text to include the award of the Mercury Prize to Reprazent and brings new perspectives to the story of the UK's most crucial subterranean scene.

'Cogent, well researched and hardly oblivious to the nutty charisma of jungle's lexicon and nomenclature. The first serious attempt to document the drum & bass realm is a total success.' **SELECT**

'Exceedingly well researched, endlessly authoritative and undeniably ace...' **MELODY MAKER**

"Martin James comes up trumps with an in-depth examination of jungle's roots, history and even a recommended listening guide." **MUZIK**

"Essential reading for anyone who is interested not only in the jungle scene... but in dance in general, in the music industry as a whole or even British society and its infrastructures." **DJ**

"An acutely perceptive and thought provoking account of the circumstances and celebrities surrounding the development of a modern music that we can finally call our own." **THE SCOTSMAN**

"Well worth rattling through if you can track it down." **FACT**

velocitypress.uk/state-of-bass

FIN